The Dead Sea Scrolls
Major Publications and Tools for Study

Revised Edition

SOCIETY OF BIBLICAL LITERATURE
Resources for Biblical Study

Edited by
W. Lee Humphreys

Number 20
The Dead Sea Scrolls
Major Publications and Tools for Study

by
Joseph A. Fitzmyer, S.J.

THE DEAD SEA SCROLLS
Major Publications and Tools for Study

Revised Edition

By
Joseph A. Fitzmyer, S.J.

Scholars Press
Atlanta, Georgia

The Dead Sea Scrolls
Major Publications and Tools for Study

© 1990
Joseph A. Fitzmyer, S.J.

Library of Congress Cataloging-in-Publication Data

Fitzmyer, Joseph A.
    The Dead Sea scrolls : major publications and tools for study / by
    Joseph A. Fitzmyer.--Rev. ed.
      p.   cm. -- (Resources for biblical study ; no. 20)
    Includes indexes.
    ISBN 1-55540-510-X (alk. paper). -- ISBN 1-55540-511-8 (pbk. :
    alk. paper)
    1. Dead Sea scrolls--Bibliography. I. Title. II. Series.
Z6371.D4F58 1990
[BM487]
016.2961'55-dc20   90-41229
                                                  CIP

Printed in the United States of America
on acid-free paper

CONTENTS

GENERAL ABBREVIATIONS

AB	Anchor Bible
ADAJ	Annual of the Department of Antiquities of Jordan
AGJU	Arbeiten zur Geschichte des antiken Judentums und des Urchristentums
ALQ	Cross, F. M., Jr., *The Ancient Library of Qumran & Modern Biblical Studies: Revised Edition* (Garden City, NY: Doubleday, 1961; repr., Grand Rapids, MI: Baker, 1980)
ALUOS	Annual of Leeds University Oriental Society
ANRW	*Aufstieg und Niedergang der römischen Welt*: II.Prinzipat (ed. H. Temporini and W. Haase; Berlin/New York: de Gruyter, 1972—)
AOAT	Alter Orient und Altes Testament
ASTI	Annual of the Swedish Theological Institute
BA	*Biblical Archaeologist*
BAC	Biblioteca de autores cristianos
BARev	*Biblical Archaeology Review*
BASOR	*Bulletin of the American Schools of Oriental Research*
BBB	Bonner biblische Beiträge
BE	J. T. Milik, *The Books of Enoch: Aramaic Fragments of Qumrân Cave 4* (with the collaboration of M. Black; Oxford: Clarendon, 1976)
BeO	*Bibbia e Oriente*
BHS	*Biblia hebraica stuttgartensia*
BHT	Beiträge zur historischen Theologie
Bib	*Biblica*
BibOr	Biblica et orientalia
BIES	*Bulletin of the Israel Exploration Society* (later renamed Yediʿot)
BIOSCS	*Bulletin of the International Organization for Septuagint and Cognate Studies*
BJRL	*Bulletin of the John Rylands (University) Library (of Manchester)*

BJS	Brown Judaic Studies
BSac	*Bibliotheca sacra*
BTB	*Biblical Theology Bulletin*
BTS	*Bible et terre sainte*
BZ	*Biblische Zeitschrift*
BZAW	Beihefte zur *ZAW*
BZNW	Beihefte zur *ZNW*
CBQ	*Catholic Biblical Quarterly*
CBQMS	Catholic Biblical Quarterly Monograph Series
CJT	*Canadian Journal of Theology*
CRAIBL	*Comptes rendus de l'Académie des Inscriptions et Belles-Lettres*
DBSup	*Dictionnaire de la Bible, Supplément*
DJD	Discoveries in the Judaean Desert (of Jordan)
DSSE	G. Vermes, *The Dead Sea Scrolls in English* (3d ed.; London: Penguin; New York: Viking Penguin, 1987)
DSSHU	E. L. Sukenik, *The Dead Sea Scrolls of the Hebrew University* (Jerusalem: Hebrew University and Magnes Press, 1955)
DSPS	J. A. Sanders, *The Dead Sea Psalms Scroll* (Ithaca, NY: Cornell University, 1967)
DTT	*Dansk Teologisk Tidsskrift*
EBib	Etudes bibliques
ESBNT	J. A. Fitzmyer, *Essays on the Semitic Background of the New Testament* (London: Chapman, 1971; paperback, Missoula, MT: Scholars Press, 1974)
EstBib	*Estudios bíblicos*
EstEcl	*Estudios eclesiásticos*
ETR	*Etudes théologiques et religieuses*
EvQ	*Evangelical Quarterly*
EvT	*Evangelische Theologie*
ExpTim	*Expository Times*
FO	*Folia orientalia*
FRLANT	Forschungen zur Religion und Literatur des Alten und Neuen Testamentes
HSM	Harvard Semitic Monographs
HSS	Harvard Semitic Studies
HTR	*Harvard Theological Review*
HTS	Harvard Theological Studies

ICASALS	International Center for Arid and Semi-Arid Land Studies
IEJ	*Israel Exploration Journal*
ILN	*Illustrated London News*
IOS	*Israel Oriental Studies*
IZBG	*Internazionale Zeitschriftenschau für Bibelwissenschaft und Grenzgebiete*
JANES	*Journal of the Ancient Near Eastern Society*
JBL	*Journal of Biblical Literature*
JEOL	*Jaarbericht ex oriente lux*
JETS	*Journal of the Evangelical Theological Society*
JJS	*Journal of Jewish Studies*
JNES	*Journal of Near Eastern Studies*
JNSL	*Journal of Northwest Semitic Languages*
JQR	*Jewish Quarterly Review*
JR	*Journal of Religion*
JSHRZ	Jüdische Schriften aus hellenistisch-römischer Zeit
JSJ	*Journal for the Study of Judaism*
JSOT	*Journal for the Study of the Old Testament*
JSOTSup	JSOT Supplements
JSP	*Journal for the Study of Pseudepigrapha*
JSPSup	JSP Supplements
JSS	*Journal of Semitic Studies*
JTC	*Journal for Theology and the Church*
JTS	*Journal of Theological Studies*
NAB	*The New American Bible* (Paterson, NJ: St. Anthony Guild, 1970)
NDBA	*New Directions in Biblical Archaeology* (ed. D. N. Freedman and J. C. Greenfield; Garden City, NY: Doubleday, 1969)
NovT	*Novum Testamentum*
NRT	*La nouvelle revue théologique*
NTA	*New Testament Abstracts*
NTAbh	Neutestamentliche Abhandlungen
NTS	*New Testament Studies*
OS	*Oudtestamentische Studiën*
PalSb	*Palestinski Sbornik*
PEQ	*Palestine Exploration Quarterly*

RB	*Revue biblique*
RechBib	Recherches bibliques
REJ	*Revue des études juives*
RHPR	*Revue d'histoire et de philosophie religieuses*
RHR	*Revue de l'histoire des religions*
RevQ	*Revue de Qumran*
RivB	*Rivista biblica*
RSR	*Recherches de science religieuse*
RTL	*Revue théologique de Louvain*
SBFLA	Studii biblici franciscani liber annuus
SBLMS	Society of Biblical Literature Monograph Series
SBT	Studies in Biblical Theology
SE I	*Studia evangelica I* (= TU 73 [1959])
Sem	*Semitica*
SJLA	Studies in Judaism in Late Antiquity
SJOT	*Scandinavian Journal of the Old Testament*
SP	*Studia papyrologica*
SPB	Studia postbiblica
SR	*Studies in Religion/Sciences religieuses*
ST	*Studia theologica*
STDJ	Studies on the Texts of the Desert of Judah
SUNT	Studien zur Umwelt des Neuen Testaments
SWDS	*Scrolls from the Wilderness of the Dead Sea* (Smithsonian Institution Exhibit Catalogue; Cambridge, MA: American Schools of Oriental Research, 1965)
SymBU	Symbolae biblicae upsalienses
TAG	J. A. Fitzmyer, *To Advance the Gospel: New Testament Studies* (New York: Crossroad, 1981)
TBT	*The Bible Today*
TLZ	*Theologische Literaturzeitung*
TRu	*Theologische Rundschau*
TS	*Theological Studies*
TTZ	*Trierer theologische Zeitschrift*
TU	Texte und Untersuchungen
USQR	*Union Seminary Quarterly Review*
VD	*Verbum Domini*
VT	*Vetus Testamentum*
VTSup	VT Supplements

WA	J. A. Fitzmyer, *A Wandering Aramean: Collected Aramaic Essays* (SBLMS 25; Missoula, MT: Scholars, 1979)
WF	Wege der Forschung
WTJ	*Westminster Theological Journal*
WUNT	Wissenschaftliche Untersuchungen zum Neuen Testament
ZAW	*Zeitschrift für die alttestamentliche Wissenschaft*
ZDPV	*Zeitschrift des deutschen Palästina-Vereins*
ZKT	*Zeitschrift für katholische Theologie*
ZNW	*Zeitschrift für die neutestamentliche Wissenschaft*
ZTK	*Zeitschrift für Theologie und Kirche*

(Abbreviations of the names of biblical books, apocrypha, pseudepigrapha, and early patristic writings follow the system proposed in *JBL* 90 [1971] 513-14.)

FOREWORD

The student who undertakes the study of the Dead Sea Scrolls soon realizes the vastness of this modern aspect of biblical studies. The bearing of the discovery of these texts on the technical study of the Bible is far from having been exploited. To some people the topic of Dead Sea Scrolls may seem to be "old hat," but when one realizes that we are still waiting for the publication of about 70 per cent of the texts from Qumran Cave 4, then it is evident that much important material is still to be brought to light and that the full bearing of this remarkable manuscript-discovery on the OT and NT is still to be worked out. Many are the aspects of the study of the Dead Sea Scrolls, for they contain not only forms of the text of the Hebrew, Aramaic, and Greek Scriptures, but also much other Palestinian Jewish literature of the last two centuries BC and of the first century AD. They bear upon the history and archaeology of the Roman period of Palestine, and the pertinence of them in providing a Palestinian Jewish background for many NT writings is far from having been adequately assessed.

In many graduate or divinity schools with programs devoted to biblical studies or to the study of the Northwest Semitic languages, seminars are often conducted in the reading and interpretation of the Qumran scrolls. Students in such seminars are all too frequently confronted with the problem of trying to find out where the texts to be studied have actually been published, either in a definitive or a preliminary form, and where one must go for secondary literature on them. For many of the texts have been published in partial or preliminary forms in out-of-the-way places, in different periodicals, or in *Festschriften*; and it is not easy to keep track of them.

Moreover, the very term "Dead Sea Scrolls" is used today in different ways. In a generic sense it often embraces texts coming from discoveries during the last forty years at different sites along the northwest shore of the Dead Sea. In a specific sense, however, it is restricted to the Qumran scrolls, to texts written in Hebrew, Aramaic, or Greek on papyrus and skin that were found in (to date) eleven caves in the vicinity of Khirbet Qumran. But in the wider

generic sense the term often includes texts found at Maṣada, Wadi
Murabbaʿat, Naḥal Ḥever, Naḥal Ṣeʾelim, Naḥal Mishmar, Khirbet
Mird, and even (in a few instances) texts from the Cairo Genizah.

In an effort to sort out all this material, to explain the various
sigla used for it, to indicate the places of publication of the Dead Sea
Scroll material made available to date, to explain the contents of the
texts, and to introduce the student to various tools of study, this
book has been composed. It includes not only the list of sites where
the texts have been found and the full bibliographical titles of the
major publications, but also guides to further material: bibliographies of the Dead Sea Scrolls, survey articles, other attempts to list
the material, concordances, dictionaries, and grammars for the
study of the texts, secondary collections of Qumran texts, translations in modern languages, outlines of the more important, longer
Qumran texts, and some of the more important bibliography on selected topics of scroll-study or secondary literature about them.

An effort has been made to be exhaustive in the listing of the
sites and the texts that have been published to date which come
from them. But when it comes to the secondary bibliography on the
topics treated, no effort has been made to be exhaustive. The bibliographies presented are selective, but it is hoped that at least the
more important material is represented among them and that they
will provide leads to further studies. In the case of select bibliographies there is always room for a critic's one-up-manship. However,
reviewers of this book are seriously asked for references to signifi-
cant contributions that may be lacking in these sections.

The eight sites treated here have a certain coherence, either because of the time of the discoveries or because of the period they
represent. Texts such as those of the Wadi ed-Daliyeh have not been
included, because, although they may come from a site not too far
away from Khirbet Qumran, they really have nothing to do with the
period in question. One might wonder, then, why the texts from
Khirbet Mird have been included. That is solely because of the time
of their discovery and of the association of them in the popular
mind with the so-called Dead Sea Scrolls. They are included only to
sort them out from the rest.

A word should be said about the decision to include outlines of
some of the important texts. The outlines are to a certain extent sub-
jective; others may prefer other ways of outlining the texts. But since
most of the material in this volume has grown out of an introduc-

tory course in the Dead Sea Scrolls given in recent years, I have learned the value of supplying students with outlines of the longer texts that have to be read. They are included here, therefore, for their propaedeutic value as tools for study. There is, however, another aspect of them that should be mentioned: the outlines are not uniform. This is dictated by the nature of the texts outlined. In some instances one can only list the contents (e.g., 11QPs[a] — a bare list of the biblical and apocryphal psalms as well as the prose insertions). Yet even such a list provides a ready reference for the contents of that scroll; with it one can tell immediately whether a given psalm in the canonical psalter is present in that Psalms text of Qumran Cave 11. The same is true of other problematic scrolls. Finally, the detailed list of the contents of scrolls is intended to facilitate the study of them from various standpoints (e.g., to enable one to check quickly for the Qumran texts in which some biblical book or other may be cited or used).

Full information (complete title, place of publication, publisher, etc.) is normally given only at the first occurrence. After that a brief title is used, but in the case of references to periodicals the volume number, year, and pertinent pages are included in subsequent references (after the first full listing of the information).

The reader should be aware that the sigla are not always followed by all students of, or commentators on, the Dead Sea Scrolls. Some still use the older system (see p. 8), which really should be abandoned; some who write in other modern languages sometimes use forms that are conventional to them. Thus, 11QtgHiob will not be found in the list below. Here one has to realize that the name for the Book of Job in German is different from the English name. And there are other, similar variants. The standard system, explained below, was devised by the members of the international scroll-team that worked in Jerusalem, but in recent writings J. T. Milik, a member of that team, has himself departed from it. I have, however, tried to reassign sigla to such texts as he now discusses according to the standard system (while recording as well his new, arbitrary abbreviations). An effort has been made to use the sigla that are current in English writings, but at times the definitive siglum has been assigned in French (e.g., by M. Baillet), and I have retained it.

Finally, my thanks are due to James A. Sanders, of the Claremont Graduate School, for his constructive criticism of an earlier draft of this work, to both Eugene C. Ulrich, of Notre Dame

University, and John Strugnell, of Harvard University, for their help
in tracing some recent publications, to F. García Martínez of the
Qumrân Instituut of Groningen for sending me a preliminary copy
of a similar list of Qumran texts that he has just published in *Henoch*,
from which I have learned much, to W. Lee Humphreys of the
University of Tennesee, the editor of the Resources for Biblical
Study, for his help in publishing this revision in this series, and to
Darwin Melnyk, the Associate Manager of Publications at Scholars
Press, for his help in seeing this volume through the Press.

Joseph A. Fitzmyer, S.J.
Jesuit Community
Georgetown University
Washington, DC 20057

I

THE SYSTEM OF ABBREVIATION USED FOR THE DEAD SEA SCROLLS

THE SYSTEM OF ABBREVIATION USED FOR
THE DEAD SEA SCROLLS
(Cf. J. T. Milik, "Table des sigles," DJD 1. 46-48)

The system that was first used, when only Qumran Cave 1 was known (see the abbreviations at the end of the list of those commonly used today, p. 8), soon became outmoded, especially when it was necessary to distinguish various Qumran caves and multiple copies of the same document found in the same cave. As a result a system was devised, which seems complicated, but once it is explained and studied proves to be easily followed. Five elements can make up the siglum for a given text, but not all five are always used, since the first and the fifth are commonly omitted, but they become necessary at times. The five elements in the order in which they occur are: (1) the material on which the text is written; (2) the name of the site where the text was discovered, or its provenience; (3) the title of the work; (4) which copy of that work at the given site; (5) the language in which the text is written (since sometimes the same text is found in more than one language).

MATERIAL	PROVENIENCE	TITLE OF WORK
(skin)	Q (Qumran: 1Q, 2Q, 3Q, etc.)	Gen, Exod, Lev, Num, Deut, etc.
p, pap (papyrus)		
cu (copper)	Mas (Maṣada)	paleoLev (Leviticus copied in paleo-Hebrew script)
o, os, ostr (ostracon)	Mur (Murabbaʿat)	
lign (wood)	Ḥev (Ḥever)	LXXNum (Numbers in the "Septuagint" version)
perg (parchment)	Ṣe (Ṣeʾelim)	
	Miš (Mišmar)	
	Mird (Khirbet Mird)	Samar (Samaritan version)
	C (Cairo Genizah)	
		phyl (Phylactery)

3

pHos (Pešer [commentary on] Hosea)

tgJob (targum [Aramaic translation] of Job)

apGen (apocryphon [non-canonical, literary work] based on Gen)

Sir (Sirach, Ecclesiasticus)

Tob (Tobit, Tobias)

EpJer (Epistle of Jeremy)

Jub (Jubilees)

En (Enoch)

TLevi (Testament of Levi)

TNaph (Testament of Naphtali)
(Sectarian Texts, see below)

Instead of a title, a (boldface or italic) number is often used; it corresponds to the number of the text in the volumes of DJD. Thus:

1Qphyl = 1Q**13** or
1Q*13*

The abbreviated
name of an OT
book may be
preceded by paleo
(= paleo-Hebrew
script), LXX (=
Old Greek
version), or tg (=
targum [or
Aramaic version]
of the book), or
Samar

COPY OF WORK	LANGUAGE
Superscript letters following the title or the language	nothing or hebr (= Hebrew)
	ar, aram (= Aramaic)
	arab (= Arabic)
	cpa (= Christian Palestinian Aramaic)
	gr (= Greek)
	lat (= Latin)
	nab (= Nabatean)

N.B. Normally, arabic numbers are used for caves, columns, and lines (sometimes writers use colons to separate the columns and lines, sometimes periods, sometimes commas - there is no set rule here). However, in some *fragmentary texts,* when there are several fragments and they must be numbered separately within a work, the *columns* are then designated by lower-case roman numerals. Thus, 1Q**27** 1 ii 25 (which means text 27 from Qumran Cave 1 [in DJD 1], fragment 1, column ii, line 25). In this case it is better not to use colons, periods, or commas. Similarly, 4QpIsa[c] 4-7 ii 2-4 (which means the third copy [copy c] of a pesher on Isaiah from Qumran Cave 4 [cf. 4Q163; DJD 5. 17-27], joined fragments 4 to 7, column ii, lines 2 to 4).

ABBREVIATIONS COMMONLY USED IN THIS SYSTEM

admon	admonition
ap	apocryphon
apoc	apocalypse
ar or aram	Aramaic
arab	Arabic
BA	Babatha Archive
BarC	Bar Cochba
Beat	Beatitude(s)
Ben	Benediction(s)
Ber	Berakôt
C	Cairo (Genizah)
Cal	Calendar(ic)
col	column
cpa	Christian Palestinian Aramaic
Cryptic	Cryptic Astrological Text
cu	copper (= cuprum)
D	Damascus Document
DibHam	Dibre Hammĕ᾽ôrôt (= Paroles des Luminaires)
dipl. trp.	diplomatic transcription
DM	Dires de Moïse (Sayings of Moses)
En	Enoch
Enastr	Enoch astronomical texts
Ep	Epistle, Letter
EschMidr	Eschatological Midrash(im)
Flor	Florilegium
frg(s).	fragment(s)
gr	Greek
H	Hôdāyôt (= Thanksgiving Psalms)
hebr	Hebrew
Hev	Ḥever (= Wadi Khabra)
Hym	Hymn(ic)
JN or JerNouv	Jérusalem Nouvelle (= New Jerusalem)

Jub	Jubilees, Book of
lat	Latin
lign	wood (= lignum)
Lit	Liturgy, Liturgical
LXX	Septuagint (so-called)
M	Milḥāmāh (War Scroll)
Mar	Marriage (or Mariage)
Mas	Maṣada
Melch	Melchizedek
Mess	Messianic (Text)
mez	Mezuzah
Mird	Khirbet Mird
Miš	Mišmar (Naḥal Mishmar = Wadi Mahras)
MT	Masoretic Text
Mur	Murabbaʿat (Wadi)
nab	Nabatean
o, os	ostracon
olim	formerly
Ord	Ordinances
p	pesher (= commentary); but sometimes it has been used for pap
paleo	text is written in Paleo-Hebrew script
palimp	palimpsest
PAM	Palestine Archaeological Museum (= Rock.)
pap	papyrus
par	paraphrase
PBless	Patriarchal Blessings
Pent	Pentateuch
perg	parchment (= pergamentum)
phyl	phylactery
Pr	Prayer(s)
PrNab	Prayer of Nabonidus
Proph	Prophecy, Prophetic
Ps(s)	Psalm(s), Psalter
PsAp	Apocryphal Psalms
ps-	Pseudo-
Pur	Purification
Q	Qumran
Quot	Quotidien (= daily)
Rit	Ritual

Rock.	Rockefeller Museum (formerly PAM)
S	Serek Hay-yaḥad (= Manual of Discipline)
Sa	Appendix A to 1QS (= 1Q28a): Rule of the Congregation
Sb	Appendix B to 1QS (= 1Q28b): Collection of Benedictions
Samar	Samaritan
Se	(Naḥal) Ṣeʾelim (= Wadi Seiyal)
Sec	Second
ŠirŠabb	Serek šîrôt ʿôlat haššabbāt (= Order of the Songs of the Sabbath Holocaust)
Sl 39-40	Strugnell Texts 39-40 (= Angelic Liturgy)
syr	Syriac
T	Testament
Testim	Testimonia
tg	targum
Vis	Vision(s)
Wiles	Wiles of the Wicked Woman
XII	Twelve Minor Prophets

OLDER SYSTEM OF ABBREVIATIONS

CDC	Cairo Damascus Covenant (= CD)
DSD	Dead Sea Discipline (= 1QS)
DSH	Dead Sea Habakkuk Commentary (= 1QpHab)
DSIa	Dead Sea Isaiah A (= 1QIsa[a])
DSIb	Dead Sea Isaiah B (= 1QIsa[b])
DSL	Dead Sea Lamech Apocalypse (= 1QapGen)
DST	Dead Sea Thanksgiving Psalms (= 1QH)
DSW	Dead Sea War Scroll (= 1QM)

(This older system should no longer be used. Even
though it is simpler, it tends to confuse.)

II

THE DEAD SEA SCROLLS: MAJOR PUBLICATIONS

MAJOR PUBLICATIONS

In the following list can be found all the places in which various Dead Sea Scrolls have been published. It contains not only the *editio princeps* but also the preliminary or partial publications, which contain all of a given text that has been made available in many cases. References have been added in some cases to other important articles or notes where different photos may have been published or further information on a text may have been supplied. The reader should realize that the long and tedious process of fitting fragments together and identifying them has at times meant the reordering of material, even after it has once been published in a preliminary fashion, because it has subsequently been recognized that certain pieces should be associated differently. An effort has been made here to list the material according to the present state of the question in this matter; this means that the sigla on some occasions may differ from what is given in a previous preliminary publication. The short Latin word *olim* ("formerly") has been used to indicate the change of a siglum, where this is known.

The texts are listed here according to the numbered caves with their conventional sigla. The numbered caves designate only those in which written material has been discovered, not all the caves (e.g., in the Qumran area) where artifacts and evidence of habitation have been found.

I. QUMRAN

    A. *Cave 1*
        (1) *OT Texts*

1QIsa^a   Burrows, M. (ed.), *The Dead Sea Scrolls of St. Mark's Monastery* (New Haven: American Schools of Oriental Research), 1 (1950) pls. I-LIV (contains all 66 chaps. of Isaiah with occasional lacunae, a few words missing at the bottom of some cols.).

                Cross, F. M. et al. (eds.), *Scrolls from Qumrân Cave I: The Great Isaiah Scroll, the Order of the*

Community, the Pesher to Habakkuk. From photographs by John C. Trever (Jerusalem: Albright Institute of Archaeological Research and the Shrine of the Book, 1972) [13]-[123]. (Black-and-white and colored photographs of cols. I-LIV of 1QIsa[a]; the black-and-white photographs, however, are not as good as those of the first printing of 1950.)

1QIsa[b]   Sukenik, E. L., *ʾôṣar ham-mĕgillôt hag-gĕnûzôt še-bîdê ha-ʾûnîbersîtāh ha-ʿibrît* (Jerusalem: Bialik Foundation and the Hebrew University, 1954 [but the title-page incorrectly reads 1956]), pls. 1-15. Two parts: Plates and Transcription. Modern Hebrew edition; the English version of it follows.

(*DSSHU*)   Sukenik, E. L. (posthumously edited by N. Avigad and Y. Yadin), *The Dead Sea Scrolls of the Hebrew University* (Jerusalem: Hebrew University and Magnes Press, 1955). Two parts: Plates and Transcriptions. (See also 1Q8 [DJD 1. 66-68]). Cf. E. Puech, "Quelques aspects de la restauration du Rouleau des Hymnes (1QH)," *JJS* 39 (1988) 38-55, esp. 55 n. 40 (mention of a Shrine of the Book photo [4287] that contains an unpublished frg. of 4 lines, which = part of Isa 44:23-25)

Detailed Listing of Contents of 1QIsa[b]

1Q8 1:1-8	(DJD 1. 66; pl. XII)	Isa 7:22-8:1
DSSHU frg. 1	(pl. 1)	Isa 10:17-19
1Q8 2:1-9	(DJD 1. 66; pl. XII)	Isa 12:3-13:8
DSSHU frg. 2	(pl. 1)	Isa 13:16-19
1Q8 3:1-10	(DJD 1. 67; pl. XI)	Isa 15:3-16:2
DSSHU frg. 3	(pl. 1)	Isa 16:7-11
1Q8 4:1-10	(DJD 1. 67; pl. XII)	Isa 19:7-17
DSSHU frg. 4	(pl. 1)	Isa 19:20-20:1
1Q8 5:1-10	(DJD 1. 67; pl. XII)	Isa 22:11-18
DSSHU frg. 5	(pl. 1)	Isa 22:24-23:4
1Q8 6:1-15	(DJD 1. 68; pl. XII)	Isa 24:18-25:8

DSSHU	frg. 6	(pl. 2)	Isa 26:1-5; 28:15-19
	frg. 7	(pl. 2)	Isa 29:1-8
	frg. 8	(pl. 2)	Isa 30:10-14
	frg. 9	(pl. 2)	Isa 30:21-26
	frg. 10	(pl. 2)	Isa 35:4-6
	frg. 11	(pl. 2)	Isa 37:8-12
	col. 1 + frg. 12	(pl. 3)	Isa 38:12-39:8; 40:2-3
	col. 2	(pl. 4)	Isa 41:3-23
	col. 3 + frg. 13	(pl. 5)	Isa 43:1-13,23-27
	col. 4	(pl. 6)	Isa 44:21-28; 45:1-13
	col. 5	(pl. 7)	Isa 46:3-13; 47:1-14
	col. 6	(pl. 8)	Isa 48:17-22; 49:1-15
	col. 7	(pl. 9)	Isa 50:7-11; 51:1-10
	col. 8	(pl. 10)	Isa 52:7-15; 53:1-12; 54:1-6
	col. 9	(pl. 11)	Isa 55:2-13; 56:1-12; 57:1-4
	col. 10	(pl. 12)	Isa 57:17-21; 58:1-14; 59:1-8
	col. 11	(pl. 13)	Isa 59:20-21; 60:1-22; 61:1-2
	col. 12	(pl. 14)	Isa 62:2-12; 63:1-19; 64:1,6-8
	col. 13	(pl. 15)	Isa 65:17-25; 66:1-24
1Q8	frg. 7	(DJD 1. 68; pl. XII)	Isa ?

1-5QIsa   Skehan, P. W., "IV. Littérature de Qumran.— A. Textes bibliques," *DBSup* 9. 805-22, esp. 811, where Skehan lists all the Isaiah passages represented in 1QIsa[a], 1QIsa[b], 4QIsa[a-q], and 5Q3. Cf. F. J. Morrow, *The Text of Isaiah at Qumran* (Washington, DC: Dissertation, The Catholic University of America, 1973; Ann Arbor, MI: University Microfilms [order #DA74-5079])

1QDan[a,b]   Trever, J. C. "Completion of the Publication of Some Fragments from Qumran Cave I," *RevQ* 5 (1964-66) 323-44 (it includes pls. I-VII, which belong to the texts transcribed in DJD 1. 150-55

[=1Q**71-72**]) (1QDan^a = Dan 1:10-17; 2:2-6; 1QDan^b = Dan 3:22-30)

For other OT Texts found in DJD 1, see the detailed listing of 1Q**1-72** below.

      (2) *Pesharim*

1QpHab   Burrows, M. (ed.), *The Dead Sea Scrolls of St. Mark's Monastery,* vol. 1, pls. LV-LXI (commentary on Hab 1:2-17; 2:1-20).

        Cross, F. M. et al. (eds.), *Scrolls from Qumrân Cave I,* [149]-[163] (Again, black-and white and colored photographs of 1QpHab I-XIII).

1QpMic   See 1Q**14** below
1QpZeph   See 1Q**15** below
1QpPs   See 1Q**16** below

      (3) *Apocryphal and Sectarian Texts*

1QapGen   Avigad, N. and Y. Yadin, *A Genesis Apocryphon: A Scroll from the Wilderness of Judaea. Description and Contents of the Scroll, Facsimiles, Transcription and Translation of Columns II, XIX-XXII* (Jerusalem: Magnes Press of the Hebrew University and Heikhal Ha-sefer, 1956) (see also 1Q**20** (DJD 1. 86-87]) (An Aramaic paraphrase, with inserts, of Gen 6:8-9; 9:2-3,4,20; Gen 10?; Gen 12:8-15:4.) [N.B. Fasc. 1 of vol. 2 of M. Burrows (ed.), *The Dead Sea Scrolls of St. Mark's Monastery* (see above), was reserved originally for this text; but it was published separately in Israel in 1956.]

1QH   Sukenik, E. L., *DSSHU,* pls. 35-47 (upper), 48-58; transcription 1-18, frgs. 1-66. (See also 1Q**35** (DJD 1. 136-38 = 1QH 7:27-8:13) The Thanksgiving Psalms (Hôdāyôt). Cf. *RB* 63 (1956) 64. See also E. Puech, "Un hymne essénien en partie retrouvé et les béatitudes: 1QH V 12 -VI 18 (= col. XIII-XIV 7) et 4QBéat.," *RevQ* 13 (Mémorial Jean Carmignac, 1988) 59-88, esp. 59-84.

1QJub^a	See 1Q17 below
1QJub^b	See 1Q18 below
1QM	Sukenik, E. L., *DSSHU*, pls. 16-34, 47 (lower); transcription, 1-19. (See also 1Q33 [DJD 1. 135-36]) The War Scroll (*Milḥāmāh*).
1QNoah 2, 1QPrs 2, 3	Trever, J. C., "Completion of the Publication," *RevQ* 5 (1964-66) 323-44 (+ pls. IV, VII). See 1Q19 below.
1QS	Burrows, M. (ed.), *The Dead Sea Scrolls of St. Mark's Monastery*, vol. 2, fasc. 2 ("The Manual of Discipline," 1951]), cols. I-XI.
	Cross, F. M. et al. (eds.), *Scrolls from Qumrân Cave I*, [125]-[147] (Again, black-and white and colored photographs of 1QS I-XI).
1QTLevi ar	Milik, J. T., "Testament de Lévi," DJD 1. 87-91. See 1Q21 below.
1Q1-72	Barthélemy, D. and J. T. Milik, *Qumran Cave I* (DJD 1; Oxford: Clarendon, 1955).

Detailed Listing of 1Q1-72 in DJD 1

(1) *OT Texts*

1Q1	1QGen	Genèse, 49-50 (+ pl. VIII): Gen 1:18-21; 3:11-14; 22:13-15; 23:17-19; 24:22-24 + frgs.
1Q2	1QExod	Exode, 50-51 (+ pl. VIII): Exod 16:12-16; 19:24-20:1; 20:5-6; 20:25-21:1,4-5 + frgs.
1Q3	1QpaleoLev	Lévitique et autres fragments en écriture 'phénicienne,' 51-54 (+ pls. VIII-IX): Lev 11:10-11; 19:30-34; 20:20-24; 21:24-22:6; 23:4-8; 27:30-31(?); Num 1:48-50; 36:7-8(?) + frgs. See now M. D. McLean, *The Use and Development of Paleo-Hebrew in the Hellenistic and Roman Period* (Cambridge, MA: Dissertation, Harvard University, 1982; Ann Arbor, MI: University Microfilms, 1982 [order #DA82-22670]). McLean distinguishes three different mss.:

		1QpaleoLev^a (= frgs. 1-8, 10-15); 1QpaleoLev^b (= frgs. 22-23); 1QpaleoNum (= frgs. 16-21)
1Q4	1QDeut^a	Deutéronome (premier exemplaire), 54-57 (+ pl. IX): Deut 1:22-25; 4:47-49; 8:18-19; 8:19(?); 9:27-28; 11:27-30; 13:1-4,4-6,13-14; 14:21,24-25; 16:4,6-7 + frgs.
1Q5	1QDeut^b	Deutéronome (second exemplaire), 57-62 (+ pl. X): Deut 1:9-13; 8:8-9; 9:10; 11:30-31; 15:14-15; 17:16; 21:8-9; 24:10-16; 25:13-18; 28:44-48; 29:9-11,12-20; 30:19-31:6,7-10,12-13; 32:17-21,21-22,22-29,24-25; 33:12-17,18-19,21-23,24 + frgs.
1Q6	1QJudg	Juges, 62-64 (+ pl. XI): Judg 6:20-22; 8:1(?); 9:1-4,4-6,28-31,40-42,40-43,48-49 + frgs.
1Q7	1QSam	Livres de Samuel, 64-65 (= pl. XI): 1 Sam 18:17-18; 2 Sam 20:6-10; 21:16-18; 23:9-12.
1Q8	1QIsa^b	Isaïe, 66-68 (+ pl. XII): Isa 7:22-8:1; 12:3-13:8; 15:3-16:2; 19:7-17; 22:11-18; 24:18-25:8.
1Q9	1QEzek	Ezéchiel, 68-69 (+ pl. XII): Ezek 4:16-5:1.
1Q10	1QPs^a	Psautier (premier exemplaire), 69-70 (+ pl. XIII): Pss 86:5-8; 92:12-14; 94:16; 95:11-96:2; 119:31-34,43-48,77-79 + frgs.
1Q11	1QPs^b	Psautier (second exemplaire), 71 (+ pl. XIII): Pss 126:6; 127:1-5; 128:3.
1Q12	1QPs^c	Psaume 44, 71-72 (+ pl. XIII): Ps 44:3-5,4,7,9,23-24,25 + frgs.
1Q71	1QDan^a	Daniel (premier exemplaire), 150-51: Dan 1:10-17; 2:2-6. See the article of Trever listed under 1QDan^a above.
1Q72	1QDan^b	Daniel (second exemplaire), 151-52: Dan 3:22-28,27-30.

(2) *Phylacteries*

1Q13	1Qphyl	Phylactère, 72-76 (+ pl. XIV): = Deut 5:1,3,5,7,9,14,21,23-27; 10:17-18; 10:21-11:1,8-11,12; Exod 13:2-3,7-9 + frgs.

(3) *Pesharim*

1Q14	1QpMic	Commentaire de Michée, 77-80 (+ pl. XV): Pesher on Mic 1:2-5,5-7,8-9; 4:13(?); 6:14-16; 7:6(?),8-9(?),17.
1Q15	1QpZeph	Commentaire de Sophonie, 80 (+ pl. XV): Pesher on Zeph 1:18-2:2.
1Q16	1QpPs	Commentaire de psaumes, 81-82 (+ pl. XV): Pesher on Ps 57:1,4; 68:12-13,26-27,30-31 + frgs.

(4) *Apocryphal Texts*

1Q17-18	1QJub[a,b]	Livre des Jubilés, 82-84 (+ pl. XVI): *Jub.* 27:19-21; 35:8-10 + frgs. [36:12(?)].
1Q19, 19bis	1QNoah	'Livre de Noé,' 84-86, 152 (+ pl. XVI): Book of Noah [related to *1 Enoch* 8:4-9:4; 106:9-10]. See now J. T. Milik, *BE*, 55-60.
1Q20	1QapGen	Apocalypse of Lamech, 86-87 (+ pl. XVII): part of 1QapGen
1Q21	1QTLevi ar	Testament de Lévi, 87-91 (+ pl. XVII): *T. Levi* 8:11(?), older form of Bodleian CTLevi ar.
1Q22	1QDM	'Dires de Moïse'' 91-97 (+ pls. XVIII-XIX): *Dibrê Môšeh* (Sayings of Moses).
1Q23-24	1QEnGiants	Deux apocryphes en araméen, 97-99 (+ pls. XIX-XX): "Book of the Giants"; see J. T. Milik, *BE*, 301-2, 309; also "Turfan et Qumran," *Tradition und Glaube: Das frühe Christentum in seiner Umwelt: Festgabe für K. G. Kuhn* [ed. G. Jeremias et al.; Göttingen: Vandenhoeck & Ruprecht, 1971] 120-21).

1Q25		Une prophétie apocryphe(?), 100-101 (+ pl. XX)
1Q26		Un apocryphe, 101-2 (+ pl. XX): A sapiential text, of the genre of testaments and instructions. See P. W. Skehan, "The Biblical Scrolls from Qumran and the Text of the Old Testament," *BA* 28 (1965) 87-100, esp. 90: six more copies of this text in 4Q, as yet unpublished(?).
1Q27	1QMyst	'Livre des mystères,' 102-7 (+ pls. XXI-XXII): cf. R. de Vaux, *RB* 56 (1949) 605-9 (+ pl. XVII); J. T. Milik, *VD* 39 (1952) 42-43; *RB* 63 (1956) 61. G. Vermes (*DSSE*, 239) labels this text "The Triumph of Righteousness."

(5) *Sectarian Texts*

1Q28		Annexes à la règle de la communauté, 107-30 (+ pls. XXII-XXIX): Appendixes of 1QS
1Q28a	1QSa	Règle de la Congrégation (1QSa), 108-18 (+ pls. XXIII-XXIV): Rule for all the Congregation of Israel in the End of Days
1Q28b	1QSb	Recueil des bénédictions, 118-30 (+ pls. XXV-XXIX): Collection of blessings uttered over the faithful, the high priest, the priests, the prince of the congregation
1Q29		Liturgie des 'trois langues de feu,' 130-32 (+ pl. XXX): cf. *RB* 63 (1956) 64.
1Q30-31		Textes liturgiques (?), 132-34 (+ pl. XXX): Hebrew liturgical texts
1Q32	1QJN ar	'Description de la Jérusalem nouvelle' (?), 134-35 (+ pl. XXXI) Aramaic text
1Q33	1QM frgs. 1-2	'La guerre des fils de lumière contre les fils de ténèbres' (1QM), 135-36 (+ pl. XXXI): frgs. belonging to 1QM

1Q34	1QLitPr^a	Recueil de prières liturgiques, 136 (+ pl. XXXI): collection of liturgical prayers probably related to 4QPr Fêtes (4Q507-9) and to the next text.
1Q34bis	1QLitPr^b	Recueil de prières liturgiques, 152-55.
1Q35	1QH frgs.	Recueil de cantiques d'action de grâces (1QH), 136-38 (+ pl. XXXI): Frgs. belonging to *Hôdāyôt* (1QH); cf. E. Puech, *JJS* 39 (1988) 38-55.
1Q36		Recueil d'hymnes, 138-41 (+ pl. XXXII): Frgs. of a collection of hymns
1Q37-40		Compositions hymniques (?), 141-43 (+ pls. XXXII-XXXIII): Hymnic frgs.
1Q41-62		Unidentified, tiny Hebrew frgs., 144-47 (+ pls. XXXIII-XXXV)
1Q63-67		Unidentified, tiny Aramaic frgs., 147 (+ pl. XXXV)
1Q68		Unidentified Aramaic frgs., 147-48 (+ pl. XXXV)
1Q69		Unidentified Hebrew frgs., 148 (+ pl. XXXVI)
1Q70		Tiny papyrus frgs., 148-49 (+ pl. XXXVII)
1Q70bis		Papyrus frg., 155: related to 1Q70

B.   *Caves 2-3, 5-10* (Minor Caves)

2Q1-33	Baillet, M., J. T. Milik, and R. de Vaux, *Les 'Petites*
3Q1-15	*Grottes' de Qumrân: Exploration de la falaise, Les*
5Q1-25	*grottes 2Q, 3Q, 5Q, 6Q, 7Q à 10Q, Le rouleau de*
6Q1-31	*cuivre* (DJD 3; Oxford: Clarendon, 1962). Two
7Q1-19	parts: 1. Texte; 2. Planches.
8Q1-5	
9Q1 (pap)	
10Q1 (ostr)	
3Q15	The Copper Plaque or "the Copper Rolls"

Detailed Listing of 2Q1-33 in DJD 3

(1) *OT Texts*

2Q1	2QGen	Genèse, 48-49 (+ pl. X): Gen 19:27-28; 36:6,35-37
2Q2	2QExod^a	Exode (premier exemplaire), 49-52 (+ pl. X): Exod 1:11-14; 7:1-4; 9:27-29; 11:3-7; 12:32-41; 21:18-20(?); 26:11-13; 30: 21(?),23-25; 32:32-34; + frgs.
2Q3	2QExod^b	Exode (deuxième exemplaire), 52-55 (+ pl. XI): Exod 4:31; 12:26-27(?); 18:21-22; 21:37-22:2,15-19; 27:17-19; 31:16-17; 19:9; 34:10 + frgs.
2Q4	2QExod^c	Exode (troisième exemplaire), 56 (+ pl. XII): Exod 5:3-5
2Q5	2QpaleoLev	Lévitique en écriture paléo-hébraïque, 56-57 (+ pl. XII): Lev 11:22-29
2Q6	2QNum^a	Nombres (premier exemplaire), 57-58 (+ pl. XII): Num 3:38-41; 3:51-4:3
2Q7	2QNum^b	Nombres (deuxième exemplaire), 58-59 (+ pl. XII): Num 33:47-53
2Q8	2QNum^c	Nombres (troisième exemplaire) 59 (+ pl. XII): Num 7:88
2Q9	2QNum$^{d(?)}$	Nombres (quatrième exemplaire ?), 59-60 (+ pl. XII): Num 18:8-9 (this frg. possibly belongs to 2Q7; possibly it = Lev 23:1-3)

2Q10	2QDeut^a	

2Q10   2QDeut^a   Deutéronome (premier exemplaire), 60 (+ pl. XII): Deut 1:7-9

2Q11   2QDeut^b   Deutéronome (deuxième exemplaire), 60-61 (+ pl. XII): Deut 17:12-15

2Q12   2QDeut^c   Deutéronome (troisième exemplaire), 61-62 (+ pl. XII): Deut 10:8-12

2Q13   2QJer   Jérémie, 62-69 (+ pl. XIII): Jer 42:7-11,14; 43:8-11; 44:1-3,12-14; 46:27-47:7; 48:7,25-39,43-45; 49:10 + frgs. (some doubtfully identified frgs.: 13:22; 32:24-25; 48:2-4,41-42)

2Q14   2QPs   Psautier, 69-71 (+ pl. XIII): Ps 103:2-11; 104:6-11

2Q15   2QJob   Job, 71 (+ pl. XIII): Job 33:28-30

2Q16   2QRuth^a   Ruth (premier exemplaire), 71-74 (+ pl. XIV): Ruth 2:13-14,14-19,19-22; 2:22-3:3,4-8; 4:3-4

2Q17   2QRuth^b   Ruth (second exemplaire), 74-75 (+ pl. XV): Ruth 3:13-18

2Q18   2QSir   Ecclésiastique (texte hébreu), 75-77 (+ pl. XV): Sir 6:14-15 (? or 1:19-20); 6:20-31

(2) *Apocryphal Texts*

2Q19   2QJub^a   Livre des Jubilés (premier exemplaire), 77-78 (+ pl. XV): *Jub.* 3:7-8 (cf. Gen 25:9,7-8)

2Q20   2QJub^b   Livre des Jubilés (second exemplaire), 78-79 (+ pl. xv): *Jub.* 46:1-3 (cf. Exod 1:7; Gen 50:26,22) + frgs. of uncertain relation

2Q21   2QapMoses   Un apocryphe de Moïse (?), 79-81 (+ pl. XV): Apocryphal writing about Moses

2Q22   2QapDavid   Un apocryphe de David (?), 81-82 (+ pl. XV): Apocryphal writing about David. See now E. M. Schuller, *Non-Canonical Psalms from Qumran: A Pseudepigraphic Collection* (HSS 28; Atlanta, GA: Scholars, 1986); but

		also C. Newsom, *JJS* 39 (1988) 56-73. This text may overlap with a 4Q text, not yet correctly identified, **4Q373** or **4Q379.**
2Q23	2QapProph	Une prophétie apocryphe, 82-84 (+ pl. XV): Apocryphal prophetic text
2Q24	2QJN ar	Description de la Jérusalem nouvelle, 84-89 (+ pl. XVI): Description of the New Jerusalem

(3) *Sectarian Juridical and Liturgical Texts*

2Q25	2Q?	Document juridique, 90 (+ pl. XVII): A juridical text
2Q26	2QEnGiants	Fragment de rituel (?), 90-91 (+ pl. XVII): Now known as part of the "Book of Giants" (see J. T. Milik, *BE*, 309).
2Q27-33	2Q?	Textes de caractère mal défini, 91-93 (+ pl. XVII): Tiny, unidentified frgs.

Detailed Listing of 3Q1-15 in DJD 3

	(1) OT Texts	
3Q1	3QEzek	Ezéchiel, 94 (+ pl. XVIII): Ezek 16:31-33
3Q2	3QPs	Psaume 2, 94 (+ pl. XVIII): Ps 2:6-7
3Q3	3QLam	Lamentations, 95 (+ pl. XVIII): Lam 1:10-12; 3:53-62

	(2) Pesharim	
3Q4	3QpIsa	Commentaire d'Isaïe, 95-96 (+ pl. XVIII): Pesher on Isa 1:1; cf. R. de Vaux, RB 60 (1953) 555-56.

	(3) Apocryphal Texts	
3Q5	3QJub (olim 3QapProph)	Une prophétie apocryphe, 96-98 (+ pl. XVIII): It is now considered to be a fragment of Jubilees, probably = Jub. 23:6-7,12-13,23(?); cf. R. Deichgräber, "Fragmente einer Jubiläen-Handschrift aus Höhle 3 von Qumran," RevQ 5 (1964-65) 415-22; but also A. Rofé, "Further Manuscript Fragments of the Jubilees in the Third Cave of Qumran," Tarbiz 34 (1965) 333-36
3Q6	3QHym	Hymne de louange, 98 (+ pl. XVIII): Hymn of Praise
3Q7	3QTJud	Un apocryphe mentionnant l'ange de la présence, 99 (+ pl. XVIII): Text about an Angel of the Presence. See J. T. Milik, "Ecrits préesséniens de Qumrân: D'Hénoch à Amram," Qumrân: Sa piété, sa théologie et son milieu (BETL 46; ed. M. Delcor; Gembloux: Duculot, 1978) 91-106, esp. 98-99; he thinks that frgs. 6 and 5 joined with 3 are part of a Hebrew

		text of a Testament of Judah. (Milik's siglum: 3QHJu 6 and 5+3).
3Q8	3Q?	Un texte mentionnant un ange de paix (?), 100 (+ pl. XIX): Text about an Angel of Peace
3Q9	3Q?	Un texte de la secte, 100-101 (+ pl. XIX): Sectarian text (?)
3Q10-11	3Q?	Tiny, unidentified Hebrew frgs., 101-2 (+ pl. XIX)
3Q12-13	3Q? ar	Tiny, unidentified Aramaic frgs., 102 (+ pl. XIX)
3Q14	3Q?	21 isolated frgs., 102-4 (+ pl. XIX). See J. T. Milik, *BE*, 61.
3Q15	3QTreasure	Le rouleau de cuivre provenant de la grotte 3Q (3Q15), 199-302 (+ pls. XLVIII-LXXI): Copper plaque mentioning Buried Treasure(s); see chapter XI below

Detailed Listing of 5Q1-25 in DJD 3

(1) *OT Texts*

5Q1	5QDeut	Deutéronome, 169-71 (+ pl. XXXVI): Deut 7:15-24; 8:5-9:2
5Q2	5QKgs	I Rois, 171-72 (+ pl. XXXVI): 1 Kgs 1:1,16-17,27-37
5Q3	5QIsa	Isaïe, 173 (+ pl. XXXVI): Isa 40:16,18-19
5Q4	5QAmos	Amos, 173-74 (+ pl. XXXVI): Amos 1:3-5
5Q5	5QPs	Psaume 119, 174 (+ pl. XXXVII): Ps 119:99-101,104,113-20,138-42
5Q6	5QLam^a	Lamentations (premier exemplaire), 174-77 (+ pl. XXXVII-XXXVIII): Lam 4:5-8,11-15,15-16,19-20; 4:20-5:3,4-12,12-13,16-17 + frgs.
5 Q 7	5QLam^b	Lamentations (second exemplaire), 177-78 (+ pl. XXXVIII): Lam 4:17-20
5 Q 8	5Qphyl	Phylactère, 178 (+ pl. XXXVIII): Phylactery in its case; unopenable.

(2) *Apocryphal Texts*

5Q9	5QToponyms	Ouvrage avec toponymes, 179-80 (+ pl. XXXVIII): A text with toponyms
5Q10	5QapMal	Ecrits avec citations de Malachie, 180 (+ pl. XXXVIII): Apocryphon of Malachi (? [cites Mal 1:13-14]); cf. J. Carmignac, "Vestiges d'un pesher de Malachie," *RevQ* 4 (1963-64) 97-100.
5Q11	5QS	Règle de la communauté, 180-81 (+ pl. XXXVIII): Serek hay-Yaḥad (= 1QS 2:4-7,12-14[?])
5 Q 12	5QD	Document de Damas, 181 (+ pl. XXXVIII): Damascus Document (= CD 9:7-10)
5Q13	5QRègle	Une règle de la secte, 181-83 (+ pls. XXXIX-XL): Frgs. related to 1QS, but not identical with it or with CD

5Q14	5QCurses	Ecrit contenant des malédictions, 183-84 (+ pl. XL): Liturgical composition with curses
5Q15	5QJN ar	Description de la Jérusalem nouvelle, 184-93 (+ pls. XL-XLI): Description of the New Jerusalem (includes readings from 4QJN and 11QJN); cf. J. Licht, "An Ideal Town Plan from Qumran—The Description of the New Jerusalem," *IEJ* 29 (1979) 45-59; cf. J. T. Milik, *BE*, 198.
5Q16-24	5Q?	Tiny, unidentified frgs., 193-96 (+ pls. XLI-XLII)
5Q25	5Q?	Unclassified frgs., 196-97 (+ pl. XLII)

Detailed Listing of 6Q1-31 in DJD 3

(1) *OT Texts*

6Q1	6QpaleoGen	Genèse en écriture paléo-hébraïque, 105-6 (+ pl. XX): Gen 6:13-21
6Q2	6QpaleoLev	Lévitique en écriture paléo-hébraïque, 106 (+ pl. XX): Lev 8:12-13
6Q3	6QDeut	Deutéronome (?), 106-7 (+ pl. XX): Possibly Deut 26:19
6Q4	6QKgs	Livre des Rois, 107-12 (+ pls. XX-XXII): 1 Kgs 3:12-14; 12:28-31; 22:28-31; 2 Kgs 5:26; 6:32; 7:8-10; 7:20-8:5; 9:1-2; 10:19-21 + many isolated frgs.
6Q5	6QPs	Psaume 78 (?), 112 (+ pl. XXIII): Ps 78:36-37 (?)
6Q6	6QCant	Cantique des cantiques, 112-14 (+ pl. XXIII): Cant 1:1-6,6-7
6Q7	pap6QDan	Daniel, 114-16 (+ pl. XXIII): Dan 8:16-17(?); 8:20-21(?); 10:8-16; 11:33-36,38 + frgs.

(2) *Apocryphal Texts*

pap6Q8	6QEnGiants (*olim* 6QapGen)	Un apocryphe de la Genèse, 116-19 (+ pl. XXIV): Now known to be part of the Enochic "Book of Giants"; see J. T. Milik, *BE*, 300-301, 309)
6Q9	6QapSam/Kgs	Un apocryphe de Samuel-Rois, 119-23 (+ pls. XXIV-XXV): Samuel-Kings Apocryphon (Hebrew)
pap6Q10	6QProph	Une prophétie, 123-25 (+ pl. XXVI): Hebrew prophetic text
6Q11	6QAllegory	Allégorie de la vigne, 125-26 (+ pl. XXVI): Allegory of the Vine (?) (Hebrew)
6Q12	6QapProph	Une prophétie apocryphe, 126 (+ pl. XXVI): Hebrew prophetic apocryphon
6Q13	6QPriestProph	Prophétie sacerdotale (?), 126-27 (+ pl. XXVI): Priestly prophecy (Hebrew text related to Ezra-Nehemiah [?])

6Q14   6QApoc ar   Texte apocalyptique, 127-28 (+ pl.
                             XXVI): Aramaic apocalyptic text

            (3) *Sectarian Texts*
6Q15   6QD   Document de Damas, 128-31 (+ pl.
                             XXVI): Damascus Document (= CD
                             4:19-21; 5:13-14; 5:18-6:2; 6:20-7:1 + a
                             frg. not found in CD); cf. *RB* 63
                             (1956) 513-23 (+ pl. II)
pap6Q16 6QBen   Bénédictions, 131-32 (+ p. XXVII):
                             Blessings related to 1QSb
6Q17   6QCal   Fragment de calendrier, 132-33 (+ pl.
                             XXVII): Calendar frgs.; cf. J. T.
                             Milik, *BE*, 61 n. 1.
pap6Q18 6QHym   Composition hymnique, 133-36 (+ pl.
                             XXVII): Hymnic composition
                             related to 1QM (?)

            (4) *Tiny Unidentified Fragments*
6Q19   6QGen(?) ar   Texte en rapport avec la Genèse, 136
                             (+ pl. XXVIII): Aramaic text related
                             to Gen 10:6,20 (?)
6Q20   6QDeut(?)   Texte en rapport avec le Deutéronome
                             (?), 136-37 (+ pl. XXVIII): Text
                             related to Deut 11:10(?)
6Q21   6QfrgProph   Fragment prophétique (?), 137 (+ pl.
                             XXVIII): Prophetic fragment (?)
6Q22   6Q? hebr   Texte hébreu, 137 (+ pl. XXVIII):
                             unidentified
6Q23   6Q? ar   Texte araméen, 138 (+ pl. XXVIII):
                             unidentified; J. T. Milik, *BE*, 91 now
                             relates it to the "Words of the book
                             of Michael" (cf. 4QMilMik)
6Q24-31   6Q?   Groupes et fragments divers, 138-41 (+
                             pls. XXVIII-XXIX)

Detailed Listing of 7Q1-19 in DJD 3

(1) *OT Texts*

7Q1	7QLXXExod	Exode, 142-43 (+ pl. XXX): Exod 28:4-7
7Q2	7QLXXEpJer	Lettre de Jérémie, 143 (+ pl. XXX): Vss. 43-44

(2) *Biblical Texts (?)* [all in Greek]; see chapter X/VII

7Q3		
7Q4		
7Q5		
7Q6		
7Q7		
7Q8		
7Q9		
7Q10		
7Q11		
7Q12		
7Q13-18		Very tiny papyrus frgs.
7Q19		Imprints of papyrus with writing on plaster frgs.

Detailed Listing of 8Q1-5 in DJD 3

(1) *OT Texts*

8Q1	8QGen	Genèse, 147-48 (+ pl. XXXI): Gen 17:12-19; 18:20-25
8Q2	8QPs	Psautier, 148-49 (+ pl. XXXI): Ps 17:5-9,14; 18:6-9 (= 2 Sam 22:6-9); 18:10-13 (= 2 Sam 22:10-13)
8Q3	8Qphyl	Phylactère, 149-57 (+ pls. XXXII-XXXIII): Phylactery (contains Exod 13:1-10; 13:11-16; Deut 6:4-9; 11:13; Deut 6:1-3; 10:20-22; Deut 10:12-19; Exod 12:43-51; Deut 5:1-14; Exod 20:11; Deut 10:13(?); 11:2; 10:21-22; 11:1,6-12)
8Q4	8Qmez	Mezouza, 158-61 (+ pl. XXXIV): Mezuzah (Deut 10:12-11:21)

(2) *Liturgical Text*

8Q5	8QHym	Passage hymnique, 161-62 (+ pl. XXXV): Hymnic composition

N.B. From 9Q has come only one papyrus frg. (unidentified [see DJD 3. 163 + pl. XXXV]), and from 10Q has come only one piece of inscribed pottery (ostracon ? [DJD 3.164 + pl. XXXV]).

C. Cave 4

(1) OT Texts

pap4QGen?   Baillet, M., *Qumrân Grotte 4,III (4Q482-4Q520)*
(DJD 7; Oxford: Clarendon, 1982) 2 (4Q483)
[text may be related to *Jubilees]*

4QGen-Exodª,   Davila, J. R., *Unpublished Pentateuchal Manu-*
4QGenᵇ⁻ʰ,ʲ⁻ᵏ   *scripts from Cave IV Qumran: 4QGenExª,*
4QGenᵇ⁻ʰ,ʲ⁻ᵏ (Cambridge, MA: Dissertation,
Harvard University, 1988; Ann Arbor, MI:
University Microfilms, 1988 [order #DA89-
01673])

4QExodᵇ   Cross, F. M., *ALQ*, 184-85 (transliteration of frg. 1
(*olim*   only, but see the plate opposite p. 101 in the
4QExodª)   1958 ed. [= Exod 1:1-5])

4QExodᶜ   Cross, F. M., "The Song of the Sea and Canaanite
Myth," *JTC* 5 (1968) 1-25, esp. 13-16 (= Exod
15:1b-18)

4QExodᶠ   Cross, F. M., *SWDS*, 14, 23 (= Exod 40:8-27); *ALQ*,
33, 121; cf. D. N. Freedman, "The Massoretic
Text and the Qumran Scrolls: A Study in
Orthography," *Textus* 2 (1962) 87-102.

4QpaleoExodᵐ   Sanderson, J. E., *An Exodus Scroll from Qumran:*
(*olim*   *4QpaleoExodᵐ and the Samaritan Tradition* (HSS
4QExª)   30; Atlanta, GA: Scholars, 1986). See also P. W.
Skehan, "Exodus in the Samaritan Recension
from Qumran," *JBL* 74 (1955) 182-87; see the
photograph in *BA* 28 (1965) 98; *SWDS*, 16, 26 (=
Exod 6:25-7:19). Sanderson's book is not an
edition of the text, but a study of its relation to
the Samaritan tradition; she supplies, however,
a list of the passages in Exodus that are
preserved according to the 45 cols. of the text
(pp. 321-23): 6:25-7:16; 7:16-19; 7:29-8:1,12-18;
8:19-22; 9:5-16,19-21; 9:35-10:1,2-5; 10:5-12,19-
24; 10:25-28, 11:8-12:2; 12:6-8,13-15,17-22; 12:31-
32,34-39; 13:3-7,12-13; 14:3-5,8-9; 14:25-26;
15:23-16:1,4-5,7-8; 16:31-32; 16:32-17:16; 17:16-
18:18,20-21; 18:21-19:1; 19:7-17; 19:23-20:1;

20:18-19; [20:21-21:4],5-6; 21:13-14,22-32; 22:3-4,6-7,11-13,16-18; 22:20-30, 23:15-16; 23:29-31, 24:1-4,6-11; 25:11-12,20-22; 25:22-29,31-34; 26:8-15,21-30; [26:35, 30:1-9],10, [26:36-37], 27:1-2,9-14; 27:18-19, 28:3-4,8-11; 28:22-24,26-28,30-39; 28:39-29:5; 29:20,22-25,31-34; 29:34-41,[42-46], [30:11],12-18; 30:29-31,34-38, 31:1-7; 31:7-8,13-15, 32:2-9; 32:10-19,25-30; 33:12-15; 33:16-34:3,10-13; 34:15-18,20-24,27-28; [35:1-37:9]; 37:9-16. Cols. are separated above by semicolons; col. 14 is lacking. Square brackets indicate reconstructed verses.

4QNum[b] .   Jastram, N., *The Book of Numbers from Qumran Cave IV (4QNum[b])* (Cambridge, MA: Dissertation, Harvard University, 1990). The frgs. contain parts of the following verses: Num 11:31-12:6; 12:8-11; 13:7,10-13,15-24; 15:41-16:11; 17:12-17; 18:25-19:6; 20:12-13b (= Samar addition); 20:16-17; 20:19-21:2; 21:12a (= Samar addition) - 13a (Samar addition); 21:20-21a (= Samar addition); 22:5-21, 31-34; 22:37-38; 22:41-23:4; 23:6,13-15,21-22; 23:27-24:10; 25:4-8,16-18; 26:1-5,7-10,12,14-34; 26:62-27:5 27:7-8,10,18-19,21-23b (= Samar addition); 28:13-17,28,30-31; 29:10-13,16-18,26-30; 30:1-3,5-9,15-16; 31:2-6,21b-25,30-33,35-36; 31:38,43-44; 31:46-32:1; 32:7-10,13-17, 19,23-30,35; 32:37-39,41; 33:1-4,23,25,28,31,45, 47-48,50-52; 34:4-9,19-21,23; 35:3-5,12,14-15,18-25,27-28; 35:33-36:2; 36:4-7. A noteworthy feature of this text: the following verses are written in red ink: 20:22-23;21a; 22:21; 23:13; 23:27; 31:25; 31:28; 31:48; 32:25; 33:1. Cf. F. M. Cross, *ALQ*, 32, 138; "The Development of the Jewish Scripts," (see p. 152 below); "The History of the Biblical Text" (see p. 157 below), 287; "The Evolution" (see p. 157 below), 310.

4QDeut[a,c,d] 4QDeut[f,g,i,n]   White, S. A., *A Critical Edition of Seven Manuscripts of Deuteronomy: 4QDt[a,] 4QDt[c], 4QDt[d], 4QDt[f], 4QDt[g], 4QDt[i],* and *4QDt[n]* (Cambridge, MA: Dissertation, Harvard University; Ann Arbor, MI: University Microfilms, 1988 [order #DA89-01693])

4QDeut[b,e,h,j,k,l]   Duncan, J. A., *A Critical Edition of Deuteronomy Manuscripts from Qumran. Cave IV: 4QDt[b], 4QDt[e], 4QDt[h], 4QDt[j], 4QDt[k], 4QDt[l]* (Cambridge, MA: Dissertation: Harvard University, 1989). These frgs. contain the following verses: 4QDeut[b]: Deut 29:24-27; 30:3-14; 31:9-14,15-17; 31:24-32:3. 4QDeut[e]: Deut 3:24; 7:12-16; 7:21-8:4; 8:5-16. 4QDeut[h]: Deut 1:1-17,22-23,29-39,40-41; 1:43-2:5; 2:28-30; 19:21; 31:9-11; 33:9-11. 4QDeut[j]: Deut 5:1-11,13-15,21,22-27,28; 5:29-33; 6:1-3; 8:5-10; 11:6-10,12-13; 32:7-8; Exod 12:43-46,46-51; 13:1-5. 4QDeut[k]: Deut 5:28-31; 11:6-13; 19:8-16; 20:6-19; 23:22-24:3; 25:19-26:4; 26:18-19; 32:17-18,22-23,25-27. 4QDeut[l]: Deut 10:12,14; 28:67-68; 29:2-5; 31:12; 33:1-2; 34:4-6,8.

4QDeut[m,o,p]   Duncan, J. A. has revealed that she has three other fragmentary texts of 4QDeut to edit and publish. They contain the following verses: 4QDeut[m]: Deut 3:18-21; 4:32-33; 7:19-22. 4QDeut[o]: Deut 4:31-34; 5:1-3,8-9; 28:15-18,33-35,47-49,51-52,58-62; 29:22-25. 4QDeut[p]: Deut 6:4-6,8-10.

4QDeut[n]   Cross, F. M., *SWDS*, 20, 31-32. The "All Souls Deuteronomy Scroll" (on p. 20 it bears the siglum 4QDeut[m]! This is incorrect, as F. M. Cross has informed me); cf. H. Stegemann, "Weitere Stücke von 4QpPsalm 37, von 4Q Patriarchal Blessings, und Hinweis auf eine unedierte Handschrift aus Höhle 4Q mit Exzerpten aus dem Deuteronomium," *RevQ* 6 (1967-69) 193-227, esp. 217-27 (= Deut 5:1-6:1; 8:5-10)

4QDeut^q	Skehan, P. W., "A Fragment of the 'Song of Moses' (Deut 32) from Qumran," *BASOR* 136 (1954) 12-15; "The Qumran Manuscripts and Textual Criticism," *Volume du congrès, Strasbourg 1956* (VTSup 4; Leiden: Brill, 1957) 148-60, esp. 150 n. 1 (= Deut 32:37-43)
4QJudg^a	Trebolle Barrera, J., "Light from 4QJudg^a and 4QKgs^a on the Text of Judges and Kings," *Forty Years of Research in the Dead Sea Scrolls* (Haifa Congress; in press, 1990) (= Judg 6:2-6,11-13)
4QSam^a	Cross, F. M., "A New Qumran Biblical Fragment Related to the Original Hebrew Underlying the Septuagint," *BASOR* 132 (1953) 15-26; cf. *SWDS*, 14, 24-25; *ALQ*, 188-89 n. 40a; 191 n. 45; P. W. Skehan, *BA* 28 (1965) 96 (= 1 Sam 1:22b-2:6; 2:16-25); F. M. Cross, "The Ammonite Oppression of the Tribes of Gad and Reuben: Missing Verses from 1 Samuel 11 Found in 4QSamuel^a," *History, Historiography and Interpretation: Studies in Biblical and Cuneiform Literature* (ed. H. Tadmor and M. Weinfeld; Jerusalem: Magnes, 1983) 148-58. See E. C. Ulrich, *The Qumran Text of Samuel and Josephus* (HSM 19; Missoula, MT: Scholars, 1978); on p. 271 Ulrich lists the texts found in 4QSam^a in fragmentary form: 1 Sam 1:11-13,22-28; 2:1-6,8-11,13-36; 3:1-4,18-20; 4:9-12; 5:8-12; 6:1-7,12-13,16-18,20-21; 7:1; 8:9-20; 9:6-8,11-12,16-24; 10:3-18,25-27; 11:1,7-12; 12:7-8,14-19; 14:24-25,28-34,47-51; 15:24-32; 17:3-6; 24:4-5,8-9,14-23; 25:3-12,20-21,25-26,39-40; 26:10-12,21-23; 27:8-12; 28:1-2,22-25; 30:28-31; 31:2-4. 2 Sam 2:5-16,25-27,29-32; 3:1-8,23-29; 4:1-4,9-12; 5:1-16 [omitted 5:4-5]; 6:2-9,12-18; 7:23-29; 8:2-8; 10:4-7,18-19; 11:2-12,16-20; 12:4-5,8-9,13-20,30-31; 13:1-6,13-34,36-39; 14:1-3,18-19; 15:1-6,27-31; 16:1-2,11-13,17-18,21-23; 18:2-7,9-11; 19:7-12; 20:2-3,9-14,23-26; 21:1-2,4-6,15-17; 22:30-51; 23:1-6; 24:16-20.

4QSam^b   Cross, F. M., "The Oldest Manuscripts from Qumran," *JBL* 74 (1955) 147-72, esp. 165-72 (= 1 Sam 16:1-11; 19:10-17; 21:3-10; 23:9-17); cf. *ALQ* (1958 ed.), photograph opposite p. 101.

4QSam^c   Ulrich, E. C., "4QSam^c: A Fragmentary Manuscript of 2 Samuel 14-15 from the Scribe of the *Serek Hayyahad* (1QS)," *BASOR* 235 (1979) 1-25 (+ pls. 4-5). Cf. F. M. Cross, *IEJ* 16 (1966) 83; = 1 Sam 25:30-32; 2 Sam 14:7-21; 14:22-15:4,4-15.

4QSam^a,b,c   (Cross, F. M.), "Textual Notes" on 1-2 Samuel in Variants   *The New American Bible* (Paterson, NJ: St. Anthony Guild, 1970) 342-51 (this edition must be consulted because the textual notes are not always reproduced in other printings of the *NAB*). The variants have been used in the textual notes on 1-2 Samuel by P. K. McCarter, Jr., *I Samuel: A New Translation with Introduction, Notes & Commentary; II Samuel: A New Translation with Introduction, Notes & Commentary* (AB 8-9; Garden City, NY: Doubleday, 1980, 1984).

4QKgs^a   Trebolle Barrera, J., "Light from 4QJudg^a and 4QKings^a on the Text of Judges and Kings," *Forty Years of Research in the Dead Sea Scrolls* (Haifa Congress; in press, 1990) (= 1 Kgs 7:31-41; 8:1-9,16-18)

4QTob ar^a-d   Milik, J. T., "La patrie de Tobie," *RB* 73 (1966) 522-
4QTob hebr   30, esp. 522 n. 3, where Milik gives the list of passages in Tobit which are present in 4QTob ar^a-d and 4QTob hebr, but none of the texts. Cf. J. T. Milik, *BE*, 163, 186, 191, 197; *Dédicaces faites par des dieux (Palmyre, Hatra, Tyr) et des thiases sémitiques à l'époque romaine* (Institut français de Beyrouth, Bibl. archéol. et histor. 92; Paris: Geuthner, 1972) 149, 199, 210, 379, 384-85. 4QTob ar^a contains parts of Tob 1:17; 1:19-2:2,3; 3:5,9-15,17; 4:2-3,5-7; 4:21-5:1; 5:3,9; 6:6-8,13,15-28; 6:18-7:6,13; 12:18-22; 13:4-6,6-12; 13:12-14:3,7. 4QTob ar^b: parts of Tob 3:6-8; 4:21-

5:1,12-14; 5:19-6:12,12-18; 6:18-7:10; 8:17-19;
8:21-9:4. 4QTob ar^c: parts of Tob 14:2-6,8-11.
4QTob ar^d: parts of Tob 7:11; 14:10. 4QTob
hebr: parts of Tob 3:6,10-11; 4:3-9; 5:2; 10:7-9;
11:10-14; 12:20-13:4,13-14; 13:18-14:2.

4QpaleoJob^c   Skehan, P. W., *RB* 63 (1956) 49-67; cf. M. D.
McLean, *The Use and Development of Paleo-
Hebrew in the Hellenistic and Roman Period*
(Cambridge, MA: Dissertation, Harvard
University, 1982; Ann Arbor, MI: University
Microfilms, 1982 [order #DA82-22670]) 44, 47-
52 (= Job 13:19-20,24-27; 14:13-17)

4QPs^a-q   Sanders, J. A., *DSPS*, 143-55 (Appendix II: "Pre-
Masoretic Psalter Texts" — a catalogue and an
index of all the Qumran, Maṣada, and Ḥever
psalm-texts, in which one can quickly find
where a frg. of a given psalm may be found)

4QPs^a-s   Skehan, P. W., *DBSup* 9. 816: a list of all the psalter
mss. from 4Q and the canonical and
apocryphal psalms that they contain. See also
his article, "Qumran and Old Testament
Criticism," *Qumrân: Sa piété, sa théologie et son
milieu* (BETL 46; ed. M. Delcor; Gembloux:
Duculot; Louvain: Leuven University, 1978)
163-82: it contains a collation of 4Q psalms
texts against *BHS*. Cf. G. H. Wilson, *The Editing
of the Hebrew Psalter* (SBLDS 76; Chico, CA:
Scholars, 1985).

4QPs^a   Skehan, P.W., *DBSup* 9. 814; reported to contain
Ps 5:9-13; 6:1-4; 25:15; 31:23-25 + 33:1-12 (with
Ps 32 omitted); 34:22 + 35:2; 35:13-20,26-29;
36:1-9; 38:2-12,16-23 + 71:1-14; 47:2; 53:4-7; 54:1-
6; 56:4; 62:13(?) + 63:2-4; 66:16-20; 67:1-8; 69:1-
19; 74:1-14.

4QPs^b   Skehan, P. W., "A Psalm Manuscript from
Qumran (4QPs^b)," *CBQ* 26 (1964) 313-22; cf.
SWDS, 20, 30-31; *DBSup* 9. 814 (= Ps 91:5-8,12-
15; 92:4-8,13-15; 94:1-4,8-9,10-14,17-18,21-22;
96:2; 98:4; 99:5-6; 100:1-2; 102:10-29; 103:1-6,9-

14,20-21; 112:4-5; 115:2-3; 116:17-19; 118:1-3,6-11,18-20,23-26,29)

4QPs^c Skehan, P. W., "Qumran and Old Testament Criticism," 180-81; *DBSup* 9. 814 (= Ps 16:7-9; 17:1(?); 18:3-4,16-17,33-41; 27:12-14; 28:1-4; 35:27-28; 37:18-19; 42:5; 45:8-11; 49:1-17; 50:14-23; 51:1-5; 52:6-11; 53:1)

4QPs^d Skehan, P. W., "Qumran and Old Testament Criticism," 180-81; *DBSup* 9. 814 (= Ps 104:1-5,8-11,14-15,22-25,33-35; 106:48[?] [before 147]; 147:1-4,13-17,20)

4QPs^e Skehan, P. W., "Qumran and Old Testament Criticism," 180-82; *DBSup* 9. 815 (= Ps 76:10-12; 77:1; 78:6-7,31-33; 81:2-3; 86:10-11; 88:1-5; 89:44-47,50-53; 104:0 [refrain],1-3,20-22; 105:1-3,23-25,33-35; 109:1[?],8[?],13; 115:15-18; 116:1-3; 120:6; 125:2-5; 126:1-5; 129:8 + 130:1-6)

4QPs^f Starcky, J., "Psaumes apocryphes de la grotte 4 de Qumrân (4QPs^f VII-X)," *RB* 73 (1966) 353-71 (+ pl. XVIII); see P. W. Skehan, *DBSup* 9. 814; "Qumran and Old Testament Criticism," 166 (= Ps 22:15-17; 107:2-5,8-11,13-16,18-19,22-30,35-42; 109:4-6,24-28 + "Apostrophe to Zion" [see 11QPs^a 22] and two non-canonical compositions)

4QPs^g Skehan, P. W., "Qumran and Old Testament Criticism," 180-82; *DBSup* 9. 815 (= Ps 119:37-43,44-46,49-50,73-74,81-83,90-92)

4QPs^h Skehan, P. W., "Qumran and Old Testament Criticism," 180-82; *DBSup* 9. 815 (= Ps 119:10-21)

4QPs^j Skehan, P. W., "Qumran and Old Testament Criticism," 180-82; *DBSup* 9. 815 (= Ps 48:1-7; 49:6[?],9-12,15[?],17[?]; 51:3-5)

4QPs^k Skehan, P. W., "Qumran and Old Testament Criticism," 166, 180-82; *DBSup* 9. 815 (= Ps 99:1-5[?]; 135:7-16)

4QPs^l Skehan, P. W., "Qumran and Old Testament Criticism," 180-82; *DBSup* 9. 815 (= Ps 104:3-5,11-12)

4QPs^m	Skehan, P.W., "Qumran and Old Testament Criticism," 180-82; *DBSup* 9. 815 (= Ps 93:3-5; 95:3-7; 97:6-9; 98:4-8)
4QPs^n	Skehan, P. W., "Qumran and Old Testament Criticism," 166, 180-82; *DBSup* 9. 815 (= Ps 135:6-8,11-12 + 136:22-23)
4QPs^o	Skehan, P. W., "Qumran and Old Testament Criticism," 180-82; *DBSup* 9. 815 (= Ps 114:7-8; 115:1-4; 116:5-10)
4QPs^p	Skehan, P. W., "Qumran and Old Testament Criticism," 180-82; *DBSup* 9. 815 (= Ps 143:3-4,6-8)
4QPs^q	Milik, J. T., "Deux documents inédits du Désert de Juda," *Bib* 38 (1957) 245-68, esp. 245-55 (+ pl. I); cf. P. W. Skehan, "Qumran and Old Testament Criticism," 180-82; *DBSup* 9. 815 (= Ps 31:24-25 + 33:1-18 [Ps 32 omitted]; 35:4-20)
4QPs^r	Skehan, P. W., "Qumran and Old Testament Criticism," 180-82; *DBSup* 9. 815 (= Ps 26:7-12; 27:1; 30:9-13)
4QPs^s	Skehan, P. W., "Qumran and Old Testament Criticism," 180-82; *DBSup* 9. 815; "Gleanings from Psalm Texts from Qumrân," *Mélanges bibliques et orientaux en l'honneur de M. Henri Cazelles* (AOAT 212; Kevelaer: Butzen & Bercker, 1981) 439-52, esp. 445-48 (= Ps 5:8-13; 6:1; 88:15-17)
4QPs89	Milik, J. T., "Fragment d'une source du psautier (4Q Ps 89) et fragments des Jubilés, du Document de Damas, d'un phylactère dans la grotte 4 de Qumrân," *RB* 73 (1966) 94-106, esp. 95-98 (+ pl. I) (= Ps 89:20-22,26,23,27-28,31) (4Q236). Cf. P. W. Skehan, "Gleanings," 439-45.
4QPs122	Puech, E., "Fragments du Psaume 122 dans un manuscrit hébreu de la grotte iv," *RevQ* 9 (1977-78) 547-54 (part of Ps 122:1-9).
4QProv^a	Skehan, P. W., *RB* 63 (1956) 59 (= Prov 1:27-2:1 + parts of chaps. 14-15)

4QQoh^a	Muilenburg, J., "A Qoheleth Scroll from Qumran," *BASOR* 135 (1954) 20-28 (= Qoh 5:13-17; 6:3-8; 7:7-9)
4QIsa^a	Muilenburg, J., "Fragments of Another Qumran Isaiah Scroll," *BASOR* 135 (1954) 28-32 (= Isa 12:5-13:6; 22:13d-23:6a). The frgs. are now known to contain parts of Isa 1:1-3; 2:7-10; 4:5-6; 6:4-7; 11:12-15; 12:4-6; 13:1-16; 17:4-14; 19:24-25; 20:1-6; 21:1-2,4-16; 22:13-25; 23:1-12.
4QIsa^c	Skehan, P. W., "The Text of Isaias at Qumran," *CBQ* 17 (1955) (158)-(163)
4QIsa^{a,c}	Flint, P. W., "The Septuagint Version of Isaiah 23:1-14 and the Massoretic Text," *BIOSCS* 21 (1988) 35-54.
4QJer^a	Cross, F. M., *ALQ* (1958 ed.), 33. See now E. Tov, "The Jeremiah Scrolls from Cave 4," (Groningen meeting; Groningen: Qumrân Instituut, 1990). The frgs. contain parts of Jer 7:28-8:11,12,19; 9:1-[3],7-15; 10:9-14; 11:3-6; 12:3-6,13-16; 12:17-13:7; 14:4-7; 15:1-2; 17:8-26; 18:15-19:1; 22:4-16
4QJer^b	Cross, F. M., *ALQ* (1961 ed.), 187 (transliteration only of Jer 10:4,9,11).
4QJer^{a,b}	Janzen, J. G., *Studies in the Text of Jeremiah* (HSM 6; Cambridge, MA: Harvard University, 1973) 173-84 (Appendix D: "Hebrew Texts of Jeremiah from Qumran" (Jer^a = Jer 7:29-9:2; 9:7-14; 10:9-14; 11:3-6; 12:3-6; 12:17-13:7; 14:4-7; 15:1-2; 17:8-26; 18:15-19:1; 22:4-16. Jer^b = Jer 9:22-10:18; 43:3-9; 50:4-6). See E. Tov, "The Jeremiah Scrolls from Cave 4," (Groningen meeting; Groningen: Qumrân Instituut, 1990). Tov distinguishes 4QJer^b into three mss.: 4QJer^b (= Jer 9:21-10:22[?]); 4QJer^d (= Jer 43:2-10); 4QJer^e (= Jer 50:4-6)
4QJer^c	Tov, E., "Some Aspects of the Textual and Literary History of the Book of Jeremiah," *Le livre de Jérémie: Le prophète et son milieu* (BETL 54; ed. P.-M. Bogaert; Louvain: Peeters/Leuven

University, 1981) 146-67 (parts of Jeremiah 8, 19-22, 25-27, 30-33).

4QLam[a]   Cross, F. M., "Studies in the Structure of Hebrew Verse: The Prosody of Lamentations 1:1-22," *The Word of the Lord Shall Go Forth: Essays in Honor of David Noel Freedman in Celebration of His Sixtieth Birthday* (Winona Lake, IN: Eisenbrauns, 1983) 129-55 (= Lam 1:1-6,6-10,10-16).

4QEzek[a,b]   Lust, J., "Ezekiel Manuscripts in Qumran: Preliminary Edition of 4QEz a and b," *Ezekiel and His Book: Textual and Literary Criticism and Their Interrelation* (BETL 74; ed. J. Lust; Louvain: Peeters/Leuven University, 1986) 90-100. Photograph in W. Zimmerli, *Ezekiel* (Hermeneia; 2 vols.; Philadelphia: Fortress, 1979, 1983). See L. A. Sinclair, *RevQ* 14 (1989) 99-105; E. Puech, "Note additionnelle," ibid., 107-8. 4QEzek[a] contains parts of Ezek 10:5-15; 10:17-11:11; 23:14-18,44-47; 41:3-6. 4QEzek[b] contains parts of Ezek 1:10,11-12,13,16-17,20-24.

4QXII[a-f]   Fuller, R. E., *The Minor Prophets Manuscripts from Qumrân, Cave IV* (Cambridge, MA: Dissertation, Harvard University, 1988; Ann Arbor, MI: University Microfilms, 1988 [order #DA89-01676]). The seventh manuscript (4QXII[g]) will be published separately. Cf. F. M. Cross, *RB* 63 (1956) 57; *ALQ* (1961 ed.), 164.

4QXII[c]   Cross, F. M., *RB* 63 (1956) 57: he speaks of it as containing parts of Hosea, Joel, Amos, Zephaniah, and Malachi.

4QXII[d]   Cross, F. M., *RB* 63 (1956) 57: parts of Hosea. See L. A. Sinclair, "A Qumran Biblical Fragment: Hosea 4QXII[d] (Hosea 1:7-2:5)," *BASOR* 239 (1980) 61-65; photograph in H. W. Wolff, *Hosea: A Commentary on the Book of the Prophet Hosea* (tr. G. Stansell; Hermeneia; Philadelphia: Fortress, 1974) v; cf. G.-W. Nebe, "Ein neue Hosea-Handschrift aus Höhle 4 von Qumran," *ZAW* 91 (1979) 292-94.

4QXII[e]   Cross, F. M., *RB* 63 (1956) 57: parts of Zechariah.

4QXII[f]   Cross, F. M., *RB* 63 (1956) 57: parts of Jonah.

4QXII[g]   Skehan, P. W., *RB* 63 (1956) 59

4QXII?   Testuz, M., "Deux fragments inédits des manuscrits de la Mer Morte," *Sem* 5 (1955) 37-38 (= Hos 13:15b-14:1a,3-6)

4QDan[a]   Ulrich, E., "Daniel Manuscripts from Qumran. Part 1: A Preliminary Edition of 4QDan[a]," *BASOR* 268 (1987) 17-37. 4QDan[a] contains 4Q112 with fragmentary texts of Dan 1:16-20; 2:9-11,19-49; 3:1-2; 4:29-30; 5:5-7,12-14,16-19; 7:5-7,25-28; 8:1-5; 10:16-20; 11:13-16. Cf. F. M. Cross, *RB* 63 (1956) 58.

4QDan[b,c]   Ulrich, E., "Daniel Manuscripts from Qumran. Part 2: Preliminary Editions of 4QDan[b] and 4QDan[c]," *BASOR* 274 (1989) 3-26 (PAM 43.083, 43.080). 4QDan[b] contains 4Q113 with fragmentary texts of Dan 5:10-12,14-16,19-22; 6:8-21,27-29; 7:1-6,11(?),26-28; 8:1-8,13-16. 4QDan[c] contains 4Q114 with fragmentary texts of Dan 10:5-9,11-16,21; 11:1-2,13-17,25-29. Cf. S. P. Jeansonne, *The Old Greek Translation of Daniel 7-12* (CBQMS 19; Washington, DC: Catholic Biblical Association of America, 1988).

4QDanSus ar   Milik, J. T., "Daniel et Susanne à Qumrân ?" *De la Tôrah au Messie: Etudes d'exégèse et d'herméneutique bibliques offertes à Henri Cazelles* ... (ed. M. Carrez et al.; Paris: Desclée, 1981) 337-59 (with photo of PAM 43.594 on p. 355).

4QLXXLev[a]   Skehan, P. W., "The Qumran Manuscripts and Textual Criticism," *Volume du Congrès, Strasbourg 1956* (VTSup 4; Leiden: Brill, 1957) 148-60, esp. 159-60 (+ pl.); cf. *SWDS*, 15, 25 (= Lev 26:2-16) (4Q119)

4QLXXLev[b]   Skehan, P. W., "The Qumran Manuscripts," VTSup 4, 157-58 (4Q120). Cf. E. Ulrich, "The Greek Manuscripts of the Pentateuch from Qumrân, Including Newly-Identified Fragments of Deuteronomy (4QLXXDeut)," *De Septuaginta: Studies in Honour of John William*

Wevers on His Sixty-fifth Birthday (ed. A. Pietersma and C. Cox; Mississauga, Ont.: Benben, 1984) 71-82, esp. 71-72, 79-80 (= Lev 2:3-5,7; 3:4,9-13; 4:4-8,10-11,18-20,26-29; 5:8-10,18-24; 6:2-4)

4QLXXNum   Skehan, P. W., "4QLXXNum: A Pre-Christian Reworking of the Septuagint," *HTR* 70 (1977) 39-50 (= Num 3:40-42,50-51[?]; 4:1,[2-4],5-9,[10],11-16); cf. "The Qumran Manuscripts," VTSup 4, 155-57; see the photograph in *BA* 28 (1965) 91 (4Q121)

4QLXXDeut   Ulrich, E., "The Greek Manuscripts of the Pentateuch from Qumrân" (see above), 71-82 (4Q122) (= Deut 11:4 + frgs.)

pap4QparExod gr   Ulrich, E., "A Greek Paraphrase of Exodus on Papyrus from Qumran Cave 4," *Festschrift Robert Hanhart* (Göttingen: Vandenhoeck & Ruprecht, 1990).

(2) *Phylacteries* (Detailed Listing of 4Q128-4Q157 in DJD 6)

4Q128	4Qphyl^a (*olim* 4Qphyl^c)	Vaux, R. de and J. T. Milik, *Qumrân Grotte 4, II: I. Archéologie; II. Tefillin, mezuzot et targums (4Q128—4Q157)* (DJD 6; Oxford: Clarendon, 1977): "Phylactère A," 48-51 (+ pls. VII-VIII). See also K. G. Kuhn, *Phylakterien aus Höhle 4 von Qumran* (Abhandlungen der Heidelberger Akademie der Wissenschaften, Philos.-hist. Kl., 1957/1; Heidelberg: C. Winter, 1957) 15-16 (Deut 5:1-14; 5:27-6:3; 10:12-11:17 [recto]; Deut 11:18-21; Exod 12:43-13:7 [verso])
4Q129	4Qphyl^b	"Phylactère B," 51-52 (+ pl. IX); also K. G. Kuhn, *Phylakterien*, 11-15 (Deut 5:1-6:5 [recto]; Exod 13:9-16 [verso])
4Q130	4Qphyl^c	"Phylactère C," 53-55 (+ pls. X-XI) (Exod 13:1-16; Deut 6:4-9; 11:13-21)
4Q131	4Qphyl^d	"Phylactère D-F," 56 (+ pl. XII) (Deut 11:13-21)
4Q132	4Qphyl^e	"Phylactère D-F," 56-57 (+ pl. XIII) (Exod 13:1-10)
4Q133	4Qphyl^f	"Phylactère D-F," 57 (+ pl. XIV) (Exod 13:11-16)
4Q134	4Qphyl^g	"Phylactère G-I," 58-60 (+ pl. XV) (Deut 5:1-21 [recto]; Exod 13:11-12 [verso])
4Q135	4Qphyl^h (*olim* 4Qphyl^d)	"Phylactère G-I," 60-62 (+ pl. XVI); see also K. G. Kuhn, *Phylakterien*, 16-20 (Deut 5:22-6:5 [recto]; Exod 13:14-16 [verso])
4Q136	4Qphylⁱ	"Phylactères G-I," 62-63 (+ pl. XVII); see also J. T. Milik, "Fragment d'une source du Psautier (4QPs 89) et fragments des *Jubilés*, du *Document de Damas*, d'un phylactère dans la grotte 4 de Qumrân," *RB* 73 (1966) 94-106, esp. 106 (+ pl. IIb) (Deut

		11:13-21; Exod 12:43-13:10 [recto]; Deut 6:6-7[?] [verso])
4Q137	4Qphyl^j (*olim* 4Qphyl^a)	"Phylactères J-K," 64-67 (+ pls. XVIII-XIX); see also K. G. Kuhn, *Phylakterien*, 5-11 (Deut 5:1-24 [recto]; Deut 5:24-32; 6:2-3 [verso])
4Q138	4Qphyl^k	"Phylactères J-K," 67-69 (+ pl. XX) (Deut 10:12-11:7 [recto]; Deut 11:7-12 [verso])
4Q139	4Qphyl^l	"Phyiactères L-N," 70 (+ pl. XXII) (Deut 5:7-24)
4Q140	4Qphyl^m	"Phylactères L-N," 71-72 (+ pl. XXI) (Exod 12:44-13:10 [recto]; Deut 5:33-6:5 [verso])
4Q141	4Qphylⁿ	"Phylactères L-N," 72-74 (+ pl. XXII) (Deut 32:14-20,32-33)
4A142	4Qphyl^o	"Phylactère O," 74-75 (+ pl. XXII) (Deut 5:1-16 [recto]; Deut 6:7-9 [verso])
4Q143	4Qphyl^p	"Phylactère P," 75-76 (+ pl. XXII) (Deut 10:22-11:3 [recto]; Deut 11:18-21 [verso])
4Q144	4Qphyl^q	"Phylactère Q," 76 (+ pl. XXIII) (Deut 11:4-8 [recto]; Exod 13:4-9 [verso])
4Q145	4Qphyl^r	"Phylactère R," 77-78 (+ pl. XXIII) (Exod 13:1-7 [recto]; Exod 13:7-10 [verso])
4Q146	4Qphyl^s	"Phylactère S," 78 (+ pl. XXIII) (Deut 11:19-21)
4Q147	4Qphyl^t	"Phylactères T-U," 79 (+ pl. XXIV) (could not be unrolled)
4Q148	4Qphyl^u	"Phylactères T-U," 79 (+ pl. XXV) (?)
	(3) *Mezuzot*	
4Q149	4Qmez^a	"Mezuza A," 80-81 (+ pl. XXVI) (Exod 20:7-12 [cf. Deut 5:11-16])
4Q150	4Qmez^b	"Mezuza B," 81 (+ pl. XXVI) (Deut 6:5-6; 10:14-11:2)
4Q151	4Qmez^c	"Mezuza C," 82-83 (+ pl. XXVII) (Deut 5:27-6:9; 10:12-30)

4Q152	4Qmez^d	"Mezuza D," 83 (+ pl. XXVI) (Deut 5:6-7)
4Q153	4Qmez^e	"Mezuza E," 83 (+ pl. XXVI) (Deut 11:17-18)
4Q154	4Qmez^f	"Mezuza F," 83-84 (+ pl. XXVI) (Exod 13:1-4)
4Q155	4Qmez^g	"Mezuza G," 84-85 (+ pl. XXV) (Exod 13:11-16)

(4) *Targumim*

4Q156	4QtgLev	"Targum du Lévitique," 86-89 (+ pl. XXVIII); see also appendix (M. M. Kasher), 92-93 (Lev 16:12-15,18-21)
4Q157	4QtgJob	"Targum de Job," 90 (+ pl. XXVIII) (Job 3:5-9; 4:16-5:4)

(5) *Pesharim*

4Q158-186 Allegro, J. M. (with the collaboration of A. A. Anderson), *Qumrân Cave 4,I (4Q158-4Q186)* (DJD 5; Oxford: Clarendon, 1968). This publication must be used with caution. Some frgs. have not been properly identified or joined; many readings are questionable; the numbering of plates is confusing; the secondary literature on the fifteen texts in it that were previously published in partial or preliminary form has normally been neglected. Essential for further work on these texts are the following: J. Strugnell, "Notes en marge du volume V des 'Discoveries in the Judaean Desert of Jordan,'" *RevQ* 7 (1969-71) 163-276; J. A. Fitzmyer, "A Bibliographical Aid to the Study of Qumrân Cave IV Texts 158-86," *CBQ* 31 (1969) 59-71. The preliminary publications are listed below; for the biblical passages on which these pesharim comment, see the detailed listing further on, p. 62. Criticism of this volume has been severe: "Überhaupt ist DJD V die schlechteste und unzuverlässigste Q-Edition, die seit dem Beginn der Funde dem Leser zugemutet wurde" (K. Müller, "Die Handschriften" [see chapter V below] 310). "'R' habet italicum liber hic, habet atque Pelasgum, Necnon hebraeum, praetereaque nihil!" (J. Strugnell, *RevQ* 7 [1969-71] 276; cf. *America* 123 [26 Sept. 1970] 207).

4QpIsa[a] Allegro, J. M., "Further Messianic References in Qumran Literature," *JBL* 75 (1956) 174-87, esp. 177-82 (Document III, 4 frgs., pls. II-III); DJD 5. 11-15; pls. IV-V (4Q161). Pesher on Isa 10:20-21,22,24-27,28-32,33-34; 11:1-5

4QpIsa[b] Allegro, J. M., "More Isaiah Commentaries from Qumran's Fourth Cave," *JBL* 77 (1958) 215-21, esp. 215-18 (+ pl. 1); DJD 5. 15-17; pl. VI (4Q162). Pesher on Isa 5:5-6,11-14,24-25,29-30; 6:9(?)

pap4QpIsa^c

Allegro, J. M., "More Isaiah Commentaries," *JBL* 77 (1958) 218-20 (+ pl. 2); DJD 5. 17-27; pls. VII-VIII (4Q**163**). Pesher on Isa 8:7-8,9(?); 9:11(?), 14-20; 10:12-13,19(?),20-24; 14:8,26-30; 19:9-12; 29:10-11,15-16,19-23; Zech 11:11; Isa 30:1-5,15-18; Hos 6:9; Isa 30:19-21; 31:1; 32:5-6. Cf. M. Baillet, "Groupe en petite écriture," DJD 7. 299-300 (4Q**515**)

4QpIsa^d

Allegro, J. M., "More Isaiah Commentaries," *JBL* 77 (1958) 220-21 (+ pl. 3); DJD 5. 27-28; pl. IX (3 frgs., upper) (4Q**164**). Pesher on Isa 54:11-12.

4QpIsa^e

Allegro, J. M., DJD 5. 28-30; pl. IX (10 frgs., lower) (4Q**165**). Pesher on Isa 1:1(?); 40:12; 14:19; 15:4-6; 21:2(?),11-15; 32:5-7.

4QpHos^a (*olim* 4QpHos^b)

Allegro, J. M., "A Recently Discovered Fragment of a Commentary on Hosea from Qumran's Fourth Cave," *JBL* 78 (1959) 142-47; DJD 5. 31-32; pl. X (4Q**166**). Pesher on Hos 2:8-9,10-14

4QpHos^b (*olim* 4QpHos^a)

Allegro, J. M., "Further Light on the History of the Qumran Sect," *JBL* 75 (1956) 89-95, esp. 93 (+ pl. 2); DJD 5. 32-36; pls. X-XI (4Q**167**). Pesher on Hos 5:13-15; 6:4,7,9-10; 8:6-7,13-14.

4QpMic(?)

Allegro, J. M., DJD 5. 36; pl. XII (4 frgs., upper left) (4Q**168**). Pesher on Mic 4:8-12.

4QpNah

Allegro, J. M., "Further Light," *JBL* 75 (1956) 90-93 (+ pl. 1); "More Unpublished Pieces of a Qumran Commentary on Nahum (4QpNah)," *JSS* 7 (1962) 304-8; cf. *SWDS*, 17, 26-27; DJD 5. 37-42; pls. XII (upper right and lower frgs.), XIII, XIV (upper frgs.) (4Q**169**). Pesher on Nah 1:3-6; 2:12-14; 3:1-5,6-9,10-12,14.

4QpZeph

Allegro, J. M., DJD 5. 42; pl. XIV (center) (4Q**170**). Pesher on Zeph 1:12-13.

4QpPs^a (*olim* 4QpPs 37)

Allegro, J. M., "A Newly Discovered Fragment of a Commentary on Psalm XXXVII," *PEQ* 86 (1954) 69-75; "Further Light," *JBL* 75 (1956) 94-95 (+ pl. 4); *The People of the Dead Sea Scrolls in Text and Pictures* (Garden City, NY: Doubleday, 1958) 86-87 (pls. 48, 50); DJD 5. 42-51; pls. XIV (lower frgs.), XV, XVI, XVII (4Q**171**). Pesher on

	Ps 37:7,8-19a,19b-26,28c-40; 45:1-2; 60:8-9 (108:8-9). Cf. H. Stegemann, "Der Pešer Psalm 37 aus Höhle 4 von Qumran (4Q p Ps 37)," *RevQ* 4 (1963-64) 235-70; "Weitere Stücke von 4QpPsalm 37,...," *RevQ* 6 (1967-69) 193-210.
4QpPs[b]	Allegro, J. M., DJD 5. 51-53; pl. XVIII (5 frgs., center) (4Q**173**). Pesher on Ps 127:2-3,5; 129:7-8; 118:26-27(?).
4QpUnid	Allegro, J. M., DJD 5. 50-51; pl. XVIII (14 frgs., upper) (4Q**172**) [an unidentified pesher] Cf. M. P. Horgan, *Pesharim: Qumran Interpretations of Biblical Books* (CBQMS 8; Washington, DC: Catholic Biblical Association, 1979)

(4) *Apocryphal and Sectarian Texts*

4QAdmon	Newsom, C. A., "4Q**370**: An Admonition Based on the Flood," *RevQ* 13 (Mémorial Jean Carmignac, 1988) 23-43 (+ pl. I, PAM 42.506). This text is related to 4Q**185** 1-2 i 13 - ii 3.
4QAgesCreat	Allegro, J. M., "Some Unpublished Fragments of Pseudepigraphical Literature from Qumran's Fourth Cave," ALUOS 4 (1962-63) 3-5; DJD 5. 77-80; pls. XXVII (5 frgs., upper), XVIII (3 frgs., lower) (4Q**180-81**). See J. T. Milik, "Milkî-ṣedeq et Milkî-rešaᶜ dans les anciens écrits juifs et chrétiens," *JJS* 23 (1972) 95-144, esp. 109-26; also J. T. Milik, *BE*, 248-53 (4QBook of Periods). Cf. D. Dimant, "The 'Pesher on the Periods' (4Q180) and 4Q181," *IOS* 9 (1979) 77-102.
4QAh ar	Starcky, J., "Les quatre étapes du messianisme à Qumrân," *RB* 70 (1963) 492
4QᶜAmram[a-e]	Milik, J. T., "4Q Visions de ᶜAmram et une citation d'Origène," *RB* 79 (1972) 77-97, esp. 78-92 (+ pl. I [= 4QᶜAmram[b]]; cf. J. A. Fitzmyer, *ESBNT*, 101-4.
pap4QAp ar	Baillet, M., "Un apocryphe en araméen," DJD 7 .10 (4Q**488**)
4QapLam[a]	Allegro, J. M., "Lamentations," DJD 5. 75-77; pl. XXVI (upper) (4Q**179**) (N.B. This is not a copy

of canonical Lamentations; it is now labelled
4QapLam^a in view of the following text.)

4QapLam^b   Baillet, M., "Lamentation," DJD 7. 79-80 (4Q501; it
is labelled 4QapLam^b because of the preceding
text)

4QapPs   Schuller, E. M., *Non-Canonical Psalms from
Qumran: A Pseudepigraphic Collection* (HSS 28;
Atlanta, GA: Scholars, 1986). Text, translation,
and commentary on 4Q380 and 4Q381 (PAM
43.224-26, 43.362)

pap4QApoc ar   Baillet, M., "Un apocalyptique en araméen (?),"
DJD 7. 10-11 (4Q489); see also 4Q490, "Groupe
de fragments à rapprocher du précédent (?)."

4QApocWeeks   Milik, J. T., *BE*, 256: The Apocalypse of Weeks
(4Q247): related to Enochic literature.

4QAstrCrypt   Milik, J. T., *BE*, 68-69 (4Q317): Astronomic cryptic
text in Hebrew, 1 ii 2-14

4QBeat   Puech, E., "Un hymne essénien en partie retrouvé
et les béatitudes: 1QH V 12-VI 18 (= col. XIII-
XIV 7) et 4QBéat.," *RevQ* 13 (Mémorial Jean
Carmignac, 1988) 59-88, esp. 84-87. Cf. J.
Starcky, *RB* 63 (1956) 67.

4QBen   Baillet, M., "Bénédiction," DJD 7. 78-79 (4Q500).
Cf. J. M. Baumgarten, "4Q500 and the Ancient
Exegesis of the Lord's Vineyard," *JJS* 40 (1989)
1-6.

4QBer^{a,b}   Milik, J. T., "Milkî-ṣedeq et Milkî-reša' dans les
anciens écrits juifs et chrétiens," *JJS* 23 (1972)
95-144, esp. 130-35 (+ pl. II) (4Q286, 4Q287). G.
Vermes (*DSSE*, 160) labels these texts "Curses
of Satan and His Lot." Milik reveals that there
are probably three other copies of this text.

4QBibPar   Allegro, J. M., "Biblical Paraphrase: Genesis,
Exodus," DJD 5. 1-6; pl. I (4Q158)

4QBookPeriods   Milik, J. T., "Book of Periods," *BE*, 248-53 (cf.
4Q180-81 [4QAgesCreat]); cf. J. T. Milik,
"Milkî-ṣedeq et Milkî-reša'," *JJS* 23 (1972) 95-
144, esp. 109-24, 138.

4QCatena^a Allegro, J. M., "Catena (A)," DJD 5. 67-74; pls. XXIV-XXV (upper) (4Q**177**) [apocalyptic view of a victory of the community)

4QCatena^b Allegro, J. M., "Catena (B)," DJD 5. 80-81; pls. XXVII (2 frgs., lower) (4Q**182**)

4QCryptic Allegro, J. M., "An Astrological Cryptic Document from Qumran," *JSS* 9 (1964) 291-94; DJD 5. 88-91; pl. XXXI (4Q**186**). (Possibly related to Enoch literature; see J. T. Milik, *HTR* 64 [1971] 366)

4QD^a (*olim* 4QD^b) Milik J. T., "Fragment d'une source," *RB* 73 (1966) 103, 105 (+ pl. III) (A part of the Damascus Document that is not in CD, but that is found in three other copies of 4QD. Milik here calls it 4Q**226**, but in the following entry it is listed as 4Q**266** [typographical error or change of siglum?]. 4QD^a 1 xvii 1-16 contains halakhah related to Leviticus 13 and 15). See J. T. Milik, *Ten Years*, 38-39, 58, 103, 124-25; DJD 3. 181, 226; cf. "Numérotation des feuilles des rouleaux dans le scriptorium de Qumrân," *Sem* 27 (1977) 75-81, esp. 79 (text of 1 i 5-24).

4QD^{b,e} Milik, J. T., "Milkî-ṣedeq et Milkî-rešaʿ," *JJS* 23 (1972) 134-36 (4Q**266**, 4Q**270**)

4QDibHam^a Baillet, M., "Paroles des luminaires (premier exemplaire: DibHam^a)," DJD 7. 137-68 (+ pls. XLIX-LIII, 4Q**504**). Cf. "Un recueil liturgique de Qumrân, grotte 4: 'Les paroles des luminaires,'" *RB* 68 (1961) 195-250 (+ pls. XXIV-XXVIII); "Remarques sur l'édition des 'paroles des luminaires,'" *RevQ* 5 (1964-66) 23-42; cf. *SWDS*, 18, 28-29.

4QDibHam^b Baillet, M., "Paroles des luminaires (deuxième exemplaire: DibHam^b)," DJD 7. 168-70 (4Q**505**)

pap4QDibHam^c Baillet, M., "Paroles des luminaires (troisième exemplaire: DibHam^c)," DJD 7. 170-75 (4Q**506**)

4QEn^a Milik, J. T., *BE*, 22-41 (The Book of Watchers), 139-63, 340-43 (dipl. trp. of the frgs.) (+ pls. I-V). The frgs. = 1 *Enoch* 1:1-6; 2:1-5:6; 6:4-8:1; 8:3-9:3,6-8; 10:3-4; 10:21-11:1 + 12:4-6.

4QEn^b

Milik, J. T., *BE*, 22-41, 164-78, 344-46 (dipl. trp.) (+ pls. VI-IX). The frgs. = *1 Enoch* 5:9-6:4 + 6:7-8:1; 8:2-9:4; 10:8-12; 14:4-6.

4QEn^c (*olim* 4QHen^b)

Milik, J. T., *BE*, 22-58, 178-217, 346-53 (dipl. trp.) (+ pls. IX-XV). The frgs. = *1 Enoch* 1:9- 5:1; 6:7; 10:13-19 + 12:3; 13:6-14:16; 14:18-20 + 15:11(?); 18:8-12; 30:1-32:1; 35 + 36:1-4; 89:31-37; 104:13-106:2; 106:13-107:2. Frgs. 2-3 of this text = 4QEnGiants^a 9-10 (see *BE*, 316-17). See J. T. Milik, "Hénoch au pays des aromates (ch. xxvii à xxxii): Fragments araméens de la grotte 4 de Qumran," *RB* 65 (1958) 70-77, esp. 70-73, 77 (what was published there as 4QHen^b 1:1-8 is now 4QEn^c 1 xii 23-30; and what was 4QHen^b 2:1-8 is now 4QEn^c 1 xiii 23-30)

4QEn^d

Milik, J. T., *BE*, 22-47, 217-25, 353-55 (dipl. trp.) (+ pls. XVI-XVII). The frgs. = *1 Enoch* 22:13-24:1; 25:7-27:1; 89:11-14,29-31,43-44.

4QEn^e (*olim* 4QHen^d)

Milik, J. T., *BE*, 22-47, 225-44, 355-59 (dipl. trp.) (+ pls. XVIII-XXI). The frgs. = *1 Enoch* 18:15(?); 21:2-4; 22:3-7; 28:3-29:2 + 31:2-32:3,6 + 33:3-34:1; 88:3-89:6,7-16,26-30. Frgs. 2-3 may contain a text which = 4QEnGiants^e (see *BE*, 236-38). Cf. *RB* 65 (1958) 70-77 (what was published there as 4QHen^d 1:1-8 is now 4QEn^e 1 xxvi 14-21).

4QEn^f

Milik, J. T., *BE*, 22-47, 244-45, 359 (dipl. trp.) (+ pl. XXI). The frg. = *1 Enoch* 86:1-3.

4QEn^g

Milik, J. T., *BE*, 47-58 (Epistle of Enoch), 245-72, 360-62 (dipl. trp.) (+ pls. XXI-XXIV). The frgs. = *1 Enoch* 91:10(?) + 91:18-19 + 92:1-2; 92:5-93:4; 93:9-10 + 91:11-17; 93:11-94:2. Cf. J. T. Milik, "Problèmes de la littérature hénochique," *HTR* 64 (1971) 333-78 (passim).

4QEnastr^a (*olim*   Milik, J. T., *BE*, 7-22, 273 (description only of the
   4QHen astr^b)   Astronomical Book; no text of the 36 frgs.
                   supplied; cf. "Problèmes de la littérature
                   hénochique," *HTR* 64 [1971] 333-78; cf. M.
                   Black, "The Fragments of the Aramaic Enoch
                   from Qumran," *La littérature juive entre Tenach
                   et Mischna: Quelques problèmes* [RechBib 9; ed.
                   W. C. van Unnik; Leiden: Brill, 1974) 15-28]).

4QEnastr^b (*olim*   Milik, J. T., *BE*, 7-22, 273-74, 278-84, 288-91, 293-96
   4QHen astr^a)   (+ pls. XXV-XVII, XXX). Some of the frgs. = 1
                   Enoch 76:13-77:4; 78:4,9-12; 79:3-6 + 78:16-79:2;
                   82:2(?),9-13. Cf. *RB* 65 (1958) 70-77, esp. 76
                   (what was published there as 4QHen astr^a is
                   now 4QEnastr^b 23:6-9); *HTR* 64 (1971) 338-39,
                   342.

4QEnastr^c (*olim*   Milik, J. T., *BE*, 7-22, 274, 284-88, 292-93 (+ pls.
   4QHen astr^c)   XXVIII, XXX). The frgs. = *1 Enoch* 76:3-10;
                   76:13-77:4; 78:6-8. Cf. *RB* 65 (1958) 70-77, esp.
                   76 (what was published there as 4QHen astr^c
                   6-9 is now 4QEnastr^a 1 ii 16-18)

4QEnastr^d   Milik, J. T., *BE* 7-22, 274, 296-97 (+ pl. XXIX). The
                   frgs. follow after *1 Enoch* 82:20.

4QEnGiants^a   Milik, J. T., *BE*, 57-58, 298-339, esp. 310-17 (10
                   frgs., originally the second part of the same
                   scroll as 4QEn^c) (+ pls. XXX-XXXII). Cf. J. T.
                   Milik, "Turfan et Qumran: Livre des Géants
                   juif et manichéen," *Tradition und Glaube: Das
                   frühe Christentum in seiner Umwelt: Festgabe für
                   Karl Georg Kuhn zum 65. Geburtstag* (eds. G.
                   Jeremias et al.; Göttingen: Vandenhoeck &
                   Ruprecht, 1971) 117-27 (+ pl. I)

4QEnGiants^b   Milik, J. T., *BE*, 303-7 (Starcky's lot, as yet
                   unpublished); cf. "Turfan et Qumran," 121-25;
                   HTR 64 (1971) 367.

4QEnGiants^c   Milik, J. T., *BE*, 307-9 (Starcky's lot)

4QEnGiants^d   Milik, J. T., *BE*, 309 (one of the "two groups of
                   small fragments entrusted to the Starcky
                   edition")

4QEnGiants^e   Milik, J. T., *BE*, 237, 309 ("a third manuscript from
                   the Starcky collection")

4QEnGiants[f]	Milik, J. T., *BE*, 309 (one of the "two groups..."). N.B. A list of passages of *1 Enoch* which are preserved in the Aramaic texts of Qumran can be found in *BE*, 365-66.
4QEn hebr	Milik, J. T., *BE*, 12: Enoch in Hebrew (4Q**227**); cf. *Jub.* 4:17-24.
4QFlor (*or* 4QEschMidr)	Allegro, J. M., "Further Messianic References," *JBL* 75 (1956) 176-77 (Document II, "Florilegium," pl. 1); "Fragments of a Qumran Scroll of Eschatological Midrašim," *JBL* 77 (1958) 350-54; DJD 5. 53-57; pls. XIX-XX (4Q**174**)
4QHalakah[a]	Milik, J. T., "Addenda à 3Q15," DJD 3. 299-302, esp. 300
pap4QHymPr	Baillet, M., "Hymnes ou prières," DJD 7. 74-77 (4Q**499**)
pap4QHymSap	Baillet, M., "Fragments hymniques ou sapientiels (?)," DJD 7. 73-74 (4Q**498**)
4QJN	Starcky, J., "Jérusalem et les manuscrits de la Mer Morte," *Le Monde de la Bible* 1 (1977) 38-40 (photo + partial translation). See J. T. Milik on 5Q**15** (= 5QJN) in DJD 3. 184-93; cf. J. Starcky, *RB* 63 (1956) 66.
4QJN hebr	Milik, J. T., *BE*, 59 (= 4Q**232**; report, no text)
4QJub[e]	Milik, J. T., DJD 3. 226 (he quotes a phrase from one frg. 1:7 [= *Jub.* 25:12])
4QJub[f]	Milik, J. T., "Fragment d'une source," *RB* 73 (1966) 104 (+ pl. IIa) (4Q**221**; = *Jub.* 21:22-24)
4QJub[?]	Milik, J. T., *BE*, 12, 14, 25, 60 (4Q**227**; = *Jub.* 4:17-24)
4QJub[?]	Kister, M., "Newly Identified Fragments of the Book of Jubilees: Jub. 23: 21-23, 30-31," *RevQ* 12 (1985-87) 529-36. Kister identifies frgs. 19-21 of 4Q**176** (= 4QTanh) as part of *Jubilees*. Possibly these frgs. belong to 4QJub[f].
pap4QJub[?]	Baillet, M., "Livre des Jubilés (?)," DJD 7. 1-2 (4Q**482**) (= *Jub.* 13:29[?]; 36:9[?])
pap4QJub[?]	Baillet, M., "Genèse ou Livre des Jubilés (?)," DJD 7. 2 (4Q**483**) (possibly *Jub.* 2:14)
4QM[a]	Hunzinger, C.-H., "Fragmente einer älteren Fassung des Buches *Milḥamā* aus Höhle 4 von

Qumrān," *ZAW* 69 (1957) 131-51; cf. *SWDS*, 18, 29 (= 1QM 14:3-16+). What Hunzinger published here in preliminary form corresponds to frgs. 8-9 of 4QMᵃ. For the full publication, see M. Baillet, "La règle de la guerre (premier exemplaire: Mᵃ)," DJD 7. 12-44 (+ pls. V-VI; 4Q491)

4QMᵇ   Baillet, M., "La règle de la guerre (deuxième exemplaire: Mᵇ)," DJD 7, 45-49 (+ pl. VII; 4Q492) (= 1QM 19:1-4; frgs. 2, 8; and 1Q33)

4QMᶜ   Baillet, M., "La règle de la guerre (troisième exemplaire: Mᶜ)," DJD 7, 49-53 (+ pl. VIII; 4Q493) (= nothing in 1QM)

4QMᵈ   Baillet, M., "La règle de la guerre (quatrième exemplaire: Mᵈ)," DJD 7, 53-54 (+ pl. VIII; 4Q494) (= 1QM 2:1-2)

4QMᵉ, pap4QMᶠ Baillet, M., ,"Débris de textes sur papyrus de la grotte 4 de Qumran (Pl. XIV-XV)," *RB* 71 (1964) 353-71, esp. 356-59, 365-71 (+ pl. XV); "Les manuscrits de la règle de la guerre de la grotte 4 de Qumran," *RB* 79 (1972) 217-26 (see esp. p. 225 for a list of 4QMᵃ⁻ᶠ frgs. and their relation to 1QM; cf. J. T. Milik, "Milkî-ṣedeq et Milkî-rešaʿ," *JJS* 23 [1972] 140). Cf. M. Baillet, "La règle de la guerre (cinquième exemplaire: Mᵉ)," DJD 7, 54-56 (+ pl. VIII; 4Q495); "La règle de la guerre (sixième exemplaire: Mᶠ)," DJD 7, 56-68 (+ pls. X, XII, XIV, XVI, XVIII [lower], XXIV [lower]; 4Q496). 4QMᵉ = 1QM 10:9-10; 13:9-12; 4QMᶠ = 1QM 1:4-9,11-17; 2:5-6,9-12,13-14,17(?),?-3:2,6-7,9-11,11-15; 3:?-4:2; 9:5-9(?)

pap4QMᵍ⁽ʔ⁾   Baillet, M. "Texte ayant quelque rapport avec la règle de la guerre (?)," DJD 7, 69-72 (+ pl. XXVI; 4Q497)

4QMess ar   Starcky, J., "Un texte messianique araméen de la grotte 4 de Qumrân," *Ecole des langues orientales anciennes de l'Institut Catholique de Paris: Mémorial du cinquantenaire 1914-1964* (Travaux de l'Institut Catholique de Paris 10; Paris: Bloud et

Gay, 1964) 51-66 (misnamed; it is not "messianic." See J. A. Fitzmyer, "The Aramaic 'Elect of God' Text from Qumran Cave IV," *ESBNT*, 127-60). Cf. F. García Martínez, "4Q Mes. Aram. y el libro de Noé," *Salmanticensis* 28 (1981) 195-232; J. T. Milik, *BE*, 56.

4QMilMik Milik, J. T., *BE*, 91 (*Millê Mîkāʾēl*, "Words of Michael": "Words of the book which Michael addressed to the angels"); cf. J. Starcky, *RB* 63 (1956) 66.

4QMišm Milik, J. T., "Le travail d'édition des manuscrits du Désert de Juda," *Volume du Congrès, Strasbourg 1956* (VTSup 4; Leiden: Brill, 1957) 17-26, esp. 24-26; cf. his *Ten Years*, 107-8, 152; *BE*, 61-65.

4QMMT (*olim* 4QMish- [nique]) Qimron, E. and J. Strugnell, "An Unpublished Halakhic Letter from Qumran," *Biblical Archaeology Today: Proceedings of the International Congress on Biblical Archaeology, Jerusalem, April 1984* (Jerusalem: Israel Exploration Society, 1985) 400-407 (a report about the text, Miqsāt Maʿăśê Tôrāh, of which there are six copies [4Q394-99]; see also E. Qimron and J. Strugnell, "An Unpublished Halakhic Letter from Qumran," *Israel Museum Journal* 4 (1985) 9-12. Cf. J. T. Milik, DJD 3. 221-25; "Le travail," VTSup 4, 24.

4QOrd[a] (*olim* 4QOrd) Allegro, J. M., "An Unpublished Fragment of Essene Halakah (4Q Ordinances)," *JSS* 6 (1961) 71-73; DJD 5. 6-9; pl. II (4Q159). Cf. Y. Yadin, *IEJ* 18 (1968) 250-52; F. Weinert, *JSJ* 5 (1974) 179-207.

4QOrd[b] Baillet, M., "Ordonnances (deuxième exemplaire: Ord[b])," DJD 7. 287-95 (4Q513)

4QOrd[c] Baillet, M., "Ordonnances (troisième exemplaire: Ord[c]) (?)," DJD 7. 295-98 (4Q514)

4QPBless (*olim* 4QpGen 49)	Allegro, J. M., "Further Messianic References," *JBL* 75 (1956) 174-76 (Document I, "Patriarchal Blessings," pl. 1). (Contains Gen 49:10). Omitted from DJD 5; see J. A. Fitzmyer, *CBQ* 31 [1969] 71; cf. H. Stegemann, "Der Pešer Psalm 37 aus Höhle 4 von Qumran (4 Q p Ps 37)," *RevQ* 4 [1963-64] 235-70); "Weitere Stücke von 4 Q p Psalm 37, von 4 Q Patriarchal Blessings und Hinweis auf eine unedierte Handschrift aus Höhle 4 Q mit Exzerpten aus dem Deuteronomium," *RevQ* 6 (1967-69) 193-227, esp. 211-17.
4QPentPar[a]	Strugnell, J., "Letter," quoted by F. García Martínez, "La 'Nueva Jerusalen' y el templo futuro de los mss. de Qumran," *Salvación en la palabra: Targum — derash — berith: En memoria del profesor Alejandro Díez Macho* (Madrid: Cristiandad, 1986) 563-64 n. 2 (4Q364). See Y. Yadin, *The Temple Scroll*, Sup., pls. 38*, 40*
4QPrFêtes[a]	Baillet, M., "Prières pour les fêtes (premier exemplaire: PrFêtes[a])," DJD 7. 175-77 (4Q507)
4QPrFêtes[b]	Baillet, M., "Prières pour les fêtes (deux exemplaire: PrFêtes[b])," DJD 7. 177-84 (4Q508)
4QPrFêtes[c]	Baillet, M., "Prières pour les fêtes (troisième exemplaire: PrFêtes[c])," DJD 7. 184-215 (4Q509)
pap4QPrLit[b]	Baillet, M., "Débris de textes," *RB* 71 (1964) 354-55, 360-65; "Psaumes, hymnes, cantiques et prières dans les manuscrits de Qumrân," *Le psautier: Ses origines. Ses problèmes littéraires. Son influence: Etudes présentées aux XIIe Journées Bibliques (29-31 août 1960)* (Orientalia et biblica lovaniensia 4; Louvain: Publications universitaires, 1962) 389-405.
4QPrNab (*or* 4QṣNab)	Milik, J. T., "'Prière de Nabonide et autres écrits d'un cycle de Daniel, fragments de Qumrân 4," *RB* 63 (1956) 407-15, esp. 407-11. Cf. F. M. Cross, "Fragments of the Prayer of Nabonidus," *IEJ* 34 (1984) 260-64
pap4QPrQuot	Baillet, M., "Prières quotidiennes," DJD 7. 105-36 (4Q503)

pap4QProph	Baillet, M., "Texte prophétique ou sapientiel," DJD 7. 4 (4Q485)
4QPsAp^{a-c}	Starcky, J., "Psaumes apocryphes de la grotte 4 de Qumrân (4QPs^f VII-X)," *RB* 73 (1966) 353-71 (+ pl. XIII)
4QpsDan ar^{a-c}	Milik, J. T., "'Prière de Nabonide,'" *RB* 63 (1956) 411-15.
4QpsDan ar^a (*olim* 4QpsDan A)	Milik, J. T., Public Lecture at Harvard University, December 1972 (cf. J. A. Fitzmyer, "The Contribution of Qumran Aramaic to the Study of the New Testament," *NTS* 20 [1973-74] 382-407, esp. 391-94) (*olim* 4Q243, now 4Q246, according to J. T. Milik, *BE*, 60, 213, 261)
4QPsJosh^{a,b}	Newsom, C., "The 'Psalms of Joshua' from Qumran Cave 4," *JJS* 39 (1988) 56-73 (4Q378 and 4Q379). Cf. P. A. Spijkerman, "Chronique du Musée de la Flagellation," *SBFLA* 12 (1961-62) 323-33, esp. 325 (photograph contains a six-line frg. [now known as 4Q379 1 or 4QPsJosh^b], acquired by the Studium Biblicum Franciscanum in 1958; also another photograph of an unidentified piece of wisdom literature); cf. 4QTestim (below).
pap4QRitMar	Baillet, M., "Rituel de mariage," DJD 7. 81-105 (4Q502). Cf. J. M. Baumgarten, "4Q502, Marriage or Golden Age Ritual?" *JJS* 34 (1983) 125-35.
pap4QRitPur	Baillet, M., "Rituel de Purification," DJD 7. 262-86 (4Q512)
4QS^{a-j}	Milik, J. T., Review of P. Wernberg-Møller, *The Manual of Discipline Translated and Annotated* (STDJ 1; Leiden: Brill, 1957), *RB* 67 (1960) 410-16, esp. 412-16 (a list of the most significant variants in 4QS^{a-j} from that of 1QS)
4QS^b	Milik, J. T., *BE*, 61 n. 1, 62-64 (on 4Q260B 1 vi 6-13). Milik here reveals that further calendaric texts are found in as yet unpublished 4Q293, 4Q319-37. See his article, "Ecrits préesséniens de Qumrân: d'Hénoch à Amram," *Qumrân: Sa piété, sa théologie et son milieu* (BETL 46; ed. M.

	Delcor; Gembloux: Duculot, 1978) 91-106, esp. 93-94.
4QS^d	Milik, J. T., "Numérotation," *Sem* 27 (1977) 78-79 (text of 2 i 1-13)
pap4QSap^a	Baillet, M., "Ouvrage sapientiel (?)," DJD 7. 4-5 (4Q486)
pap4QSap^b	Baillet, M., "Ouvrage sapientiel (?)," DJD 7. 5-10 (4Q487)
4QSecEzek^a	Milik, J. T., *BE*, 254-55. Milik refers to 4Q384-390 of Strugnell's lot and gives various phrases of 4Q390. See now J. Strugnell and D. Dimant, "4Q Second Ezekiel," *RevQ* 13 (Mémorial Jean Carmignac, 1988) 45-58. Frgs. 2 and 3 of 4Q385 (PAM 43.503) are presented here with readings from overlaps in other related copies (4QSecEzek^{a-i}).
4QŠir^a	Baillet, M., "Cantiques du Sage (premier exemplaire: Shir^a)," DJD 7. 215-19 (4Q510)
4QŠir^b	Baillet, M., "Cantiques du Sage (second exemplaire: Shir^b)," DJD 7. 219-62 (4Q511)
4QŠirŠabb^{a-h} (*olim* 4QSl 39-40)	Strugnell, J., "The Angelic Liturgy at Qumrân— 4Q Serek šîrôt ʿôlat Haššabbāt," *Congress Volume, Oxford, 1959* (VTSup 7; Leiden: Brill, 1960) 318-45 (= 4QŠirŠabb^d). See now the full publication of these texts: C. Newsom, *Songs of the Sabbath Sacrifice: A Critical Edition* (HSS 27; Atlanta, GA: Scholars, 1985). This edition contains the texts of 4Q400, 4Q401, 4Q402, 4Q403, 4Q404, 4Q405, 4Q406, 4Q407, MasŠirŠabb, and 11QŠirŠabb.
4QTanh	Allegro, J. M., "Tanhûmîm," DJD 5. 60-67; pls. XXII-XXIII (4Q176); contains Ps 79:2-3; Isa 40:1-5; 41:8-9; 49:7,13-17; 43:1-2,4-6; 51:22-23; 52:1-3; 54:4-10; 52:1-2; Zech 13:9. See comment on 4QJub? above.
4QTeharot B	Milik, J. T., "Milkî-ṣedeq et Milkî-rešaʿ," *JJS* 23 (1972) 129-30 (4Q275). There are five or six other copies of this text from 4Q, as yet unpublished.

4QTeharot D   Milik, J. T., "Milkî-ṣedeq et Milkî-rešaᶜ," *JJS* 23 (1972) 126-29 (+ pl. I) (4Q280); cf. G. Vermes, *DSSE*, 161.

4QTemple[a]   Texts related to 11QTemple[a] (?); see B. Z. Wacholder, *The Dawn of Qumran: The Sectarian Torah and the Teacher of Righteousness* (Cincinnati, OH: Hebrew Union College, 1983) 200 (Strugnell's lot[?]); cf. J. van der Ploeg, "Une *halakha* inédite de Qumrân" (see 11QHalakha below), 71.

4QTestim   Allegro, J. M., "Further Messianic References," *JBL* 75 (1956) 182-87 (Document IV, "Testimonia," pl. 4),; DJD 5. 57-60; pl. XXI (4Q175). It contains a proto-Samaritan text of Exod 20:21 (conflating Deut 5:28-29 and 18:18-19 [see P. W. Skehan, *CBQ* 19 (1957) 435-40]); Num 24:15-17; Deut 33:8-11; Josh 6:26 and PsJosh (see above 4QPsJosh).

4QTher   Allegro, J. M., *The Dead Sea Scrolls and the Christian Myth* (Devon, UK: Westbridge Books [David & Charles], 1979; repr., Buffalo, NY: Prometheus Books, 1984) 235-40 (Appendix 1: 4QTherapeia). The frg. is genuine (infrared photo, PAM 43.407). But what Allegro has published here as a would-be report of "medical" activity is highly questionable. See J. Naveh, "A Medical Document or a Writing Exercise? The So-called 4Q Therapeia," *IEJ* 36 (1986) 52-55. Beware of the followup on Allegro's publication written by J. H. Charlesworth, *The Discovery of a Dead Sea Scroll (4Q Therapeia): Its Importance in the History of Medicine and Jesus Research* (ICASALS Publ. 85-1; Lubbock, TX: Texas Tech University, 1985); cf. J. C. Greenfield, *IEJ* 36 (1986) 118-19; F. García Martínez, *JSJ* 17 (1986) 242-44. Charlesworth now admits that he misunderstood the text; see "A Misunderstood Recently Published Dead Sea Scroll (4QM 130)," *Explorations* (American Institute for the

	Study of Religious Cooperation, Philadelphia, PA) 1/2 (1987) 2.
4QTJos ar	Milik, J. T., "Ecrits préesséniens de Qumrân: d'Hénoch à 'Amram," *Qumrân: Sa piété, sa théologie et son milieu* (ed. M. Delcor; BETL 46; Gembloux: Duculot; Louvain: Leuven University, 1978) 91-106, esp. 101-3 (PAM 42.443 and ?.286 [Milik's siglum: 4QAJo]).
4QTJud ar	Milik, J. T., "Ecrits préesséniens," 97-102 (PAM 41.890 and 41.945 [Milik's siglum: 4QAJu])
pap4QTJud?	Baillet, M., DJD 7. 3 (4Q484). Cf. 3Q7.
4QTLevi ar[a] (*olim* 4QTLevi ar[b])	Milik, J. T., "Le Testament de Lévi en araméen: Fragment de la grotte 4 de Qumrân," *RB* 62 (1955) 398-406; cf. *SWDS*, 16, 25-26 (related to CTLevi ar, Bodleian). For text of 8 iii 2-8, see J. T. Milik, *BE*, 23-24; cf. *RB* 62 (1955) 399; *HTR* 64 (1971) 344-45
4QTLevi ar[b]	As yet unpublished (see *RB* 86 [1979] 215).
4QTLevi ar[c]	As yet unpublished (see *RB* 86 [1979] 215).
4QTNaph	Milik, J. T., "Ecrits préesséniens," 97 (text in Hebrew, as yet unpublished [Milik's siglum: 4QHN]).
4QTQahat	Milik, J. T., "4Q Visions de 'Amram," *RB* 79 (1972) 97
4QVisJac ar (*olim* 4QTestuz ar)	Testuz, M., "Deux fragments inédits des manuscrits de la Mer Morte," *Sem* 5 (1955) 37-38, esp. 38 (figures are upside down and the labels are confused). According to J. T. Milik ("Ecrits préesséniens," 103-4), this is part of the Visions of Jacob (his siglum: 4QAJa I a-d).
4QVisSam	Allegro, J. M., "The Vision of Samuel," DJD 5. 9-11; pl. III (4Q160)
4QWiles	Allegro, J. M., "The Wiles of the Wicked Woman: A Sapiential Work from Qumran's Fourth Cave," *PEQ* 96 (1964) 53-55; DJD 5. 82-85; pl. XXVIII (4Q184)
4Q?	Allegro, J. M., DJD 5. 74-75; pl. XXV (13 frgs., lower) (4Q178)
4Q?	Allegro, J. M., DJD 5. 81-82; pl. XXVI (3 frgs., lower) (4Q183)

4Q?	Allegro, J. M., DJD 5. 85-87; pls. XXIX-XXX (4Q185). See note on 4QAdmon. G. Vermes (*DSSE*, 242-43) labels this text "Exhortation to Seek Wisdom."
pap4Q?	Baillet, M., "Fragments divers," DJD 7. 300 (4Q516); "Fragments non classés inscrits sur une face," DJD 7. 301-4 (4Q517); "Fragments non classés sur les deux faces. Recto," DJD 7. 304-6 (4Q518); "Fragments non classés sur les deux faces. Verso," DJD 7. 307-9 (4Q519); "Fragments non classés inscrits seulement au verso," DJD 7. 309-12 (4Q520).

Detailed Listing of 4Q158-186 in DJD 5

(A)   *Pesharim*

4Q161	4QpIsa[a]	Commentary on Isaiah (A), 11-15 (+ pls. IV-V): on Isa 10:20-21,22,24-27,28-32,33-34; 11:1-5 (partly published in *JBL* 75 [1956] 177-82)
4Q162	4QpIsa[b]	Commentary on Isaiah (B), 15-17 (+ pl. VI): Isa 5:5-6,11-14,24-25,29-30; 6:9(?) (published in *JBL* 77 [1958] 215-18)
4Q163	4QpIsa[c]	Commentary on Isaiah (C), 17-27 (+ pls. VII-VIII): Isa 8:7,8,9(?); 9:11(?),14-20; 10:12,13,19(?),20-24; 14:8,26-30; 19:9-12; 29:10-11,15-16,19-23; Zech 11:11; Isa 30:1-5,15-18; Hos 6:9; Isa 30:19-21; 31:1; 32:5-6 + 30 tiny frgs. (partly published in *JBL* 77 [1958] 218-20)
4Q164	4QpIsa[d]	Commentary on Isaiah (D), 27-28 (+ pl. IX [upper]): Isa 54:11,12 (partly published in *JBL* 77 [1958] 220-21)
4Q165	4QpIsa[e]	Commentary on Isaiah (E), 28-30 (+ pl. IX [lower]: Isa 1:1(?); 40:12; 14:19; 15:4-6; 21:2(?),11-15; 32:5-7 + frgs.
4Q166	4QpHos[a]	Commentary on Hosea (A), 31-32 (+ pl. X [upper]): Hos 2:8-9,10-14 (published in *JBL* 78 [1959] 142-47)
4Q167	4QpHos[b]	Commentary on Hosea (B), 32-36 (+ pls. X [lower]-XI Hos 5:13-15; 6:4,7,9-10; 8:6-7, 13-14 + frgs. (partly published in *JBL* 75 [1956] 93)
4Q168	4QpMic	Commentary on Micah (?), 36 (+ pl. XII [upper left]: Mic 4:8-12
4Q169	4QpNah	Commentary on Nahum, 37-42 (+ pls. XII-XIV): Nah 1:3-6; 2:12-14; 3:1-5,6-9,10-12,14 (partly published in *JBL* 75 [1956] 90-93 and in *JSS* 7 [1962] 304-8)
4Q170	4QpZeph	Commentary on Zephaniah, 42 (+ pl. XIV [middle]): Zeph 1:12-13

4Q171	4QpPs^a	Commentary on Psalms (A), 42-50 (+ pls. XIV [left side]-XVII): Ps 37:7,8-19a,19b-26,28c-40; 45:1-2; 60:8-9 (108:8-9) (partly published in *PEQ* 86 [1954] 69-75 and in *JBL* 75 [1956] 93-95)
4Q172	4QpUnid	Commentary on Unidentified Texts, 50-51 (+ pl. XVIII [upper])
4Q173	4QpPs^b	Commentary on Psalms (B), 51-53 (+ pl. XVIII [center]): Ps 127:2-3,5; 129:7-8; 118: 26-27(?)

(B)	*Other Texts Using Biblical Passages*	
4Q158	4QBibPar	Biblical Paraphrase: Genesis, Exodus, 1-6 (+ pl. I): on Gen 32:25-32,31(?); Exod 4:27-28; 3:12; Gen 24:4-6; Exod 19:17-23; 20:19-22; Deut 5:29; 18:18-20,22; Exod 20:12,16,17; Deut 5:30-31; Exod 20:22-26; 21:1,3,4,6,8,10; 21:15,16,18,20,22,25,32,34,35-37; 22:1-11,13; 30:32,34 (frg. 6 of 4Q158 has been identified by R. Weiss as a Proto-Samaritan form of Exod 20:19ff.; see his review in *Kirjath Sepher* 45 [1970] 61).
4Q159	4QOrd^a	Ordinances, 6-9 (+ pl. II) (partly published in *JSS* 6 [1961] 71-73)
4Q160	4QVisSam	The Vision of Samuel, 9-11 (+ pl. III): see 1 Sam 3:14-17
4Q174	4QFlor	Florilegium, 53-57 (+ pls. XIX-XX): Quotations from 2 Sam 7:10-14 (1 Chr 17:9-13); Exod 15:17-18; Amos 9:11; Ps 1:1; Isa 8:11; Ezek 37:23(?); Ps 2:1; Dan 12:10; 11:32 (intervening comments); Deut 33:8-11,12(?),19-21 + frgs. (partly published in *JBL* 75 [1956] 176-77 and 77 [1958] 350-54)
4Q175	4QTestim	Testimonia, 57-60 (+ pl. XXI): Quotations from Deut 5:28-29; 18:18-19 (= Samaritan Pentateuch

		Exod 20:21); Num 24:15-17; Deut 33:8-11; Josh 6:26 (+ comments = 4QPsJosh) (published in *JBL* 75 [1956] 182-87)
4Q176	4QTanh	Tanhûmîm, 60-67 (+ pls. XXII-XXIII): Quotations from Ps 79:2-3; Isa 40:1-5; 41:8-9; 49:7,13-17; 43:1-2,4-6; 51:22-23,23c-e; 52:1-3; 54:4-10 (+ pesher); 52:1-2; Zech 13:9 + frgs. of comments. Frgs. 19-21 of this text have been identified as part of *Jubilees*; see M. Kister, "Newly Identified Fragments of the Book of Jubilees: Jub. 23: 21-23, 30-31," *RevQ* 12 (1985-87) 529-36.
4Q177	4QCatena[a]	Catena (A), 67-74 (+ pls. XXIV-XXV [upper]): Text possibly related to 4QFlor (see J. Strugnell, *RevQ* 7 [1969-71] 236-37)
4Q178	4Q?	(Unnamed), 74-75 (+ pl. XXV [lower])
4Q179	4QapLam[a]	Lamentations, 75-77 (+ pl. XXVI [upper]): Allusions to canonical Lamentations 1 and 4
4Q180	4QAgesCreat	The Ages of Creation, 77-79 (+ pl. XXVII). J. T. Milik believes that this and the following text are part of the "Book of Periods" (see *BE*, 248-53) (partly published by J. M. Allegro in ALUOS 4 [1962-63] 3-5)
4Q181	4Q?	(Unnamed), 79-80 (+ pl. XVIII [lower]); see comment on 4Q180 (partly published in ALUOS 4 [1962-63] 3-5). G. Vermes (*DSSE*, 159) labels this text "The Wicked and the Holy."
4Q182	4QCatena[b]	Catena (B), 80-81 (+ pl. XXVII [lower]): On Enemies of the Community
4Q183	4Q?	(Unnamed), 81-82 (+ pl. XXVI [lower]): On desecration of the Temple (?)

4Q184	4QWiles	(Unnamed), 82-85 (+ pl. XXVIII): Instruction of sapiential genre (partly published in *PEQ* 96 [1964] 53-55; frg. 2 is in the Oriental Institute Museum, University of Chicago, No. A30303, photo #47799)
4Q185	4Q?	(Unnamed), 85-87 (+ pls. XXIX-XXX): Sapiential text
4Q186	4QCryptic	(Unnamed), 88-91 (+ pl. XXXI): possibly related to the Enoch literature; see J. T. Milik, *HTR* 64 (1971) 366; *BE*, 56 (partly published in *JSS* 9 [1964] 291-94)

Detailed Listing of 4Q482-4Q520 in DJD 7

4Q482	pap4QJub?	Livre des Jubilés (?), 1-2 (+ pl. I [upper]): *Jub.* 13:29; 36:9
4Q483	pap4QJub?	Genèse ou Livre des Jubilés (?), 2 (+ pl. I [middle]): *Jub.* 2:14 (or possibly Gen 1:28 [cf. pap4QGen?])
4Q484	pap4QTJud?	Testament de Juda (?), 3 (+ pl.I [lower]): *T. Judah* 25:1-2 (?)
4Q485	pap4QProph	Texte prophétique ou sapientiel, 4 (+ pl. II [upper])
4Q486	pap4QSap^a	Ouvrage sapientiel (?), 4-5 (+ pl. I [middle])
4Q487	pap4QSap^b	Ouvrage sapientiel (?), 5-10 (+ pls. III-IV)
4Q488	pap4QAp ar	Un apocryphe en araméen, 10 (+ pl. II [middle])
4Q489	pap4QApoc ar	Un apocalyptique en araméen, 10-11 (+ pl. II [middle])
4Q490		Groupe de fragments à rapprocher du précédent (?), 11 (+ pl. II [lower])
4Q491	4QM^a	La règle de la guerre (premier exemplaire: M^a), 12-44 (+ pls, V-VI)
4Q492	4QM^b	La règle de la guerre (deuxième exemplaire: M^b), 45-49 (+ pl. VII)

4Q493	4QM^c	La règle de la guerre (troisiènme exemplaire: M^c), 49-53 (+ pl. VIII [upper])
4Q494	4QM^d	La règle de la guerre (quatrième exemplaire: M^d), 53-54 (+ pl. VIII [lower])
4Q495	4QM^e	La règle de la guerre (cinquième exemplaire: M^e), 54-56 (+ pl. VIII [lower])
4Q496	pap4QM^f	La règle de la guerre (sixième exemplaire: M^f), 56-68 (+ pls. X, XII, XIV, XVI, XVIII [lower], XXIV [lower])
4Q497	pap4QM^g(?)	Texte ayant quelque rapport avec la règle de la guerre (?), 69-72 (+ pl. XXVI)
4Q498	pap4QHymSap	Fragments hymniques ou sapientiels (?), 73-74 (+ pl. XXVII [upper])
4Q499	pap4QHymPr	Hymnes ou prières, 74-77 (+ pl. XXV)
4Q500	pap4QBen	Bénédiction, 78-79 (+ pl. XXVII [lower])
4Q501	4QapLam^b	Lamentation, 79-80 (+ pl. XXVIII [upper])
4Q502	pap4QRitMar	Rituel de mariage, 81-105 (+ pls. XXIX-XXXIV)
4Q503	pap4QPrQuot	Prières quotidiennes, 105-36 (+ pls. XXXV, XXXVII, XXXIX, XLI, XLIII, XLV, XLVII)
4Q504	4QDibHam^a	Paroles des luminaires (premier exemplaire: DibHam^a), 137-68 (+ pls. XLIX-LIII)
4Q505	4QDibHm^b	Paroles des luminaires (deuxième exemplaire: DibHam^b), 168-70 (+ pl. XXIII)
4Q506	4QDibHam^c	Paroles des luminaires (troisième exemplaire: DibHam^c), 170-75 (+ pls. XVIII [upper], XX and XXIV [upper])

4Q507	4QPrFêtes[a]	Prières pour les fêtes (premier exemplaire: PrFêtes[a]), 175-77 (+ pl. XXVIII [lower])
4Q508	4QPrFêtes[b]	Prières pour les fêtes (deuxième exemplaire: PrFêtes[b]), 177-84 (+ pl. LIV)
4Q509	4QPrFêtes[c]	Prières pour les fêtes (troisième exemplaire: PrFêtes[c]), 184-215 (+ pls. IX, XI, XIII, XV, XVII, XIX, XXI, XXII)
4Q510	4QŠir[a]	Cantiques du Sage (premier exemplaire: Shir[a]), 215-19 (+ pl. LV)
4Q511	4QŠir[b]	Cantiques du Sage (second exemplaire: Shir[b]), 219-62 (+ pls. LVI-LXXI)
4Q512	pap4QRitPur	Rituel de purification, 262-86 (+ pls. XXXVI, XXXVIII, XL, XLII, XLIV, XLVI, XLVIII)
4Q513	4QOrd[b]	Ordonnances (deuxième exemplaire: Ord[b]), 287-95 (+ pls. LXXII-LXXIII)
4Q514	4QOrd[c]	Ordonnances (troisième exemplaire: Ord[c]) (?), 295-98 (+ pl. LXXIV)
4Q515	pap4Q?	Groupe en petite écriture, 299-300 (+ pl. LXXV [upper])
4Q516	pap4Q?	Fragments divers, 300 (+ pl. LXXV [lower])
4Q517	pap4Q?	Fragments non classés inscrits sur une face, 301-4 (+ pls. LXXVI-LXXVII)
4Q518	pap4Q?	Fragments non classés inscrits sur les deux faces. Recto, 304-6 (+ pl. LXXVIII)
4Q519	pap4Q?	Fragments non classés inscrits sur les deux faces. Verso, 307-9 (+ pl. LXXIX)
4Q520	pap4Q?	Fragments non classés inscrits seulement au verso, 309-12 (+ pl. LXXX)

D. Cave 11

(1) *OT Texts*

11QLev   Ploeg, J. P. M. van der, "Lev. IX,23-X,2 dans un
                  texte de Qumran," *Bibel und Qumran: Beiträge
                  zur Erforschung der Beziehungen zwischen Bibel-
                  und Qumranwissenschaft: Hans Bardtke zum 22. 9.
                  1966* (ed. S. Wagner; Berlin: Evangelische
                  Haupt-Bibelgesellschaft, 1968) 153-55 (= Lev
                  9:23-10:2). Van der Ploeg has published another
                  frg. of this text in "Les manuscrits de la grotte
                  XI de Qumrân," *RevQ* 12 (1985-87) 3-15, esp. 10
                  (= part of Lev 13:58-59), but A. S. van der
                  Woude (*RevQ* 13 [1988] 89 n. 3) maintains that
                  the latter frg. is part of 11QTemple[b] (see
                  below).

11QpaleoLev   Freedman, D. N. and K. A. Mathews (with
                  contributions by R. S. Hanson), *The Paleo-
                  Hebrew Leviticus Scroll (11QpaleoLev)*
                  (Philadelphia: American Schools of Oriental
                  Research, 1985 [distributed by Eisenbrauns,
                  Winona Lake, IN]). Contains parts of Lev 4:24-
                  26; 10:4-7; 11:27-32; 13:3-9; 13:39-43; 14:16-21;
                  14:52-15:5/16:2-4; 16:34-17:5; 18:27-19:4; 20:1-6;
                  21:6-11; 22:21-27; 23:22-29; 24:9-14; 25:28-36;
                  26:17-26; 27:11-19. Cf. D. N. Freedman,
                  "Variant Readings in the Leviticus Scroll from
                  Qumran Cave 11," *CBQ* 36/4 (Patrick W.
                  Skehan Festschrift, 1974) 525-34 (+ photo of
                  Lev 14:53-15:5); gives variants in Lev 15:3; 17:2-
                  4; 18:27-19:3; 20:2-3; 21:6-9; 22:22-25; 24:9-10;
                  25:29-35; 26:20-24; 27:13-17. See E. Puech,
                  "Notes en marge, de 11QpaleoLevitique: Le
                  fragment L, des fragments inédits et une jarre
                  de 1a grotte 11,"*RB* 96 (1989) 161-83.

11QDeut   Ploeg, J. P. van der, *RevQ* 12 (1985-87) 3-15, esp. 10
                  (= part of Deut 13:7-11).

11QEzek   Brownlee, W. H., "The Scroll of Ezekiel from the
                  Eleventh Qumran Cave," *RevQ* 4 (1963-64) 11-

28 (+ pls. I-II) (= part of Ezek 4:3-5; 5:11-17; 7:9-12; 10:11).

11QPs^a Sanders, J. A., *The Psalms Scroll of Qumran Cave 11 (11QPsª)* (DJD 4; Oxford: Clarendon, 1965); *The Dead Sea Psalms Scroll* (Ithaca: Cornell University, 1967). The postscript of the latter book (pp. 155-65) contains the text of an additional fragment (E), on which see Y. Yadin, "Another Fragment (E) of the Psalms Scroll from Qumran Cave 11 (11QPsª), *Textus* 5 (1966) 1-10 (+ pls. I-V). See the detailed analysis of this scroll below, p. 73)

11QPs^b Ploeg, J. van der, "Fragments d'un manuscrit de psaumes de Qumran (11QPs^b)," *RB* 74 (1967) 408-12 (+ pl. XVIII) (= the Plea for Deliverance of 11QPsª [19:1-15]; Ps 141:10 [last word only], followed by Ps 133:1-3; Ps 144:1-2; Ps 118:1[?], 15-16)

11QPs^c Ploeg, J. P. M. van der, "Fragments d'un psautier de Qumrân," *Symbolae biblicae et mesopotamicae Francisco Mario Theodoro de Liagre Böhl dedicatae* (ed. M. A. Beek et al.; Leiden: Brill, 1973) 308-9 (+ pl.). The frgs. = Ps 17:9-15; 18:1-12. Van der Ploeg now reveals that there are further small frgs. with Ps 2:1-8; 9:3-7; 12:5-13:6; 14:1-6; 43:1-3; 77:18-78:1; and perhaps Ps 36:13-37:4; 86:11-14; 18:15-16 (*RevQ* 12 [1985-87] 13). Published as yet?

11QPs^d Ploeg, J. P. M. van der, *RevQ* 12 (1985-87) 13. Frgs. contain parts of Ps 39:13-40:1; 43:1-3; 59:5-8; 68:1-5,16-18; 78:5-12; 81:4-10. Published as yet?

11QPs^e Ploeg, J. P. M. van der, *RevQ* 12 (1985-87) 13. Frgs. contain Ps 37:1-4. Published as yet?

11QPsAp^a Ploeg, J. van der, "Le psaume xci dans une recension de Qumran," *RB* 72 (1965) 210-17 (+ pls. VIII-IX) (= Ps 91:1-16, which follows on apocryphal psalms); "Un petit rouleau de psaumes apocryphes (11 QPsApª)," *Tradition und Glaube: Das frühe Christentum in seiner Umwelt: Festgabe für Karl Georg Kuhn zum 65.*

Geburtstag (ed. G. Jeremias et al.; Göttingen:
Vandenhoeck & Ruprecht, 1971) 128-39 (+ pls.
II-VII) (= the apocryphal psalms which precede
Psalm 91 published in the preceding entry). Cf.
RevQ 12 (1985-87) 12; also E. Puech, "Les deux
derniers psaumes davidiques du rituel
d'exorcisme 11QPsApª," Forty Years of Research
in the Dead Sea Scrolls (Haifa Congress; 1990).

(2) Targum

11QtgJob   Ploeg, J. P. M. van der, and A. S. van der Woude,
                  Le targum de Job de la grotte XI de Qumrân, édité
                  et traduit avec la collaboration de B. Jongeling
                  (Koninklijke nederlandse Akademie van
                  Wetenschappen; Leiden: Brill, 1971). A
                  fragmentary Aramaic translation of Job 17:14-
                  18:4; 19:11-19; 19:29-20:6; 21:2-10; 21:20-27; 22:3-
                  9; 22:16-22; 24:12-17; 24:24-26:2; 26:10-27:4;
                  27:11-20; 28:4-13; 28:20-28; 29:7-16; 29:24-30:4;
                  30:13-20; 30:25-31:1; 31:8-16; 31:26-32; 31:40-
                  32:3; 32:10-17; 33:6-16; 33:24-32; 34:6-17; 34:24-
                  34; 35:6-15; 36:7-16; 36:23-33; 37:10-19; 38:3-13;
                  38:23-34; 39:1-11; 39:20-29; 40:5-14(15?); 40:23-
                  31; 41:7-17; 41:25-42:6; 42:9-11. See E. Puech and
                  F. García, "Remarques sur la colonne XXXVIII
                  de 11 Q tg Job," RevQ 9 (1977-78) 401-7. Cf. M.
                  Sokoloff, The Targum to Job from Qumran Cave
                  XI (Bar-Ilan Studies in Near Eastern Languages
                  and Culture; Ramat-Gan: Bar-Ilan University,
                  1974).

                  Ploeg, J. van der, "Le targum de Job de la grotte 11
                  de Qumran (11QtgJob), Première commu-
                  nication," Mededelingen der koninklijke
                  nederlandse Akademie van Wetenschappen, Afd.
                  Letterkunde, nieuwe reeks, deel 25, no. 9 (Am-
                  sterdam: N. V. NoordHollandsche Uitgevers
                  Maatschappij, 1962) 543-57 (prelimimary report
                  on the preceding entry)

(3) *Apocryphal and Sectarian Texts*

11QBer   Woude, A. S. van der, "Ein neuer Segensspruch
       aus Qumran (11QBer)," *Bibel und Qumran:*
       Beiträge zur Erforschung der Beziehungen
       zwischen Bibel- und Qumranwissenschaft: Hans
       Bardtke zum 22. 8. 1966 (ed. S. Wagner; Berlin:
       Evangelische Haupt-Bibelgesellschaft, 1968)
       253-58 (+ pl.). Cf. the review of this volume by
       J. Strugnell, *RB* 77 (1970) 267-68.

11QHalakha   Ploeg, J. van der, "Une *halakha* inédite de
       Qumrân," *Qumrân: Sa piété, sa théologie et son*
       milieu (ed. M. Delcor; BETL 46; Gembloux:
       Duculot; Louvain: Leuven University, 1978)
       107-13. "Having read this paper at [the
       Journées Bibliques of] Louvain, Prof. Yadin,
       who was present, took the floor to tell us, to
       our great surprise, that he knew well the
       fragments that we had analysed above and that
       they belong to a copy of the scroll that he had
       seized, at the time of the Six-Day War, from M.
       Kando at Bethlehem. . . ." (p. 112). See
       11QTemple[a] 20-21. Cf. 11Temple[b] below; and J.
       P. M. van der Ploeg, "Les manuscrits de la
       grotte XI de Qumrân," *RevQ* 12 (1985-87) 3-15,
       esp. 9.

11QHym[a]   Ploeg, J. P. M. van der, *RevQ* 12 (1985-87) 3-15,
       esp. 11 (PAM 44.003)

11QHym[b]   Ploeg, J. P. M. van der, *RevQ* 12 (1985-87) 3-15,
       esp. 12 (PAM 40.006)

11QJN ar   Jongeling, B., "Publication provisoire d'un
       fragment provenant de la grotte 11 de Qumran
       (11Q Jér Nouv ar)," *JSJ* 1 (1970) 58-64; "Note
       additionnelle," ibid., 185-86. Cf. J. P. M. van der
       Ploeg, *RevQ* 12 (1985-87) 13-14.

11QJub   Woude, A. S. van der, "Fragmente des Buches
       Jubiläen aus Qumran Höhle XI (11 Q Jub),"
       Tradition und Glaube: Das frühe Christentum in
       seiner Umwelt: Festgabe für Karl Georg Kuhn zum
       65. Geburtstag (eds. G. Jeremias et al.;

Göttingen: Vandenhoeck & Ruprecht, 1971)
140-46 (+ pl. VIII). Cf. J. T. Milik, "A propos de
11QJub," *Bib* 54 (1973) 77-78. This text may =
Jub. 3:25-27; 4:7-11,13-14,16-17,29-30; 5:1-2;
6:12(?); 12:15-17,28-29.

11QMelch Woude, A. S. van der, "Melchisedech als
himmlische Erlösergestalt in den neu-
gefundenen eschatologischen Midraschim aus
Qumran Höhle XI," *OS* 14 (1965) 354-73. Cf. M.
de Jonge and A. S. van der Woude, "11Q
Melchizedek and the New Testament," *NTS* 12
(1965-66) 301-26 (improved reading of the text);
see also J. T. Milik, "Milkî-ṣedeq et Milkî-rešaᶜ,"
JJS 23 (1972) 95-144, esp. 96-109, 124-26; P. J.
Kobelski, *Melchizedek and Melchirešaᶜ* (CBQMS
10; Washington, DC: Catholic Biblical
Association of America, 1981); E. Puech,
"Notes sur le manuscrit de XIQMelkîsédeq,"
RevQ 12 (1985-87) 483-513.

11QŠirŠabb Newsom, C., *Songs of the Sabbath Sacrifice: A
Critical Edition* (HSS 27; Atlanta, GA: Scholars,
1985) 361-87 (+ pls. XVII-XIX). Cf. A. S. van der
Woude, "Fragmente einer Rolle der Lieder für
das Sabbatopfer aus Höhle XI von Qumran
(11QŠirŠabb)," *Von Kanaan bis Kerala: Festschrift
für Prof. Mag. Dr. Dr. J. P. M. van der Ploeg zur
Vollendung des siebzigsten Lebensjahres am 4. Juli
1979* (ed. W. C. Delsman et al.; AOAT 211;
Kevelaer: Butzon & Bercker; Neukirchen-
Vluyn: Neukirchener-V., 1982) 311-37 (+ 6 pls.).
Cf. 4QŠirŠabb above.

11QTemple[a] Yadin, Y., *Mgylt-hmqdš: Hhdyr wṣyrp mbwʾ wpyrwš*
(3 vols. with a supplement; Jerusalem: Israel
Exploration Society, Archaeological Institute of
the Hebrew University, Shrine of the Book,
1977). The scroll was also published in an
English edition, *The Temple Scroll* (3 vols. with a
supplement; Jerusalem [as above], 1983).
11QTemple[a] contains 67 fragmentary cols.
Some of the lines have been restored on the

basis of the frgs. of 11QTemple[b]. Cf. *NDBA*, 139-48 + figs. 56-57.

11QTemple[b]   See 11QHalakha above, which is one of the frgs. that Y. Yadin has published in *The Temple Scroll*, Supplementary plates, 34*-40*: Yadin labels the frgs. Rock. (= PAM) 42.178; 43.366; 43.975; 43.976; 43.976B; 43.978; 44.008; 44.010 (see F. García Martínez, *EstBib* 45 [1987] 402 for a list of cols. in 11QTemple[a] that such frgs. have helped to interpret). 11QHalakha[a] corresponds to PAM 43.975 (see Y. Yadin, *The Temple Scroll*, suppl. pl. 37/1). According to J. P. M. van der Ploeg (*RevQ* 12 [1985-87] 9), Yadin has used 35 frgs. of 11QTemple[b], but was unaware of some others. What van der Ploeg labels here as "Fragments du Lévitique" has now been identified by A. S. van der Woude as another frg. of 11QTemple[b]: "Ein bisher unveröffentlichtes Fragment der Tempelrolle," *RevQ* 13 (Mémorial Jean Carmignac, 1988) 89-92, esp. 89 n. 3. In this article A. S. van der Woude publishes yet another frg. of 11QTemple[b] (from PAM 43.976), which corresponds to 11QTemple[a] 54:19-21 and 55:02-05, with some interesting variant readings of Deut 13:7-11. See further M. O. Wise, "A New Manuscript Join in the 'Festival of Wood Offering' (Temple Scroll XXIII)," *JNES* 47 (1988) 113-21. Cf. 4QTemple[a] (above).

Detailed Listing of the Contents of 11QPs[a] in DJD 4

Frgs. A,B,Ci	Ps 101:1-8; 102:1-2 (see DJD 4. 19-49)
frg. C ii	Ps 102:18-29; 103:1
frg. D	Ps 109:21-31
frg. E i	Ps 118:25-29; 104:1-6 (see J. A. Sanders, *DSPS*, 160-65)
ii	Ps 104:21-35; 147:1-2
iii	Ps 147:18-20; 105:?, 1-11

col. i	Ps 105:25-45
ii	Ps 146:9-?-10; 148:1-12
iii	Ps 121:1-8; 122:1-9; 123:1-2
iv	Ps 124:7-8; 125:1-5; 126:1-6; 127:1
v	Ps 128:4-6; 129:1-8; 130:1-8; 131:1
vi	Ps 132:8-18; 119:1-6
vii	Ps 119:15-28
viii	Ps 119:37-49
ix	Ps 119:59-73
x	Ps 119:82-96
xi	Ps 119:105-20
xii	Ps 119:128-42
xiii	Ps 119:150-64
xiv	Ps 119:171-76; 135:1-9
xv	Ps 135:17-21; 136:1-16
xvi	Ps 136:26b(?); 118:1(?),15,16,8,9,?,29(?); 145:1-7
xvii	Ps 145:13-21+?
xviii	Syriac Ps II:3-19 (in Hebrew) [= Psalm 154]
xix	Plea for Deliverance (lines 1-18)
xx	Ps 139:8-24; 137:1
xxi	Ps 137:9; 138:1-8; Sir 51:13-20b
xxii	Sir 51:30; Apostrophe to Zion (lines 1b-15); Ps 93:1-3
xxiii	Ps 141:5-10; 133:1-3; 144:1-7
xxiv	Ps 144:15; Syriac Ps III:1-18 (in Hebrew) [= Psalm 155]
xxv	Ps 142:4-8; 143:1-8
xxvi	Ps 149:7-9; 150:1-6; Hymn to the Creator (lines 9-15)
xxvii	2 Sam 23:7 (line 1); David's Compositions (lines 2-11); Ps 140:1-5
xxviii	Ps 134:1-3; LXX 151 A (Syriac Ps I) (lines 3-12), B (lines 13-14) (in Hebrew)

(See J. A. Sanders, "The Qumran Psalms Scroll [11QPsᵃ] Reviewed," *On Language, Culture, and Religion: In Honor of Eugene A. Nida* [eds. M. Black and W. A. Smalley; The Hague: Mouton, 1974] 79-99; A. S. van der Woude, "Die fünf syrischen Psalmen," *Poetische Schriften* [JSHRZ 4; Gütersloh: Mohn, 1974] 29-47; F. García Martínez, "Texts from Cave 11," *Forty Years of Research in the Dead Sea Scrolls* [Haifa Congress; 1990].

E.   *Unidentified Cave*

(1) *Phylacteries*

XQPhyl 1-4   Yadin, Y., "*Tpylyn-šl-rʾš mqwmrʾn* (X Q Phyl 1-4),"
                 W. F. Albright Volume (Eretz-Israel 9; Jerusalem:
                 Israel Exploration Society, 1969) 60-85

                 Yadin, Y., *Tefillin from Qumran* (X Q Phyl 1-4)
                 (Jerusalem: Israel Exploration Society and the
                 Shrine of the Book, 1969) (an English and
                 modern Hebrew edition of the phylacteries).
                 Cf. M. Baillet, "Nouveaux phylactères de
                 Qumrân (X Q Phyl 1-4): A propos d'une
                 édition récente," *RevQ* 7 (1969-71) 403-15.

II. MAṢADA

(See L. H. Feldman, "Masada: A Critique of Recent Scholarship," *Christianity, Judaism and Other Greco-Roman Cults* [SJLA 12/3; ed. J. Neusner; Leiden: Brill, 1975] 218-48)

(1) *OT Texts*

MasGen	Yadin, Y., *Masada: Herod's Fortress and the Zealots'*
MasLev	*Last Stand* (New York: Random House, 1966)
MasDeut	179, 187-89 (preliminary report only).
MasEzek	Yadin, Y., "The Excavation of Masada — 1963/64:
MasPs	Preliminary Report," *IEJ* 1-120 (+ pls. 1-24),

esp. 81-82, 103-4 (= Ps 81:3-85:10; Lev 4:3-8; Gen 46:7-11)

Yadin, Y., Report in *Jerusalem Post*, 20 December 1964 (discovery of MasPs frg. with Ps 150:1-6)

Sanders, J. A., "Pre-Masoretic Psalter Texts," *DSPS*, 143-49, 152

MasSir   Yadin, Y., "*Mgylt bn-Syrʾ šntglth bmṣdh*," *The E. L. Sukenik Memorial Volume* (Eretz-Israel 8; Jerusalem: Israel Exploration Society, 1965) 1-45

Yadin, Y., *The Ben Sira Scroll from Masada: With Introduction, Emendations and Commentary* (Jerusalem: Israel Exploration Society and the Shrine of the Book, 1965) (an English and modern Hebrew edition of the text) (= Sir 39:27-44:17c)

Milik, J. T., "Un fragment mal placé dans l'édition du Siracide de Masada," *Bib* 47 (1966) 425-26

Yadin, Y., "The Excavation of Masada," *IEJ* 15 (1965) 108-9; *The Excavation of Masada 1963/64: Preliminary Report* (Jerusalem: Israel Exploration Society, 1965) 103-14

Strugnell, J., "Notes and Queries on 'The Ben Sira Scroll from Masada,'" *W. F. Albright Volume* (Eretz-Israel 9; Jerusalem: Israel Exploration Society, 1969) 109-19

(2) *Apocryphal Texts*

MasJub   Yadin, Y., *Masada: Herod's Fortress*, 179

MasŠirŠabb   Yadin, Y., "The Excavation of Masada," *IEJ* 15
                  (1965) 81-82, 105-8. See now the full publication
                  of this text in C. Newsom, *Songs of the Sabbath
                  Sacrifice: A Critical Edition* (HSS 27; Atlanta, GA:
                  Scholars, 1985) 167-84 (+ pl. 16). Cf. C. Newsom
                  and Y. Yadin, "The Masada Fragment of the
                  Qumran Songs of the Sabbath Sacrifice," *IEJ* 34
                  (1984) 77-88 (+ pl. 9). See also E. Puech, "Notes
                  sur le manuscrit des Cantiques du Sacrifice du
                  Sabbat trouvé à Masada," *RevQ* 12 (Mémorial
                  Jean Carmignac, 1985-87) 575-83. Cf. 4QŠirŠabb
                  above.

(3) *Ostraca, etc.*

MasOstr   Yadin, Y., *Masada: Herod's Fortress*, 82, 110-14

papMasEp gr   Yadin, Y., *Masada: Herod's Fortress*, 189-91

papMas lat

III. MURABBA'AT

Mur 1-173		Benoit, P., J. T. Milik, and R. de Vaux, *Les grottes de Murabba'at* (DJD 2; Oxford: Clarendon, 1961). Two parts: 1. Texte; 2. Planches. (Though five caves were discovered, only three yielded written material: 1Mur: texts 2, 78; 2Mur: texts 3-77, 79-87, 89-173; 5Mur: text 88 (see DJD 2. 50). But it is customary not to distinguish them by cave in this instance, and the texts are simply designated by Mur and numbered consecutively according to genre.)

Bardtke, H., *Die Handschriftenfunde in der Wüste Juda* (Berlin: Evangelische Haupt-Bibelgesellschaft, 1962) 81-93. German transl. of Mur 19-25, 29-30, 38, 42-46, 72, 115.

Koffmahn, E., *Die Doppelurkunden aus der Wüste Juda: Recht und Praxis der jüdischen Papyri des 1. und 2. Jahrhunderts n. Chr. samt Übertragung der Texte und deutsche Übersetzung* (STDJ 5; Leiden: Brill, 1968)

Detailed Listing of Mur 1-173 in DJD 2

A. *Murabba'at Cave 1*

Mur 2	MurDeut	Deut 10:1-3; 11:2-3; 12:25-26; 14:29-15:1 or 2
Mur 78	MurABC	Ostracon with inscribed partial alphabet

B. *Murabba'at Cave 2*

(1) *OT Texts*

Mur 1	MurGen, MurExod, MurNum	Gen 32:4-5,30; 32:33-33:1; 34:5-7; 34:30-35:1,4-7; Exod 4:28-31; 5:3; 6:5-11; Num 34:10; 36:7-11
Mur 3	MurIsa	Isa 1:4-14
Mur 4	MurPhyl	Exod 13:1-10,11-16; Deut 11:13-21; 6:4-9
Mur 5	MurMez(?)	Illegible

(2) *Literary Texts (?)*

Mur 6	Mur?	Non-biblical literary text
Mur 72	Mur?	Aramaic narrative text (written on an ostracon)
Mur 108 gr	Mur?	Fragmentary philosophical(?) text (on papyrus)
Mur 109-12 gr	Mur?	Fragmentary literary texts (on papyrus)

(3) *Non-Literary Documents and Letters*

Mur 7		Contract (very fragmentary, in Hebrew)
Mur 8 ar		Account of cereals and vegetables (in Aramaic)
Mur 9		List (with numerical ciphers)
Mur 10	MurPalimp^a	List of Names with accounts; Abecedary
Mur 11		Abecedary
Mur 12-16		Non-classified frgs.
Mur 17	MurPalimp^b	Palimpsest Letter (8th c. BC [Milik]); List of persons
Mur 18 ar		IOU (dated in 2d year of Nero Caesar, AD 55/56) (in Aramaic)
Mur 19 ar		Writ of divorce (in Aramaic, dated AD 111)
Mur 20 ar		Marriage contract (in Aramaic, dated AD 117)
Mur 21 ar		Marriage contract (in Aramaic, date missing [Milik is inclined to date it "avant la Première Révolte")
Mur 22		Deed of sale of land (in Hebrew, dated AD 131)
Mur 23 ar		Deed of sale (?) (in Aramaic, AD 132[?])
Mur 24		Farming contracts (*diastrōmata*, in Hebrew, AD 133), texts A-F: more or less complete; texts G-L: quite fragmentary
Mur 25 ar		Deed of sale of land (in Aramaic, AD 133)

Mur 26 ar		Deed of sale (in Aramaic)
Mur 27 ar		Deed of sale (in Aramaic)
Mur 28 ar		Deed about some property (in Aramaic)
Mur 29		Deed of sale (in Hebrew, dated AD 133)
Mur 30		Deed of sale of land (in Hebrew, dated AD 134)
Mur 31 ar		Deeds of sale, various frgs. (in Aramaic)
Mur 32 ar		Deed about money (in Aramaic)
Mur 33 ar		Deed about money (in Aramaic)
Mur 34-35 ar		Frgs. of Aramaic contracts
Mur 36		Frgs. of a Hebrew contract
Mur 37-40		Scraps of contracts and signatures
Mur 41		List of persons
Mur 42	MurEpBeth-Mashiko	Letter of the administrators of Beth-Mashiko to Yeshuaᶜ ben Galgulaᵓ
Mur 43	MurEpBarCᵃ	Letter of Shimᶜon ben Kosibah to Yeshuaᶜ ben Galgulaᵓ
Mur 44	MurEpBarCᵇ	Letter of Shimᶜon to Yeshuaᶜ ben Galgulaᵓ
Mur 45		Letter (fragmentary)
Mur 46	MurEpJona-than	Letter of Jonathan ben X to Joseph [ben...], sent from ᶜEn-Gedi
Mur 47		Fragmentary letter (in Hebrew)
Mur 48		Fragmentary letter (in Hebrew)
Mur 49-52		Fragments of letters
Mur 53-70		Non-classified fragments
Mur 71 nab		Fragment of a text written in Nabatean script
Mur 73		Abecedary and list of personal names on an ostracon
Mur 74		List of persons on an ostracon
Mur 75-77		Lists of persons on ostraca
Mur 79-80		Abecedaries on ostraca
Mur 81-86		Non-classified frgs. of ostraca
Mur 87		Personal name on an ostracon
Mur 89 gr		Account of money (in Greek, on skin)

Mur 90 gr	Account of cereals and vegetables (in Greek, on skin)
Mur 91 gr	Account of cereals and vegetables (in Greek, on skin)
Mur 92 gr	Account of cereals (in Greek, on skin)
Mur 93 gr	An account of (?) (in Greek, on skin)
Mur 94 gr	Recapitulation of accounts (in Greek, on skin)
Mur 95 gr	List of names (in Greek, on skin)
Mur 96 gr	Account of cereals and vegetables (in Greek, on skin)
Mur 97 gr	Account of cereals (in Greek, on skin)
Mur 98-102 gr	Fragments of accounts (?)
Mur 103-7 gr	"Coins de feuilles et onglets" (in Greek, on skin)
Mur 113 gr	Proceedings of a lawsuit
Mur 114 gr	IOU (in Greek, on papyrus, dated AD 171[?])
Mur 115 gr	Contract of remarriage (in Greek, *Doppelurkunde* on papyrus, dated AD 124)
Mur 116 gr	Contract of marriage (in Greek, on papyrus)
Mur 117 gr	Extracts of official ordinances (in Greek, on papyrus, end of 2d c. AD)
Mur 118 gr	An account (fragmentary, on papyrus, in Greek)
Mur 119 gr	List (fragmentary, on papyrus, in Greek)
Mur 120 gr	List (fragmentary, on papyrus, in Greek)
Mur 121 gr	List (fragmentary, on papyrus, in Greek)
Mur 122 gr	List or a schoolboy's exercise (in Greek, on papyrus)
Mur 123-25 gr	Fragments of lists
Mur 126-32 gr	Fragments in literary or notarial script
Mur 133-54	Fragments in cursive script
Mur 155 gr	Fragments of a document

Mur 156 gr	Christian liturgical fragment (11th c. AD[?])
Mur 157 gr	Fragmentary magical text (10th c. AD)
Mur 158-59 lat	Fragmentary texts of official nature (in Latin, on papyrus)
Mur 160-63 lat	Fragments (in Latin, on papyrus)
Mur 164 gr	Document in Greek shorthand (as yet undeciphered)
Mur 165-68	Ostraca texts (very fragmentary) in Greek or Latin
Mur 169-73	Arabic texts (from the 9th-10th c. AD)

C. *Murabbaʿat Cave 5*

(1) *OT Text*

Mur 88   MurXII   col.

i	Joel 2:20
ii	Joel 2:26-4:16
iii	Amos 1:5-2:1
iv-v	(missing)
vi	Amos 6 (only a few letters left)
vii	Amos 7:3-8:7
viii	Amos 8:11-9:15
ix	Obad 1-21
x	Jonah 1:1-3:2
xi	Jonah 3:2 — Mic 1:5
xii	Mic 1:5-3:4
xiii	Mic 3:4-4:12
xiv	Mic 4:12-6:7
xv	Mic 6:11-7:17
xvi	Mic 7:17 — Nah 2:12
xvii	Nah 2:13-3:19
xviii	Hab 1:3-2:11
xix	Hab 2:18 — Zeph 1:1
xx	Zeph 1:11-3:6
xxi	Zeph 3:8 — Hag 1:1
xxii	Hag 1:12-2:10
xxiii	Hag 2:12 — Zech 1:4

The Dead Sea Scrolls

D. *Possibly a Murabbaʿat Cave*

Mur(?) Gen

Puech, E., "Fragment d'un rouleau de la Genèse provenant du Désert de Juda (*Gen.*, 33,18-34,3)," *RevQ* 10 (1979-81) 163-66.

IV. NAḤAL ḤEVER (WADI KHABRA)

> See *The Expedition to the Judean Desert, 1960-1961* (= *IEJ* 11-12 [1961-62]); cf. M. Broshi, "Recherches archéologiques israéliennes dans la région de Qumrân," *DBSup* 9 (1979) 1475-79 (on Naḥal Ḥever, Naḥal Ṣeʾelim, and Maṣada)

(1) *OT Texts*

?ḤevGen
Burchard, C., "Gen 35:6-10 und 36:5-12 MT aus der Wüste Juda (Naḥal Ḥever, Cave of the Letters?)," *ZAW* 78 (1966) 71-75 (The photograph is published in ADAJ 2 [1953] pl. XII)

5/6ḤevNum
Yadin, Y., "Expedition D — The Cave of the Letters," *IEJ* 12 (1962) 227-57, esp. 229 (+ pl. 48; = Num 20:7-8)

5/6ḤevPs
Yadin, Y., "Expedition D," *IEJ* 11 (1961) 36-52, esp. 40 (= Ps 15:1-5; 16:1 [and even 7:14-31:22; cf. J. A. Sanders, *JBL* 86 (1967) 439])

8ḤevXII gr
Barthélemy, D., *Les devanciers d'Aquila: Première publication intégrale du texte des fragments du Dodécaprophéton trouvés dans le Désert de Juda, précédée d'une étude sur les traductions et recensions grecques de la Bible réalisées au premier siècle de notre ère sous l'influence du rabbinat palestinien* (VTSup 10; Leiden: Brill, 1963) 163-78

8ḤevXII gr
Lifshitz, B., "The Greek Documents from the Cave of Horror," *IEJ* 12 (1962) 201-7 (+ pl. 32B); *Yediʿot* 26 (1962) 183-90 (9 more frgs. belonging to the text that Barthélemy published, discovered in March 1961, establishing the provenience of the text). Barthélemy (*Les devanciers d'Aquila*, 168, n. 9) differs with Lifshitz's identification of the frgs. and proposes the following identification:

frg. 1   Nah 3:13 (Lifshitz: Hos 2:8)
frg. 2   Amos 1:5(?) (Lifshitz: Amos 1:5)
frg. 3   Nah 1:14 (Lifshitz: Joel 1:14)
frg. 4   Jonah 3:2-5 (also Lifshitz)

frg. 5   Nah 1:13-14 (Lifshitz: Nah 1:9)
frg. 6   ? (certainly not Nah 2:8-9 [so
          Lifshitz]; see above)
frg. 7   Zech 3:1-2 (also Lifshitz)
frg. 8   Nah 3:3 (Lifshitz: 3:1-2)
frg. 9   Zech 2:11-12 (Lifshitz: Zech 4:8-9)

Tov, E. (in collaboration with R. A. Kraft), *The Greek Minor Prophets Scroll from Naḥal Ḥever (8ḤevXIIgr)* (DJD 8; The Seiyâl Collection I; Oxford: Clarendon, 1990)

Detailed Listing of Contents of 8ḤevXII gr

col.	
ii	Jonah 1:14-16; 2:1-7
iii	Jonah 3:2-5,7-10; 4:1-2,5
iv	Mic 1:1-7a
v	Mic 1:7b-8
vi	Mic 2:7-8; 3:5-6
vii	Mic 4:3-5
viii	Mic 4:6-10; 5:1-4(5)
ix	Mic 5:4(5)-6(7)
xiii	Nah 1:13-14
xiv	Nah 2:5-10,14
xv	Nah 3:6-17
xvi	Hab 1:5-11
xvii	Hab 1:14-17; 2:1-8a
xviii	Hab 2:13-20
xix	Hab 3:9-15
xx	Zeph 1:1-6a
xxi	Zeph 1:13-18
xxii	Zeph 2:9-10
xxiii	Zeph 3:6-7
xxviii	Zech 1:1-4
xxix	Zech 1:12-15
xxx	Zech 1:19-2:4,7-12
xxxi	Zech 2:16-3:7
B1	Zech 8:19-23a
B2	Zech 8:23b-9:5

(2) *Letters and Contracts*

pap5/6HevA nab	Starcky, J., "Un contrat nabatéen sur papyrus," *RB* 61 (1954) 161-81; cf. Y. Yadin, "Expedition D — The Cave of the Letters," *IEJ* 12 (1962) 227-57, esp. 229 (on the provenience of the contract)
pap?HevB ar	Milik, J. T ., "Un contrat juif de l'an 134 après J.-C.," *RB* 61 (1954) 182-90; "Deux documents inédits du Désert de Juda," *Bib* 38 (1957) 245-68, esp. 264-68 (+ pl. IV)
pap?HevC ar	Milik, J. T., "Deux documents," *Bib* 38 (1957) 255-64 (+ pls. II-III)
5/6HevEp 1-15	Yadin, Y., "Expedition D," *IEJ* 11 (1961) 36-52 (+ pl. 22); *BIES* (= *Yediʿot*) 25 (1961) 49-64; "Expedition D — The Cave of the Letters," *IEJ* 12 (1962) 227-57. Cf. E. Y. Kutscher, "The Languages of the Hebrew and Aramaic Letters of Bar Kokhba and His Contemporaries, *Lešonénu* 25 (1960-61) 117-33; 26 (1961-62) 7-23 [texts of various letters with brief modern Hebrew commentary]
5/6HevBA	Yadin, Y., "Expedition D — The Cave of Letters," *IEJ* 12 (1962) 227-57, esp. 235-57 (mostly a preliminary report, but with some texts of the Babatha archive). See now N. Lewis (ed.), *The Documents from the Bar Kokhba Period in the Cave of Letters: Greek Papyri* (Jerusalem: Israel Exploration Society, 1989). In this volume 37 Greek legal texts are published. The subscriptions on some documents in Aramaic or Nabatean or both have been presented by Y. Yadin and J. C. Greenfield.
5/6HevBA	Polotsky, H. J., "*Šlwš tʿwdwt mʾrkywnh šl Bbth bt Šmʿwn*," *The E. L. Sukenik Memorial Volume* (Eretz Israel 8; Jerusalem: Israel Exploration Society, 1967) 46-51 (3 documents of the Babatha archive); cf. N. Lewis "Two Greek Documents from Provincia Arabia," *Illinois Classical Studies* 3 (1978) 100-114

Yadin, Y., "The Nabataean Kingdom, Provincia Arabia, Petra and En-Geddi in the Documents from Naḥal Ḥever," *JEOL* 17 (1963) 227-41

Polotsky, H. J., "The Greek Papyri from the Cave of the Letters," *IEJ* 12 (1962) 258-62; *Yediʿot* 26 (1962) 237-41

Yadin, Y., *Bar-Kokhba: The Rediscovery of the Legendary Hero of the Second Jewish Revolt against Rome* (London: Weidenfeld and Nicolson, 1971) 124-253

P. Yadin 18   Lewis, N., R. Katzoff, and J. C. Greenfield, "*Papyrus Yadin* 18: I. Text, Translation and Notes; II. Legal Commentary; III. The Aramaic Subscription," *IEJ* 37 (1987) 229-50

5/6ḤevEp gr   Lifshitz, B., "Papyrus grecs du désert de Juda," *Aegyptus* 42 (1962) 240-56 (+ 2 pls.); cf. Y. Yadin, *Bar-Kokhba*, 130-31 (2 Greek letters of Bar Cochba or his lieutenant)

8ḤevEp gr   Aharoni, Y., "Expedition B — The Cave of Horror, *IEJ* 12 (1962) 186-99, esp. 197; cf. B. Lifshitz, "The Greek Documents," *IEJ* 12 (1962) 206-7 (+ pl. 32A)

V. NAḤAL ṢEʾELIM (WADI SEIYAL)

34ṢePhyl   Aharoni, Y., "Expedition B," *IEJ* 11 (1961) 11-24, esp. 22-23 (+ pl. 11); *Yediʿot* 25 (1961) 19-33; cf. *ILN*, 20 February 1960, p. 230 (Photograph); London *Times*, 16 February, 1960 (= 2 phylactery frgs., Exod 13:2-10,11-16)

34ṢeEp   Aharoni, Y., "Expedition B," *IEJ* 11 (1961) 11-24, esp. 24

pap34Ṣe gr 1-8   Lifshitz, B., "The Greek Documents from Nahal Seelim and Nahal Mishmar," *IEJ* 11 (1961) 53-62, esp. 53-58 (+ pl. 23), 205; *BIES* (= *Yediʿot*) 25 (1961) 65-73 (lists of Greek names)

VI. NAHAL MISHMAR (WADI MAHRAS)

papMiš gr   Bar Adon, P., "Expedition C," *IEJ* 11 (1961) 25-35;
                 BIES 25 (1961) 34-38
                 Lifshitz, B., "The Greek Documents from Naḥal
                 Ṣeelim and Naḥal Mishmar," *IEJ* 11 (1961) 53-
                 62, esp. 59-60 (papyrus lists of names)

VII. KHIRBET MIRD

papMird A   Milik, J. T., "Une inscription et une lettre en araméen christo-palestinien," *RB* 60 (1953) 526-39; cf. *Bib* 42 (1961) 21-27

Mird Acts cpa Perrot, C., "Un fragment christo-palestinien découvert à Khirbet Mird (Actes des Apôtres, X, 28-29; 32-41)," *RB* 70 (1963) 506-55 (+ pls. XVIII, XIX)

MirdAmul cpa Baillet, M., "Un livret magique en christo-palestinien à l'Université de Louvain," *Muséon* 76 (1963) 375-401.

papMird 1-100 arab   Grohmann, A., *Arabic Papyri from Ḫirbet el-Mird* (Bibliothèque du Muséon 52; Louvain: Publications universitaires, 1963)

VIII. CAIRO GENIZAH

Though not discovered in the vicinity of the Dead Sea, these texts are medieval copies of some of the documents that have been discovered in the Qumran caves or at Maṣada and are thus related to them. These texts were actually found at the end of the 19th century in a genizah of the Ezra synagogue in Old Cairo.

CSir	Schechter, S. and C. Taylor, *The Wisdom of Ben Sira: Portions of the Book Ecclesiasticus from Hebrew Manuscripts in the Cairo Genizah Collection Presented to the University of Cambridge by the Editors* (Cambridge, UK: University Press, 1899)
CD	Schechter, S., *Documents of Jewish Sectaries: Volume 1: Fragments of a Zadokite Work* (Cambridge, UK: University Press, 1910) [reprinted with a prolegomenon by J. A. Fitzmyer; New York: Ktav, 1970].
	Zeitlin, S., *The Zadokite Fragments: Facsimile of the Manuscripts in the Cairo Genizah Collection in the Possession of the University Library, Cambridge, England* (*JQR*, Monograph Series 1; Philadelphia: Dropsie College, 1952).
	Rabin, C., *The Zadokite Documents: I. The Admonition; II. The Laws, Edited with a Translation* (Oxford: Clarendon, 1954; 2d rev. ed., 1958)
CTLevi ar	Known to exist in two sources: (a) Cambridge University Genizah Frg. T-S 16.94; (b) Bodleian Library Genizah Frg., Ms Heb c 27 f 56.
	Pass, H. L. and J. Arendzen, "Fragment of an Aramaic Text of the Testament of Levi," *JQR* 12 (1899-1900) 651-61 (= Cambridge frg.; no photograph).
	Charles, R. H. and A. Cowley, "An Early Source of the Testaments of the Patriarchs," *JQR* 19 (1906-7) 566-83 (= Bodleian frg. with photograph + text of Cambridge frg. [without photograph]).

Greenfield, J. C. and M. E. Stone, "Remarks on the Aramaic Testament of Levi from the Geniza," *RB* 86 (1979) 214-30 (+ pls. XIII-XIV [photograph of the Cambridge frg.])

Grelot, P., "Le testament araméen de Lévi, est-il traduit de l'hébreu? A propos du fragment de Cambridge, col. c 10 à d 1," *REJ* 114 (1955) 91-99. Cf. *RB* 62 (1955) 398-406.

III

BIBLIOGRAPHIES OF THE DEAD SEA SCROLLS

Amussin, J. D., "Bibliography," *RevQ* 14 (1989-90) 121-26.

Amussin, J. D., "*1 Enoch* and the Figure of Enoch: A Bibliography of Studies 1970-1988," *RevQ* 14 (1989-90) 149-74.

Burchard, C., *Bibliographie zu den Handschriften vom Toten Meer* (BZAW 76; Berlin: Töpelmann, 1957) [Alphabetical arrangement by authors]

Burchard, C., *Bibliographie zu den Handschriften vom Toten Meer, II: Nr. 1557-4459* (BZAW 89; Berlin: Töpelmann, 1965) [Continuation of the preceding; up to 1962]

Fitzmyer, J. A., "A Bibliographical Aid to the Study of the Qumran Cave IV Texts 158-186," *CBQ* 31 (1969) 59-71 (serves as a supplement to DJD 5) [Arranged according to texts]

Fröhlich, I., "Bibliographie des recherches hongroises sur les manuscrits de la Mer Morte, *FO* 25 (1988) 79-83.

García Martínez, F. and E. J. C. Tigchelaar, "*1 Enoch and the Figure of Enoch: A Bibliography of Studies 1970-1988,*" *RevQ* 14 (1989) 149-74.

Habermann, A. M., "*Byblywgrpyh lḥr mgylwt mdbr yhwdh wšᵓr hmmṣᵓym šnmṣᵓw šm*" [title varies in different installments], *Beth Mikra* (Jerusalem) 1 (1956) 116-21; 2 (1957) 92-97; 3 (1958) 103-11; 4 (1959) 91-95; 5 (1960) 89-93; 6 (1961) 87-91; 13 (1962) 126-33; 16 (1963) 147-51; Nos. 18-19 (1964) 215-19; Nos. 23-24 (1965) 125-33; No. 27 (1966) 162-67; No. 32 (1967) 134-36; No. 35 (1968) 134-40; No. 41 (1969-70) 208-16; (nothing in Nos. 42-51 [1972]) [Alphabetical arrangement]

Jongeling, B., *A Classified Bibliography of the Finds in the Desert of Judah 1958-1969* (STDJ 7; Leiden: Brill, 1971). (Sequel to LaSor's *Bibliography*; topical arrangement; updated supplement is in preparation)

Kapera, Z. J., "Selected Polish Subject Bibliography of the Dead Sea Discoveries," *FO* 23 (1985-86) 269-338

Koester, C., "A Qumran Bibliography: 1974-1984," *BTB* 15 (1985) 110-20.

LaSor, W. S., *Bibliography of the Dead Sea Scrolls 1948-1957* (Fuller Library Bulletin 31; Pasadena: Fuller Theological Seminary Library, 1958) [Topical arrangement]

Nober, P., "Elenchus bibliographicus," *Bib*, each year up to 1967, section IV/c, "Qumranica et praemishnica"; since 1968 the bibliography has been published separately as *Elenchus bibliographicus biblicus* (Rome: Biblical Institute), see chapter IV/3 (until 60 [1979], when R. North took over *EBB*). Since 61 (1980) "Qumran Surveys" appears in section K3. *EBB* changed its name after 65 (1984). It is now called *Elenchus of Biblica 1985* (Elenchus of Biblical Bibliography 1; Rome: Biblical Institute, 1988). [Alphabetical arrangement by authors]

(Various Authors), "Bibliographie," *RevQ* 1 (1958-59) 149-60 (J. Carmignac), 309-20 (J. C.), 461-79 (C. Burchard), 547-626 (C. B.); 2 (1959-60) 117-51 (C. B.), 299-312 (J. C.), 459-72 (W. S. LaSor), 587-601 (W. S. L.); 3 (1961-62) 149-60 (W. S. L.), 313-20 (W. S. L.), 467-80 (W. S. L.), 593-602 (W. S. L.); 4 (1963-64) 139-59 (W. S. L.), 311-20 (W. S. L.), 467-80 (W. S. L.), 597-606 (J. C.); 5 (1964-66) 149-60 (W. S. L.), 293-320 (W. S. L.), 463-79 (J. C.), 597-607 (J. C.); 6 (1967-69) 301-20 (J. C.), 457-79 (J. C.); 7 (1969-71) 131-59 (J. C.), 305-19 (J. C.), 463-80 (J. C.); 8 (1972-75) 131-59 (J. C.), 299-319 (J. C.), 459-79 (J. C.); 9 (1977-78) 139-60 (J. C.), 293-319 (J. C.), 463-79; 10 (1979-81) 129-59 (J. C.), 455-79 (J. C.); 11 (1982-84) 119-59 (F. García Martínez), 295-320 (F. G. M.), 461-78 (F. G. M.); 12 (1985-87) 129-60 (F. G. M.), 293-315 (F. G. M.), 455-80 (F. G. M.). [Neither alphabetical nor topical arrangement; listed by periodicals from which the entries are culled (?!). But the indexes of each volume can be consulted for authors' names.]

Yizhar, M., *Bibliography of Hebrew Publications on the Dead Sea Scrolls 1948-1964* (HTS 23; Cambridge, MA: Harvard University, 1967) [Topical arrangement; see my review, *JBL* 87 (1968) 116]

IV

SURVEY ARTICLES AND PRELIMINARY REPORTS
ON UNPUBLISHED MATERIALS

SURVEY ARTICLES AND PRELIMINARY REPORTS ON UNPUBLISHED MATERIALS
(arranged by date of publication)

Starcky, J. and J. Milik, "L'Etat actuel du déchiffrement des manuscrits du Désert de Juda et le plan de leur publication," *CRAIBL* 1954, 403-9.

Benoit, P. et al., "Le travail d'édition des fragments manuscrits de Qumrân," *RB* 63 (1956) 49-67 (Report on 2-6Q); "Editing the Manuscript Fragments from Qumran," *BA* 19 (1956) 75-96 (An English version of the preceding).

Milik, J. T., "Le travail d'édition des manuscrits du Désert de Juda," *Volume du Congrès, Strasbourg 1956* (VTSup 4; Leiden: Brill, 1957) 17-26 (Report on Murabbaʿat, Ḥever, Minor Caves, 4Q texts)

Milik, J. T., *Ten Years of Discovery in the Wilderness of Judaea* (SBT 26; London: SCM; Naperville, IL: Allenson, 1959) 20-43 ("The Qumran Library").

Hunzinger, C. H., "Qumran," *Evangelisches Kirchenlexikon* (Göttingen: Vandenhoeck & Ruprecht), 3 (1959) 420-30

Cross, F. M., *The Ancient Library of Qumran and Modern Biblical Studies* (rev. ed.; Anchor Books A 272; Garden City, NY: Doubleday, 1961; repr., Grand Rapids, MI: Baker, 1980) 30-47 ("A Catalogue of the Library of Qumran").

Avigad, N. et al., *The Expedition to the Judean Desert, 1961* (= *IEJ* 12/3-4; Jerusalem: Israel Exploration Society, 1962)

Aviram, J. et al., *The Judean Desert Caves Archaeological Survey, 1961* (= *Yediʿot* 26/3-4; Jerusalem: Hebrew University and Department of Antiquities, 1963) [in modern Hebrew]

Skehan, P. W., "The Biblical Scrolls from Qumran and the Text of the Old Testament," *BA* 28 (1965) 87-100

Driver, G. R., *The Judaean Scrolls: The Problem and a Solution* (Oxford: Blackwell, 1965) (to be used with discretion, see R. de Vaux, *NTS* 13 [1966-67] 89-104).

Cross, F. M., *Die antike Bibliothek von Qumran und die moderne biblische Wissenschaft: Ein zusammenfassender Überblick über die Handschriften vom Toten Meer und ihre einstigen Besitzer*

101

(Neukirchener Studienbücher 5; Neukirchen/Vluyn: Neukirchener Verlag, 1967) (An updated form of *ALQ*)

Yadin, Y., *Bar-Kokhba: The Rediscovery of the Legendary Hero of the Second Jewish Revolt against Rome* (London: Weidenfeld and Nicolson, 1971) 124-253

Rost, L., *Judaism Outside the Hebrew Canon: An Introduction to the Documents* (Nashville: Abingdon, 1971) 129-90.

Sanders, J. A., "The Dead Sea Scrolls—A Quarter Century of Study," *BA* 36 (1973) 110-48

Vermes, G., "The Impact of the Dead Sea Scrolls on Jewish Studies during the Last Twenty-Five Years," *JJS* 26 (1975) 1-14; repr., *Approaches to Ancient Judaism* (ed. W. S. Green; BJS 1; Missoula, MT: Scholars, 1978) 201-14.

Vermes, G., *The Dead Sea Scrolls: Qumran in Perspective* (rev. ed.; London: Collins, 1977; Philadelphia: Fortress, 1981)

Soggin, J. A., *I manoscritti del Mar Morto* (Civiltà scomparse 22; Rome: Newton Compton Editori, 1978)

Grözinger, K. E. et al., *Qumran* (WF 410; Darmstadt: Wissenschaftliche Buchgesellschaft, 1981)

Nickelsburg, G. W. E., *Jewish Literature between the Bible and the Mishnah: A Historical and Literary Introduction* (Philadelphia: Fortress, 1981) 122-42, 231-41, 263-65.

Delcor, M. and F. García Martínez, *Introducción a la literatura esenia de Qumrán* (Academia cristiana 20; Madrid: Cristiandad, 1982)

Wise, M., "The Dead Sea Scrolls: Part 1, Archaeology and Biblical Manuscripts," *BA* 49 (1986) 140-54; "The Dead Sea Scrolls: Part 2, Nonbiblical Manuscripts," ibid., 228-43.

Fujita, N. S., *A Crack in the Jar: What Ancient Jewish Documents Tell Us about the New Testament* (Mahwah, NJ/New York: Paulist, 1986). Misentitled: The book treats of more than the influence of the Scrolls on the NT.

Schürer, E., *The History of the Jewish People in the Age of Jesus Christ (175 B.C.-A.D. 135)* (3 vols.; rev. ed., G. Vermes et al.; Edinburgh: Clark) III/1 (1986) passim.

Vermes, G., "Biblical Studies and the Dead Sea Scrolls 1947-1987: Retrospects and Prospects," *JSOT* 39 (1987) 113-28

García Martínez, F., "Estudios Qumránicos 1975-1985: Panorama crítico (I)," *EstBib* 45 (1987) 125-206; (II), ibid., 361-402; (III), *EstBib* 46 (1988) 325-74; (IV), ibid., 527-48; (V), *EstBib* 47 (1989) 93-118; (VI), ibid., 225-67.

Woude, A. S. van der, "Fünfzehn Jahre Qumranforschung (1974-1988)," *TRu* 54 (1989) 221-61 (to be continued).

Brown, R. E., "Apocrypha; Dead Sea Scrolls; Other Jewish Literature," *The New Jerome Biblical Commentary* (eds. R. E. Brown, J. A. Fitzmyer, and R. E. Murphy; Englewood Cliffs, NJ: Prentice-Hall, 1990), art. 67 (pp. 1068-79)

V

LISTS OF THE DEAD SEA SCROLLS
AND FRAGMENTS

LISTS OF THE DEAD SEA SCROLLS AND FRAGMENTS

The lists mentioned below are similar to that of chapter II above, but they are often less complete; some, however, include notice of texts known to exist but not yet published. Each list has its advantages and disadvantages, and the mode of listing in one reveals aspects of the study not found in others. The lists are arranged according to the date of publication.

Burchard, C., *Bibliographie II* (see chapter III above), 313-59: "Register: Ausgaben und Übersetzungen der neugefundenen Texte, Antike Essenerberichte"

Sanders, J. A., "Pre-Masoretic Psalter Texts," *CBQ* 27 (1965) 114-23

Stegemann, H., "Anhang," *ZDPV* 83 (1967) 95-100 (a supplement to Burchard's list)

Sanders, J. A., *DSPS*, 143-49: "Appendix II: Pre-Masoretic Psalter Texts," (cf. *JBL* 86 [1967] 439 for corrections)

Sanders, J. A., "Palestinian Manuscripts 1947-67," *JBL* 86 (1967) 431-40

Müller, K., "Die Handschriften und Editionen der ausserbiblischen Qumranliteratur," *Einführung in die Methoden der biblischen Exegese* (ed. J. Schreiner; Würzburg: Echter Verlag, 1971) 303-10

Sanders, J. A., "Palestinian Manuscripts 1947-1972," *JJS* 24 (1973) 74-83

Fitzmyer, J. A., *The Dead Sea Scrolls: Major Publications and Tools for Study* (SBLSBS 8; Missoula, MT: Scholars, 1975; with an Addendum, 1977) (earlier forms of the present work).

García Martínez, F., "Lista de mss procedentes de Qumran," *Henoch* 11 (1989) 149-232. (This list includes mention of many fragmentary texts of 4Q known to exist but not yet published,)

Brown, R. E., "Apocrypha" (see chapter IV above), 1068-70.

VI

CONCORDANCES, DICTIONARIES,
AND GRAMMARS FOR THE STUDY OF
THE DEAD SEA SCROLLS

CONCORDANCES, DICTIONARIES, AND GRAMMARS FOR THE STUDY OF THE DEAD SEA SCROLLS

These books are intended for use in the study of the original texts (in Aramaic, Hebrew, or Greek). They presuppose the use of ordinary concordances, dictionaries, and grammars in the study of these biblical languages.

Carmignac, J., "Concordance de la 'Regle de la Guerre,'" *RevQ* 1 (1958-59) 7-49.

Lignée, H., "Concordance de '1 Q Genesis Apocryphon,'" *RevQ* 1 (1958-59) 163-86.

Habermann, A. M., *Megilloth Midbar Yehuda: The Scrolls from the Judean Desert, Edited with Vocalisation, Introduction, Notes and Concordance* (Tel Aviv: Machbaroth Lesifruth, 1959) [1]-[175]

Kuhn, K. G. et al., *Konkordanz zu den Qumrantexten* (Göttingen: Vandenhoeck & Ruprecht, 1960). (All extrabiblical texts of 1Q; 4QIsa^{a-d}, 4QHos^{a,b}, 4QpNah, 4QpPs37, 4QPBless, 4QFlor, 4QTestim, 4QM^a, 6QD, CD)

Kuhn, K. G. et al., "Nachträge zur 'Konkordanz zu den Qumrantexten,'" *RevQ* 4 (1963-64) 163-234 (4QpNah, 4QpPs37, 4QFlor, 4QŠirŠabb, 4QDibHam, 4QOrd^a)

Qimron, E., *The Hebrew of the Dead Sea Scrolls* (HSS 29; Atlanta, GA: Scholars, 1986)

Richter, H. P., "Konkordanz zu XIQMelkîsédeq (éd. E. Puech)," *RevQ* 12 (1985-87) 515-18

Kuhn, K. G. et al., *Rückläufiges hebräisches Wörterbuch* (Göttingen: Vandenhoeck & Ruprecht, 1958). (A reverse-index of words in biblical and Qumran Hebrew writings; it lists the words spelled backwards as an aid to the restoration of lacunae in texts)

VII

SECONDARY COLLECTIONS OF QUMRAN TEXTS

SECONDARY COLLECTIONS OF QUMRAN TEXTS

Listed here are manuals which have brought together various texts of Qumran in convenient form. Sometimes they are accompanied by translations into a modern language; sometimes they are vocalized.

Bardtke, H., *Hebräische Konsonantentexte aus biblischem und ausserbiblischem Schrifttum für Übungszwecke ausgewählt* (Leipzig: Harrassowitz, 1954). (Parts of 1QIsa[a], 1QS, 1QpHab, 1QH, CD, Mur 42, 43)

Beyer, K., *Die aramäischen Texte vom Toten Meer, samt den Inschriften aus Palästina, dem Testament Levis aus der Kairoer Genisa, der Fastenrolle und den alten talmudischen Zitaten: Aramaistische Einleitung, Text, Übersetzung, Deutung: Grammatik/Wörterbuch, Deutsch-aramäische Wortliste, Register* (Göttingen: Vandenhoeck & Ruprecht, 1984). Contains the Aramaic texts of 1QapGen, 4QVisJac, 4QTJud, 4QTJos, 1QTLevi, 4QTLevi, CTLevi, 4QTQahat, 4Q'Amram, 1QJN, 2QJN, 4QJN, 5QJN, 11QJN, 4QprNab, 4QpsDan, 1QNoah, 4QEnastr, 4QEnGiants, 4QEn, 4QMess, 4QMilMik, 4QtgLev, 4QtgJob, 11QtgJob, 4QTob, 4QJer (10:11), 1QDan; Mur 18, Mur 19, Mur 20, Mur 21, Mur 23, Mur 25, Mur 26, Mur 27, Mur 28, Mur 31, Mur 32, Mur 33, Mur 38, Mur 43, Mur 44, Mur 72; 5/6HevBA, pap?HevB, pap?HevC. The texts are accompanied by translations and bibliographies. One must, however, note the differences in readings that Beyer often proposes; his readings have to be checked against the photographs in the *editiones principes*.

Boccaccio, P. and G. Berardi (eds. of a series, "Materiale didattico"):

Srk h'dh: *Regula congregationis* (Fani, Italy: Seminarium Picenum; Rome: Biblical Institute, 1956) (1QSa)

Mlḥmt bny 'wr bbny ḥwšk: *Bellum filiorum lucis contra filios tenebrarum: Fasc. A: Transcriptio et versio latina* (Fani: Seminarium Picenum, 1956) (1QM)

Pšr ḥbqwq: *Interpretatio Habacuc (1QpHab: Transcriptio et versio latina) (Appendix: Interpretatio Naḥum [2, 12b- 14])* (Fani: Seminarium Picenum, 1958). (1QpHab) (Second printing also contains *Interpretatio Ps 37.8-11, 19b-26* [Fani: Seminarium Picenum; Rome: Biblical Institute, 1958]) (4QpPs^a)

Srk hyḥd: Regula unionis seu manuale disciplinae (1QS): Transcriptio et versio latina (3d ed.; Fani: Seminarium Picenum; Rome: Biblical Institute, 1958)

Fitzmyer, J. A. and D. J. Harrington, *A Manual of Palestinian Aramaic Texts (Second Century B.C.—Second Century A.D.)* (BibOr 34; Rome: Biblical Institute, 1978). Contains the Aramaic texts of 1QDan, 1QapGen (+ 1Q20), 1QTLevi, 1QJN, 1QEnGiants, 2QJN, 2QEnGiants, 4QJer^b, 4QprNab, 4QpsDan; parts of 4QEnastr, 4QEnGiants, and 4QEn; 4QTLevi, 4Q'Amram, 4QTQahat, 4QMess, 4QVisJac (*olim* 4QTestuz), unidentified frgs. of 1Q, 3Q, 5Q, 6Q; MasOstr; Mur 8, Mur 19, Mur 20, Mur 21, Mur 23, Mur 25, Mur 26, Mur 27, Mur 28, Mur 31, 33-35, Mur 72; pap?ḤevB, pap?ḤevC, 5/6Ḥev 1,2,4,8,10,11,14,15, 5/6ḤevBA 1-2, 5/6Ḥev nab. Texts are accompanied by a translation and secondary bibliography.

Habermann, A. M., *'Edah we-'eduth: Three Scrolls from the Judaean Desert: The Legacy of a Community, Edited with Vocalisation, Introduction, Notes and Indices* (Jerusalem: Machbaroth Lesifruth, 1952). (Contains 1QpHab, 1QS, CD, and a text from the Cairo Genizah, published by I. Levi, *REJ* 65 [1913] 24-31)

Habermann, A. M., *Megilloth Midbar Yehudah* (see section 6 above). (The texts incorporated here [1QpHab, 1QS, CD, 1QM, 1QH, 4QPBless, 4QFlor, 4QpIsa^a, 1QpMic, 4QpNah, 1QpZeph, 4QpPs^a, 1QMyst, 1Q30-31, 1QSb, 1QLitPr, 1Q29] are pointed.)

Jongeling, B., C. J. Labuschagne, and A. S. van der Woude, *Aramaic Texts from Qumran, with Translations and Annotations* (Semitic Study Series 4; Leiden: Brill, 1976). Contains the Aramaic texts of 11QtgJob, 1QapGen, 4QprNab; the translations are accompanied by brief notes.

Licht, J., *Mgylt hsrkym: Srk hyḥd, srk lkwl 'dt yśr'l l'ḥryt hymym, srk hbrkwt* (Jerusalem: Student Association of Hebrew University, 1961-62) (Annotated unpointed Hebrew text of 1QS, 1QSa, 1QSb)

Lohse, E., *Die Texte aus Qumran: Hebräisch und deutsch, mit masoretischer Punktation, Übersetzung, Einführung und Anmerkungen* (Munich: Kösel; Darmstadt: Wissenschaftliche

Buchgesellschaft, 1964; 2d ed., 1971). Contains the pointed Hebrew texts of 1QS, 1QSa, 1QSb, CD, 1QH, 1QM, 1QpHab, 4QPBless, 4QTestim, 4QFlor, 4QpNah, 4QpPs^a with a German translation and brief notes.

Vegas Montaner, L., *Biblia del Mar Muerto: Profetas Menores: Edición crítica según manuscritos hebreos procedentes del Mar Muerto* (Textos y Estudios "Cardenal Cisneros" 29; Madrid: Instituto "Arias Montano," 1980). (This publication brings together the texts of the canonical Minor Prophets as they appear in 1QpHab, 1QpMic, 1QpZeph, 4QpHos^{a,b}, 4QpMic, 4QpNah, 4QpZeph, 4QFlor, 4QTanh, 4QCatena^a, 4QapLam, 4QXII? [Testuz], 5QAmos, 5QpMal [= 5Q10], Mur 88.)

Weiss, R., *Hmqr> bqwmr>n* (Jerusalem: Hebrew University, 1966) (A collection of samples of the biblical texts used at Qumran: e.g., 1QLev [= 1Q3] frgs. 1-7; 4QExod^a; QExod^m; 4QSam^a; samples of biblical quotations in non-biblical writings of Qumran; cols. 1, 29-33 of 1QIsa^a; 1QIsa^b; 11QPs^a cols. 16-19, 21-22, 24, 27-28; 1QpHab cols. 1-13; 4QpNah cols. 1-4; 4QpPs^a [= 4QpPs37] cols. 1-4; CD 3:13-4:21; 5:12-6:13; 7:9-21; 1QS cols. 1-11; 1QH col. 5)

Anon., *T<wdwt ltwldwt kt mdbr-yhwdh: Documents Bearing on the History of the Judaean Desert Sect* (Jerusalem: Hebrew University, 1966) (contains unpointed Hebrew text of CD, 1QS, 1QSa) (N.B. The title page reads: "For the use of the students of The Hebrew University but not for genaral [sic] sale.")

VIII

TRANSLATIONS OF THE DEAD SEA SCROLLS
IN COLLECTIONS

TRANSLATIONS OF THE DEAD SEA SCROLLS IN COLLECTIONS

Listed here are the books in which one finds attempts to translate into a modern language various Qumran texts known at the time, as well as the more wide-ranging discussions of the scrolls which often incorporate sizeable portions of the texts in translation. Any serious study of the texts must take such translations into consideration as well as those in the formal editions of the texts, since they often bear witness to pioneer attempts to cope with the problems of translating the Dead Sea scrolls. Translations of single texts, which form part of commentaries on such texts, are not listed here.

Allegro, J. M., *The Dead Sea Scrolls* (Pelican A376; Baltimore: Penguin, 1956; 2d ed., 1964): partial transl. of 4QSam[a], 4QDeut[a], 1QS, 1QH, Mur 42-43.

Amusin, I. D., *Nakhodki u Mertvogo moria* (Moscow: Akademia Nauk, 1964)

Amusin, I. D., *Teksty Kumrana* (Moscow: Akademia Nauk, 1971): Russian transl. of 1QpHab, 4QpNah, 4QpHos[b,a], 1QpMic, 4QpPs37, 4QFlor, 4QPBless, 11QMelch, 4QTestim, 1QMyst, 4QPrNab.

Bardtke, H., *Die Handschriftenfunde am Toten Meer: Mit einer kurzen Einführung in die Text- und Kanonsgeschichte des Alten Testaments* (2d ed.; Berlin: Evangelische Haupt-Bibelgesellschaft, 1953): German transl. of 1QS, 1QH, 1QM, 1QpHab.

Bardtke, H., *Die Handschriftenfunde am Toten Meer: Die Sekte von Qumran* (2d ed.; Berlin: Evangelische Haupt-Bibelgesellschaft, 1961): German transl. of 1QIsa[a], 1QS, 1QM, 1QH, CD, 1QapGen, 1QSa, 1QSb, 1Q34, 1QDM, 1QMyst, 1QpHab, 1QpMic, 1QpZeph, 1QpPs, 4QPrNab, 4QpNah, 4QFlor, 4QTestim.

Baron, S. W. and J. Blau, *Judaism: Post-Biblical and Talmudic Period* (Library of Religion 3; New York: Liberal Arts Press, 1954): partial English transl. of CD, 1QS, 1QH.

Bič, M., *Poklad v Judské pouti: Kumránské nálezy* (Prague: Ústřední církevní nakladaleství, 1960)

Bonsirven, J., *La Bible apocryphe: En marge de l'Ancien Testament* (Paris: Beauchesne, 1953): partial French transl. of CD, 1QpHab, 1QS, 1QM, 1QH.

Burrows, M., *The Dead Sea Scrolls* (New York: Viking, 1955): English transl. of CD, 1QpHab, 1QS, 1QM (selections), 1QH (selections).

Burrows, M., *More Light on the Dead Sea Scrolls: New Scrolls and New Interpretations with Translations of Important Recent Discoveries* (New York: Viking, 1958): transl. of 1QapGen, 1QSa, 1QSb, 1QMyst, 1QLitPr, 4QPrNab, 4QTestim, 4QFlor, 4QpPs37, 4QPBless, 4QpIsa[a], 1QpMic, 4QpNah.

Carmigmac, J., P. Guilbert, and E. Cothenet, *Les textes de Qumran traduits et annotés* (2 vols.; Paris: Letouzey et Ané, 1961, 1963): French transl. of 1QS, 1QM, 1QH, 1QSa, 1QSb, 3QpIsa, 4QpIsa[b], 4QpIsa[a], 4QpIsa[c], 4QpIsa[d], 4QpHos[b], 4QpHos[a], 1QpMic, 4QpNah, 1QpHab, 1QpZeph, 4QpPs37, CD, 1QapGen, 1QDM, 1QMyst, 1QLitPr, 4QTestim, 4QFlor, 4QPBless, 4QPrNab, 4QDibHam, 4QŠirŠabb.

Dupont-Sommer, A., *Aperçus préliminaires sur les manuscrits de la Mer Morte* (L'Orient Ancien Illustré 4; Paris: Maisonneuve, 1950): French transl. (broken up) of 1QpHab, 1QS, CD, 1QH, 1QM.

Dupont-Sommer, A., *The Dead Sea Scrolls: A Preliminary Survey* (tr. E. M. Rowley; Oxford: Blackwell, [1952]): English version of the preceding.

Dupont-Sommer, A., *Les écrits esséniens découverts près de la Mer Morte* (Bibliothèque historique; Paris: Payot, 1959; 3d ed., 1964): French transl. of 1QS, 1QSa, 1QSb, CD, 1QM, 1QH, 1QpHab, 4QpNah, 4QpPs37, 4QpIsa[a], 4QpHos[b], 1QpMic, 1QpZeph, 1QapGen, 1QDM, 4QFlor, 4QPBless, 4QTestim, 4QpsDan, 4QPrNab, 1QMyst, 1QJN, 1QLitPr.

Dupont-Sommer, A., *The Essene Writings from Qumran* (tr. G. Vermes; Oxford: Blackwell, 1961; repr., Cleveland: World, 1962; Magnolia, MA: Peter Smith, 1971): English version of the preceding.

Edelkoort, A. H., *De Handschriften van de Dode Zee* (Baarn: Bosch en Keuning, 1952; 2d ed., 1954): Dutch transl. of 1QpHab, 1QS, 1QH, 1QM, 1QJub[a].

Gaster, T. H., *The Dead Sea Scriptures: In English Translation with Introduction and Notes* (Anchor A378; Garden City, NY: Doubleday, 1956; rev. ed., 1964; 3d ed., 1976): transl. of 1QS, CD, 4QOrd^a, 1QSb, 1QH, 11QPs^a (in part), 4QDibHam, 4QŠirŠabb, 4QpIsa^a-e, 4QpHos^b, 1QpMic, 4QpNah, 1QpHab, 4QpPs^a, 1QapGen, 1QDM, 1QM, 4QCatena^a, 1QMyst, 4Q185, 11QMelch, 1QLitPr^a, 1QSa, 4QPBless, 4QTestim, 4QFlor, 4QMess ar, 4QWiles, 4Q^cAmram, 4QBookPeriods. (The translation of texts is quite free; no indication is given of cols. or lines.)

Haapa, E. (ed.), *Qumran: Kuolleen meren löydöt 1950-luvun tutkimuksessa* (Porvoo-Helsinki: W. Söderström, 1960).

De Handschriften van de Dode Zee in nederlands vertaling (Amsterdam: Proost en Brandt). Dutch transl. in a series:

Woude, A. S. van der, *De Dankpsalmen* (1957): transl. of 1QH.

Woude A. S. van der, *Bijbelcommentaren en bijbelse verhalen* (1958): transl. of 1QpHab, 1QpMic, 4QpNah, 4QpPs37, 4QpIsa^a, 4QPBless, 4QFlor, 4QTestim, 1QapGen, 1QDM.

Brongers, H. A., *De Gedragsregels der Qoemraan-Gemeente* (1958): transl. of CD, 1QS, 1QSa.

Brongers, H. A., *De Rol van de Strijd* (1960): transl. of 1QM.

Hempel, J., "Chronik," *ZAW* 62 (1949-50) 246-72: partial German transl. of 1QM, 1QH.

Knibb, M. A., *The Qumran Community* (Cambridge, UK/London/New York: Cambridge University, 1987): English transl. of CD, 1QS, 1QSa, 1QH, 1QapGen, 4QprNab, 4QpNah, 1QpHab, 4QpPs, 4QFlor, 4QTestim.

Lamadrid, A. G., *Los descubrimientos de Qumran* (Madrid: Instituto Español de Estudios Eclesiásticos, 1956): Spanish transl. of 1QS, 1QSa, CD, 1QH 3-4, 1QM (in part).

Lamadrid, A. G., *Los descubrimientos del Mar Muerto: Balance de veinticinco años de hallazgos y estudio* (BAC 317; Madrid: Editorial Católica, 1971): partial Spanish transl. of major texts.

Lambert, G ., "Traduction de quelques 'psaumes' de Qumrân et du 'pêsher' d'Habacuc," *NRT* 74 (1952) 284-97.

Lohse, E., *Die Texte aus Qumran hebräisch und deutsch* (see chapter VII above).

Maier, J., *Die Texte vom Toten Meer: I. Übersetzung; II. Anmerkungen* (2 vols.; Munich/Basel: E. Reinhardt, 1960): German transl. of 1QS, CD, 1QH, 1QM, 1QpHab, 1QapGen, 1QpMic, 1QDM,

1QMyst, 1QSa, 1QSb, 4QpNah, 4QpPs37, 4QPBless, 4QTestim, 4QFlor, 4QIsa[a,b,c,d], 4QpHos[a,b].

Maier, J., *Die Tempelrolle vom Toten Meer übersetzt und erläutert* (Munich/Basel: E. Reinhardt, 1978): German transl. of 11QTemple. *The Temple Scroll: An Introduction, Translation & Commentary* (tr. R. T. White; JSOTSup 34; Sheffield, UK: University of Sheffield, 1985): English version of the preceding.

Medico, H. E. del, *Deux manuscrits hébreux de la Mer Morte: Essai de traduction du 'Manuel de Discipline' et du 'Commentaire d'Habbakuk' avec notes et commentaires* (Paris: Geuthner, 1951): French transl. of 1QpHab, 1QS.

Medico, H. E. del, *L'énigme des manuscrits de la Mer Morte: Etude sur la provenance et le contenu des manuscrits découverts dans la grotte I de Qumrân suivi de la traduction commentée des principaux textes* (Paris: Plon, 1957): French transl. of 1QS, 1QSa, 1QSb, 1QpHab, 1QM, 1QH, 1QapGen, CD.

Medico, H. E. del, *The Riddle of the Scrolls* (tr. H. Garner; London: Burke, 1958): English version of the preceding.

Michelini Tocci, F., *I manoscritti del Mar Morto: Introduzione, traduzione e commento* (Bari: Laterza, 1967): Italian transl. of 1QS, 1QSa, 1QSb, CD, 1QM, 1QH, 4QŠirŠabb, 4QDibHam, 1QLitPr, 11QPs[a], 4QpPs37, 4QpHos, 1QpMic, 4QpNah, 1QpHab, 3QpIsa, 4QpIsa[a], 1QapGen, 4QPrNab, 1QDM, 4QTestim, 4QFlor, 4QOrd[a], 4QPBless, 11QMelch, 1QMyst, 5QJN, 4QMess ar[a], 4QCryptic, 4QWiles, 3Q15.

Milik, J. T., "Elenchus textuum ex caverna Maris Mortui," *VD* 30 (1952) 34-35, 101-9: Latin transl. of 1QJub[a], 1Q19, 1QMyst.

Molin, G., *Die Söhne des Lichtes: Zeit und Stellung der Handschriften vom Toten Meer* (Vienna/Munich: Herold, 1954): German transl. of 1QpHab, 1QpMic, 1QS, 1QH, 1QM, 1QMyst, CD.

Moraldi, L., *I manoscritti di Qumrân* (Classici delle religioni; Turin: Unione Tipografico — Editrice Torinese, 1971): Italian transl. of 1QS, 1QSa, 1QSb, CD, 1QM, 1QH, 11QPs[a], 4QpPs37, 3QpIsa, 4QpIsa[a,b,c,d,e], 4QpHos[a,b], 4QpMic, 1QpMic, 4QpNah, 1QpHab, 4QPBless, 4QFlor, 11QMelch, 4QVisSam (= 4Q160), 4QCatena[a,b], 4QTanh (= 4Q176), 4QTestim, 1QDM, 1QapGen, 1QMyst, 1QLitPr, 4QDibHam, 4QOrd[a], 4QŠirŠabb, 4QPrNab, 4QCryptic, 4QMess ar[a], 4QAgesCreat, 4QLam[a] (= 4Q179), 4QWisdom (= 4Q185), 4QWiles, 3Q15, 5QJN. This was the most comprehensive collection of translated texts up to the time of publication.

Nielsen, E. and B. Otzen, *Dødehavs teksterne: Skrifter fra den jødiske menigheid i Qumran i oversaettelse og med noter* (2d ed.; Copenhagen: G. E. C. Gad, 1959): Danish transl. of 1QpHab, 1QpMic, 4QpNah, 1QS, 1QH, 1QM, 1QSa, 1QMyst.

Reicke, B., *Handskrifterna från Qumran (eller ʿAin Feshcha) I-IV* (SymBU 14; Uppsala: Wretman, 1952): Swedish transl. of 1QpHab, 1QS.

Rosenvasser, A., "Los manuscritos descubiertos en el desierto de Judá," *Davar* (Buenos Aires) 29 (1950) 75-98; 30 (1950) 80-109: Spanish transl. of 1QM, 1QS, 1QH, 1QpHab.

Schreiden, J., *Les énigmes des manuscrits de la Mer Morte* (Wetteren: Editions Cultura, 1961; 2d ed., 1964): transl. of 1QpHab, 1QS, 1QSa, CD.

Schubert, K., "Die jüdischen und judenchristlichen Sekten im Lichte des Handschriftenfundes von ʿEn Fescha," ZKT 74 (1952) 1-62: German transl. of 1QpHab, 1QS.

Schubert, K., "Die Texte aus der Sektiererhöhle bei Jericho," *Nötscher Festschrift* (BBB 1; Bonn: Hanstein, 1950) 224-45: German transl. of 1QS, 1QH, 1QM.

Sekine, M. (ed.), *Shikai-bunsho* (Tokyo: Yamamoto Shoten, 1963): complete Japanese translation of texts published to date, with notes.

Simotas, P. N., "Ta heurēmata tou Khirbet Qumran," *Nea Sion* 47 (1952) 25-56, 141-46: Modern Greek transl. of 1QJub[a], 1QMyst, 1QM, 1QH.

Sutcliffe, E. F., *The Monks of Qumran* (Westminster, MD: Newman, 1960): English transl. of CD, 1QSa, 1QS, 1QpHab, 1QpMic, 4QpNah, 4QpPs37, 1QH, 1QSb, 1QM.

Tyloch, W., *Rekopisy z Qumran ned Morzem Martwym* (Polskie Tow. Religioznawcze, Rozprawy i Materialy 6; Warsaw: Panstowe Wyd. Naukowe, 1963): Polish transl. of 1QS, 1QSa, 1QM, 1QH, 1QpHab, CD.

Vermes, G., *Les manuscrits du Désert de Juda* (2d ed.; Paris: Desclée, 1954): French transl. of 1QpHab, 1QS, CD, 1QH, 1QM, 1QMyst, Mur 42, Mur 43.

Vermes, G., *Discovery in the Judean Desert* (New York: Desclée, 1956): English version of the preceding entry.

Vermes, G., "Quelques traditions de la communauté de Qumrân d'après les manuscrits de l'Université Hebraëque," *Cahiers sioniens* 9 (1955) 25-58: partial French transl. of 1QM, 1QH.

Vermes, G., *The Dead Sea Scrolls in English* (3d ed.; London: Penguin; New York: Viking Penguin, 1987): transl. of 1QS, CD, 1QSa, 1QM, 4QM, 11QTemple, 4Q181, 4Q286-87, 4Q280-82, 1QH, 11QPs[a], 4Q179, 4Q501, 4QDibHam, 4QŠirŠabb (= 4Q400-407), 11QŠirŠabb, 1QLitPr (= 1Q34, 34bis), 4QPrFêtes (= 4Q507-9), 4QPrQuot (= 4Q503, 1QSb, 4QRitPut (= 4Q512), 1Q27, 4QWiles (= 4Q184), 4Q185, 4Qir (= 4Q510-11), 1QapGen, 4QPBless, 4QAgesCreat, 4Q'Amram, 1QDM, 4QVisSam, 4QpIsa[a-d], 5QJN (= 5Q15), 4QprNab, 4QpsDan and 4Q246, 4QHos[a,b], 1QpMic, 4QpNah, 1QpHab, 4QpPs (= 4Q171, 173), 4QTestim, 4QOrd[a,b,c] (= 4Q159, 4Q513-14), 11QMelch, 4QTanh, 4Q186, 4QMess ar, 3Q15. This is the most comprehensive, one-volume English translation of the Scrolls to date; unfortunately the lines of the texts are not numbered, and so this translation is not easy to consult. (Earlier editions of this title appeared in 1962 [first], 1965, 1968, 1975 [2d ed.].)

Vincent, A., *Les manuscrits hébreux du Désert de Juda* (Textes pour l'histoire sacrée; Paris: A. Fayard, 1955): French transl. of 1QpMic, 1QpHab, 1QS, CD, 1QH, 1QM, 1QJub[a].

Werber, E., *Krcanstvo prije Krista?* (Zagreb: Liber, 1972): partial Yugoslav transl. of 1QS, CD, 1QpHab, 4QpNah, 4QpPs37, 1QM.

Dupont-Sommer, A. and M. Philonenko (eds.), *La Bible: Ecrits intertestamentaires* (Biblothèque de la Pléiade; Paris: Gallimard, 1987): Transl. of 1QS, 11QTemple, CD, 1QM, 1QH, 11QPs[a], 1QpHab, 4QpNah, 4QpPs37, 1QapGen, 4QFlor, 4QTestim, 11QMelch, 4QŠirŠabb, 4QWiles, 1QMyst; *1 Enoch, Jubilees, T. 12 Patr., Ps. Sol., T. Moses, Mart. Isa., Sib. Orac., 3 Apoc. Bar., 2. Enoch, Ps.-Philo, 4 Ezra, 2 Apoc. Bar., Joseph and Aseneth, T. Job, T. Abraham, Apoc. Abraham, Par. Jer., Adam and Eve, Apoc. Elijah.*

IX

OUTLINES OF SOME OF THE DEAD SEA SCROLLS
(WITH SELECT BIBLIOGRAPHY)

OUTLINES OF SOME OF THE DEAD SEA SCROLLS

In this section outlines are provided for the Manual of Discipline (1QS), the Damascus Document (CD + 4QD), the Genesis Apocryphon (1QapGen), the War Scroll (1QM), and the Temple Scroll (11QTemple^a) — the long sectarian scrolls. No attempt is made to outline the pesharim, since they follow for the most part the biblical texts on which they are commenting and cannot be divided up logically. The list of their contents and that of other scrolls, such as 11QPs^a, given in chapter II, is tantamount to an outline and should be consulted for study. The smaller texts, often because of their fragmentary character, do not lend themselves to outlining. The outlines provided are followed in some instances by bibliographical references; in others by indications where extensive bibliographies can be found.

SEREK HAY-YAḤAD: THE RULE OF THE COMMUNITY (1QS)

(I)	1:1-15	INTRODUCTION: The Aim and Purpose of the Community
(II)	1:16-3:12	ENTRANCE INTO THE COVENANT
(A)	1:16-2:18	Rite for Entrance into the Covenant
(B)	2:19-25a	Ceremony for the Assembly of Members
(C)	2:25b-3:12	Denunciation of Those Who Refuse to Enter
(III)	3:13-4:26	THE TENETS OF THE COMMUNITY
(A)	3:13-4:1	The Two Spirits
(B)	4:2-14	Activity of the Spirits in Human Life
(C)	4:15-26	Destiny and End of the Spirits
(IV)	5:1-6:23	PURPOSE AND WAY OF LIFE IN THE COMMUNITY
(A)	5:1-7a	Statement of the Purpose and the Way
(B)	5:7b-6:1a	Fidelity to the Way: Avoidance of Outsiders
(C)	6:1b-8	Rules for Community Life
(D)	6:8-13a	Rules for a Session of the Members
(E)	6:13b-23	Rules for Candidates
(V)	6:24-7:25	PENAL CODE OF THE COMMUNITY
(VI)	8:1-9:26	THE MODEL, PIONEER COMMUNITY
(A)	8:1-15a	Constitution and Negative Confession
(B)	8:15b-9:11	Conduct and Study of the Law until Messianic Times
(C)	9:12-26	Guidance for the Instructor of the Pioneer Community
(VII)	10:1-11:22	THE HYMN OF THE COMMUNITY
(A)	10:1-8a	The Creator to be Praised in Times of Worship
(B)	10:8b-11:2a	Hymn of Praise and Service
(C)	11:2b-15a	Hymn to God's Righteousness
(D)	11:15b-22	Hymn of Blessing and Thanksgiving

For the study of the structure of 1QS, see P. Guilbert, "Le plan de la Règle de la Communauté," *RevQ* 1 (1958-59) 323-44; A. R. C. Leaney, *The Rule of Qumran and Its Meaning*, 111-13; J. Licht, *The Rule Scroll*, 8-10.

Principal Commentaries or Translations of 1QS
(beyond those listed in chapter VIII above)

Brownlee, W. H., *The Dead Sea Manual of Discipline: Translation and Notes* (BASOR Supplementary Studies 10-12; New Haven: American Schools of Oriental Research, 1951). The pioneer translation.

Guilbert, P., "La règle de la Communauté," *Les textes de Qumran traduits et annotés* (ed. J. Carmignac et al., Paris: Letouzey et Ané) 1 (1961) 9-80.

Lambert, G., "Le Manuel de Discipline de la grotte de Qumrân: Traduction intégrale du 'Manuel de Discipline,'" *NRT* 73 (1951) 938-75 (also incorporated in A. Vincent, *Les manuscrits hébreux du Désert de Juda* [Paris: Fayard, 1955] 120-54)

Leaney, A. R. C., *The Rule of Qumran and Its Meaning* (New Testament Library; London: SCM; Philadelphia: Westminster, 1966)

Licht, J., *Měgillat has-Sěrākîm: The Rule Scroll: A Scroll from the Wilderness of Judaea: 1QS, 1QSa, 1QSb: Text, Introduction and Commentary* (Jerusalem: Bialik, 1965) (in modern Hebrew)

Milik, J. T., "Manuale disciplinae," *VD* 29 (1951) 129-58.

Pouilly, J., *La règle de la communauté de Qumrân: Son évolution littéraire* (Cahiers de la *RB* 17; Paris: Gabalda, 1976). An important literary analysis of 1QS.

Wernberg-Møller, P., *The Manual of Discipline* (STDJ 1; Leiden: Brill, 1957). See J. T. Milik's review of this commentary, *RB* 67 (1960) 410-16, esp. 412-16 for variant readings in the different texts of the *Serek* from Qumran Cave 4.

Of fundamental importance for the study of 1QS is the following article J. Murphy-O'Connor, "La genèse littéraire de la Règle de la Communauté," *RB* 76 (1969) 528-49. Pouilly's study listed above depends on this.

THE DAMASCUS DOCUMENT (CD AND 4QD)

This tentative outline utilizes the Cairo Genizah ms. A and the frgs. from Qumran Caves 4, 5, 6 and is arranged according to the indications given by J. T. Milik, *Ten Years*, 151-52. These indications are derived mainly from the copies of 4QD^{b,e}.

(I)   4Q Columns [missing in CD] + CD 1:1-8:21 (= 19:1-20:34)
EXHORTATION: GOD'S SAVING PLAN IN HISTORY

    (A)   Introductory Columns in 4Q Texts
    (B)   Meditation on the Lessons of History (CD 1:1-2:1)
    (C)   Predestination of the Upright and the Wicked (2:2-13)
    (D)   Second Meditation on Lessons of History (2:14-4:12a)
    (E)   The Three Nets of Belial (4:12b-6:2a [6Q15 1:1-3 = CD 4:19-21; 6Q15 2:1-2 = CD 5:13-14; 6Q15 3:1-5a = CD 5:18-6:2a])
    (F)   The Community of the New Covenant (6:2b-7:9a [6Q15 3:5 = CD 6:2b; 6Q15 4:1-4 = CD 6:20-7:1. CD 19:1-5a (ms. B) = 7:5b-9a])
    (G)   Diverse Fates of Those Who Are Faithful to the Covenant and of Those Who are Apostates (7:9b-8:21 [= (ms. B) 19:5b-34])
    (H)   Conclusion (ms. B: 19:35-20:34)

(II)   4Q Columns [missing in CD] PRESCRIPTIONS

    (A)   Cultic Purity of Priests and Sacrifices
    (B)   The Law of Diseases (cf. Lev 13:29ff.)
    (C)   The Fluxes of Men and Women (Leviticus 15)
    (D)   Laws of Marriage
    (E)   Prescriptions Relating to Agricultural Life, Payment of Tithes, Relations with Pagans, Relations between the Sexes; a Prohibition of Magic

(III)   15:1-16:20; 9:1-14:22   CONSTITUTION: LIFE IN THE
    [+ 4Q texts]   NEW COVENANT

    (A)   Rules for Entrance into the Covenant and for Oaths (15:1-16:16)

(1) The Oath by Which to Swear (15:1-5a)
(2) Admission into the Community (15:5b-19 [15: 15-17 can be restored as in 4QD^b]; see J. T. Milik, *Ten Years*, 114)
(3) Oath on Entering the Covenant (16:1-6a)
(4) The Validity of Oaths (16:6b-12)
(5) Voluntary Gifts (16:13-16)

(B) Regulations within the Community (9:1-10:10a)
(1) Fraternal Correction (9:1-6; 4QD^e 10 iii ?-20; 9:7-8a [= 5Q12 1:2])
(2) Judicial Oaths (9:8b-16a [5Q12 1:3-5 = CD 9:8b-10])
(3) Witnesses (9:16b-10:3)
(4) Judges (10:4-10a)

(C) Rites to be Observed in the Community (10:10b-12:18)
(1) Purification with Water (10:10b-13)
(2) Sabbath Regulations (10:14-11:18a)
(3) Sundry Regulations (11:18b-12:11a)
   (a) Sacrificial Offerings through an Unclean Intermediary (11:18b-21a)
   (b) Entrance into Temple in a State of Uncleanness (11:21b-23)
   (c) Defilement of the Sanctuary (12:1-3 [cf. 6Q15 5:1-5; does it belong here?])
   (d) Profanation of the Sabbath (12:3b-6a)
   (e) Killing or Robbing Pagans (12:6b-8a)
   (f) Commerce with Outsiders (12:8b-11a)
(4) Ritual Purity (12:11b-18)

(D) The Organization of the Community (12:19-14:19)
(1) Preamble (12:19-13:2a)
(2) Local Communities (13:2b-7a)
(3) The Overseer of the Camp (13:7b-14:2)
(4) Functionaries in the Community (14:3-12a)
(5) The Works of the Community (14:12b-19)

(E) The Penal Code (14:20-22)
(F) Liturgy for the Feast of the Renewal of the Covenant [4Q columns]

(IV) [4Q columns] CONCLUSION (see J. T. Milik, *RB* 63 [1956] 61)

N.B. Two mss. of CD came from the Cairo Genizah: Ms. A (10th cent.) contains 8 sheets with cols. 1-16; ms. B (12th cent.) contains one sheet with cols. 19-20. The latter cols. coincide roughly with cols. 7 and 8 of ms. A, but the last part of col. 20 corresponds to nothing in ms. A.

For an extensive bibliography on CD, see S. Schechter, *Documents of Jewish Sectaries* (with a prolegomenon by J. A. Fitzmyer; 2 vols. in one; New York: Ktav, 1970) 25-34. See further:

Davies, P. R., "The Ideology of the Temple in the Damascus Document," *JJS* 33 (1982) 287-301

Davies, P. R., *The Damascus Covenant: An Interpretation of the "Damascus Document"* (Sheffield, UK: JSOT, 1983)

Davies, P. R., "The Teacher of Righteousness and the 'End of Days,'" *RevQ* 13 (Mémorial Jean Carmignac, 1988) 313-17

Derrett, J. D. M., "'Beḥuqey hagoyim': Damascus Document IX, 1 Again," *RevQ* 11 (1982-84) 409-15

Dion, P.-E., "The Hebrew Particle ʾt in the Paraenetic Part of the 'Damascus Document,'" *RevQ* 9 (1977-78) 197-212

Greenfield, J. C., "The Words of Levi Son of Jacob in Damascus Document IV, 15-19," *RevQ* 13 (Mémorial Jean Carmignac,1988) 319-22

Huppenbauer, H. W., "Zur Eschatologie der Damaskusschrift," *RevQ* 4 (1963-64) 567-73

Kesterson, J. C., "Cohortative and Short Imperfect Forms in *Serakim* and *Dam. Doc.*," *RevQ* 12 (1985-87) 369-82

Knibb, M. A., "Exile in the Damascus Docuemtn," *JSOT* 25 (1983) 99-117

Levine, B. A., "Damascus Document IX, 17-22: A New Translation and Comments," *RevQ* 8 (1972-75) 195-96

Levy, R., "First 'Dead Sea Scroll' Found in Egypt Fifty Years before Qumran Discoveries," *BARev* 8/5 (1982) 38-52.

Milik, J. T., "Fragment d'une source du psautier (4QPs89) et fragments des Jubilés, du Document de Damas, d'un phylactère dans la grotte 4 de Qumran," *RB* 73 (1966) 94-106 (= 4QD^a 1 xvii 1-16 [corresponding to nothing in CD])

Milikowsky, C., "Again: *Damascus* in Damascus Document and in Rabbinic Literature," *RevQ* 11 (1982-84) 97-106

Murphy-O'Connor, J., "An Essene Missionary Document? CD II, 14 VI, 1," *RB* 77 (1970) 201-29

Murphy-O'Connor, J., "The Translation of Damascus Document VI,11-14," *RevQ* 7 (1969-71) 553-56

Murphy-O'Connor, J., "A Literary Analysis of Damascus Document VI, 2 —VIII, 3," *RB* 78 (1971) 210-32

Murphy-O'Connor, J., "The Critique of the Princes of Judah (CD VIII, 3-19)," *RB* 79 (1972) 200-16

Murphy-O'Connor, J., "A Literary Analysis of Damascus Document XIX, 33 —XX, 34," *RB* 79 (1972) 544-64

Murphy-O'Connor, J., "The *Damascus Document* Revisited," *RB* 92 (1985) 223-46

Nebe, G. W., "Der Gebrauch der sogenannten 'Nota Accusativi' את in Damaskusschrift XV, 5-9 und 12," *RevQ* 8 (1972-75) 257-66

Neusner, J., "'By the Testimony of Two Witnesses' in the Damascus Document IX, 17-22 and in Pharisaic-Rabbinic Law," *RevQ* 8 (1972-75) 197-217

Osten-Sacken, P. von der, "Die Bücher der Tora als Hütte der Gemeinde: Amos 5:26f. in der Damaskusschrift," *ZAW* 91 (1979) 423-35

Rosso-Ubigli, L., "Il documento di Damasco e la halakah settaria (Rassegna di studi)," *RevQ* 9 (1977-78) 357-99

Schiffman, L. H., "Legislation Concerning Relations with Non-Jews in the *Zadokite Fragments* and in Tannaitic Literature," *RevQ* 11 (1982-84) 379-89

Strickert, F. M., "Damascus Document VII, 10-20 and Qumran Messianic Expectation," *RevQ* 12 (1985-87) 327-49

Thorion-Vardi, T., "The Use of the Tenses in the Zadokite Documents," *RevQ* 12 (1985-87) 65-88

VanderKam, J. C., "Zadok and the Spr Htwrh Hḥtwm in Dam. Doc. V,2-5," *RevQ* 11 (1982-84) 561-70

Vermes, G., "Sectarian Matrimonial Halakah in the Damascus Rule," *JJS* 25 (1974) 197-202

Wacholder, B. Z., "The 'Sealed' Torah versus the 'Revealed' Torah: An Exegesis of Damascus Covenant V, 1-6 and Jeremiah 32, 10-14," *RevQ* 12 (1985-87) 351-68

Wacholder, B. Z., "Does Qumran Record the Death of the *Moreh*?: The Meaning of *heʾaseph* in *Damascus Covenant* XIX, 35, XX,14," *RevQ* 13 (Mémorial Jean Camignac, 1988) 323-30

White, S. A., "A Comparison of the 'A' and 'B' Manuscripts of the Damascus Document," *RevQ* 12 (1985-87) 537-53

Zahavy, T., "The Sabbath Code of Damascus Document X, 14-XI, 18:
    Form Analytical and Redaction Critical Observations," *RevQ*
    10 (1979-81) 589-91

THE GENESIS APOCRYPHON (1QapGen) or THE BOOK OF THE PATRIARCHS

(The beginning of the scroll is lost; see 1Q20
for some fragments of it.)

(I) THE STORY OF NOAH (1QapGen 1:? -17:?)
   (A) Lamech's Anxiety about the Conception of His Son Noah (2:1-5:?)
   (B) Noah and the Flood (6:?-10:-?)
   (C) God's Covenant with Noah (11:?)
   (D) Noah Divides the Earth among His Sons (16:?-17:?)

(II) THE STORY OF ABRAM (18:? —??)
   (A) Abram in Ur and Haran (18:?-?)
   (B) Abram in Canaan (18:?-19:9)
      (1) Abram's Journey to Bethel (19:?-6)
      (2) Abram's Journey from Bethel to Hebron (19:7-9)
   (C) Abram in Egypt (19:10-20:33)
      (1) Abram's Descent to Egypt because of a Famine (19:10-13)
      (2) Abram's Dream on Entering Egypt: The Cedar and the Date-Palm (19:14-23a)
      (3) Abram Visited by Three Nobles of the Pharaoh's Court (19:23b-27)
      (4) Sarai's Beauty Described by the Nobles to Pharaoh Zoan (20:2-8a)
      (5) Pharaoh Carries off Sarai; Abram's Prayer (20:8b-16a)
      (6) God Punishes Pharaoh and All His Household with a Plague (20:16b-21a)
      (7) Abram Cures Pharaoh Who Returns Sarai Untouched after Learning Her True Identity (20:21b-31a)
      (8) Pharaoh Sends Sarai and Abram from Egypt with Gifts and an Escort (20:31b-33)
   (D) Abram in the Promised Land (20:34-21:22)
      (1) Abram Returns with Lot to Bethel (20:34-21:4)
      (2) Lot Leaves Abram and Goes to Live in Sodom (21:5-7)

        (3)   Abram's Dream: The Promised Land (21:8-14)

        (4)   Abram Explores the Promised Land (21:15-22)

  (E)   Abram's Defeat of the Four Kings (21:23-22:26)

        (1)   Four Kings Invade and Defeat the Five
               Canaanite Kings (21:23-34a)

        (2)   Lot is Taken Captive (21:34b-22:5a)

        (3)   Abram Goes in Pursuit of the Four Kings
               (22:5b-12a)

        (4)   The Kings of Sodom and Salem Come out to
               Meet Abram on His Return from the Defeat
               of the Kings (22:12b-26)

  (F)   Abram's Vision: God Tells Him of His Heir (22:27—?)

        (1)   Eliezer, His Household Slave, Will Not Inherit
               Him (22:27-34)

Bibliography on 1QapGen can be found in my commentary: *The Genesis Apocryphon of Qumran Cave I: A Commentary* (BibOr 18; Rome: Biblical Institute, 1966; 2d rev. ed., 18A, 1971). See further:

Archer, G. L., Jr., "The Aramaic of the 'Genesis Apocryphon' Compared with the Aramaic of Daniel," *New Perspectives on the Old Testament* (ed. J. B. Payne; Waco, TX: Word Books, 1970 [appeared 1971]) 160-69

Bardtke, H., "Literaturbericht über Qumrān VI. Teil: II. Das Genesis-Apocryphon 1 QGenAp," *TRu* 37 (1972) 193-219, esp. 193-204

Batto, B. F., "The Reed Sea: *Requiescat in Pace*," *JBL* 102 (1983) 27-35.

Caquot, A., "Le livre des Jubilés, Melkisedeq et les dimes," *JJS* 33 (1982) 257-64

Cohen, S. J. D., "The Beauty of Flora and the Beauty of Sarai,"*Helios* 8 (1981) 41-53.

Coxon, P., "The Nunation Variant in the Perfect of the Aramaic Verb," *JNES* 36 (1977) 297-98.

Coxon, P. W., "The Problem of Nasalization in Biblical Aramaic in the Light of 1 Q GA and 11 Q tg Job," *RevQ* 9 (1977-78) 253-58

Dehandschutter, B., "Le rêve dans l'Apocryphe de la Genèse," *La littérature juive entre Tenach et Mischna: Quelques problèmes* (RechBib 9; Leiden: Brill, 1974) 48-55

Eichler, B. L., "ʾmry-nʾ ʾḥwty ʾt: hʿrkh ḥdšh bšmwšlwḥwt Nwzy lhʾrt hmqrʾ ('Please Say That You Are My Sister': Nuzi and Biblical Studies)," *Shnaton* 3 (1978-79) 108-15

Elmer-DeWitt, P., "When the Dead Are Revived," *TIME*, 14 March 1988, 89-81

Evans, C. A., "The Genesis Apocryphon and the Rewritten Bible," *RevQ* 13 (Mémorial Jean Carmignac, 1988) 153-65.

Freedman, D. N. and A. Ritterspach, "The Use of Aleph as a Vowel Letter in the Genesis Apocryphon," *RevQ* 6 (1967-69) 293-300

Grelot, P., "Un nom égyptien dans l'Apocryphe de la Genèse," *RevQ* 7 (1969-71) 557-66

Jongeling, B., "A propos de I Q GenAp XX, 28," *RevQ* 10 (1979-81) 301-3

Kee, H. C., *The Sources of Christianity: Sources and Documents* (Englewood Cliffs, NJ: Prentice Hall, 1973) 147-49 ("Non-Rabbinic Midrash")

Kennedy, J. M., "The Root G‛R in the Light of Semantic Analysis," *JBL* 106 (1987) 47-64

Liverani, M. "Un'ipotesi sul nome di Abramo," *Henoch* 1 (1979) 9-18.

Luria, B. Z., "Melchizedek, King of Salem, Priest of El Elyon,"*Beth Mikra* 32 (1986-87) 1-3 [in Modern Hebrew].

Miller, P. D., Jr., "El, the Creator of Earth," *BASOR* 239 (1980) 43-46.

Muraoka, T., "Notes on the Aramaic of the Genesis Apocryphon,"*RevQ* 8 (1972-75) 7-51.

Muraoka, T., "Segholate Nouns in Biblical and Other Aramaic Dialects," *JAOS* 96 (1976) 226-35, esp. 231-32

Reeves, J. C. "What Does Noah Offer in 1 QapGen X, 15?" *RevQ* 12 (1985-87) 415-19

Reif, S. C., "A Note on g‛r," *VT* 21 (1971) 241-44.

Starkova, C., "The Travels of Abraham (I Q Gen Ap XXI 8-20),"*PalSb* 28 (1986) 69-73 [Russian, with French abstract]

Stone, G. R., "Enhancing the Image of a Dead Sea Scroll," *Buried History* (Melbourne) 24 (1988) 32-35.

Tyloch, W., "Aramejski apokryf Księgi Rodzaju," *Euhemer* 81 (1971) 13-22.

VanderKam, J. C., "The Textual Affinities of the Biblical Citations in the Genesis Apocryphon," *JBL* 97 (1978) 45-55

VanderKam, J. C., "The Poetry of 1 Q Ap Gen, XX, 2-8a," *RevQ* 10 (1979-81) 57-66

Vasholz, R. I. "A Further Note on the Problem of Nasalization in Biblical Aramaic, 11 Q tg Job and 1 Q Genesis Apocryphon," *RevQ* 10 (1979-81) 95-96

Vattioni, F., "Aspetti del culto del signore dei cieli," *Augustinianum* 12 (1972) 479-515

Widengren, G., "Aramaica et syriaca," *Hommages à André Dupont-Sommer* (Paris: Maisonneuve, 1971) 221-31

Zuckerman, B. "'For Your Sake . . .': A Case Study in Aramaic Semantics," *JANES* 15 (1983) 119-29

THE WAR SCROLL (1QM)

(I) INTRODUCTION (1:1-?)
   (A) The Rule of the War to Come (1:1-7)
   (B) The Time Appointed for the Final Carnage (1:8-15)
   (C) The Annihilation of the Sons of Darkness (1:16-?)

(II) PREPARATION FOR THE FINAL WAR (1:?-2:14)
   (A) Reorganization of Worship to be Carried out during the Struggle (1:?-2:6a)
   (B) Gathering for the War (2:6b-9a)
   (C) Thirty-Five Years of the Battle and Its Operations (2:9b-14)

(III) RULES CONCERNING TRUMPETS, STANDARDS, AND SHIELDS IN THE STRUGGLE (2:15-5:2)
   (A) The Rule for the Trumpets (2:15-3:11)
      (1) The Sounding of the Trumpets (2:15-3:2a)
      (2) Inscriptions on the Trumpets (3:2b-11)
   (B) The Rule for the Standards (3:13-4:17+)
      (1) Inscriptions on the Standards of the Entire Congregation (3:13-17+)
      (2) Inscriptions on the Standards of the Clan of Merari (4:1-5)
      (3) Changes on the Standards of the Levites (4:6-8)
      (4) Changes on the Standards of the Congregation (4:9-14)
      (5) Dimensions of the Standards (4:15-17+)
   (C) The Rule for the Shields (4:?-5:2)
      (1) ? (4:?-?)
      (2) Inscriptions on the Shields (4:?-5:2)

(IV) BATTLE-ARRAY AND WEAPONS OF THE INFANTRY (5:3-6:6)
   (A) Rule for the Arming and Drawing Up of the Troops (5:3-14)
   (B) The Battle Array (5:16-6:6)

(V) ARRAY OF THE CAVALRY (6:8-17+)

(VI)   RECRUITMENT AND AGE OF THE SOLDIERS (6:?-7:7)

(VII)   ROLE OF THE PRIESTS AND LEVITES IN THE CAMP
         (7:9-9:9)

(VIII)   RULE FOR CHANGES IN BATTLE-ARRAY FOR AN
         ATTACK (9:10-18+)

(IX)   HIGH PRIEST'S EXHORTATION IN THE BATTLE-
         LITURGY (9:?-12:18+)
         (A)   Discourse of the High Priest (9:?-10:8a)
         (B)   Prayer of the High Priest (10:8b-12:18+)
               (1)   Praise of God's Power Shown in His Deeds
                     (10:8b-11:12)
               (2)   God's Power Will Accomplish New Things
                     (11:13-12:5)
               (3)   The Call for Divine Intervention (12:7-18+)

(X)   BLESSING UTTERED BY ALL LEADERS OF THE
         COMMUNITY AT VICTORY (12:?-14:1)
         (A)   God be Blest (12:?-13:3)
         (B)   Belial be Cursed (13:4-6)
         (C)   Victory for the Sons of Light Comes from God (13:7-
               16)
         (D)   ? (13:17-14:1)

(XI)   CEREMONY OF THANKSGIVING (14:2-18+)
         (A)   Blest be God (14:2-15)
         (B)   A Call for Aid (14:16-18+)

(XII)   THE LAST BATTLE AGAINST THE KITTIM (14:?-19:13)
         (A)   Beginning of the Battle (14:?-16:9)
               (1)   Arrival of the Troops (14:?-15:3)
               (2)   Exhortation Addressed to the First Troop (15:4-
                     16:1)
               (3)   Combat Engagement of the First Troop (16:3-9)
         (B)   The Second Troop (16:11-17:17+)
               (1)   Coming Forth of the Second Troop (16:11-14)
               (2)   Exhortation Addressed to the Second Troop
                     (16:15-17:3)

(3)   Exhortation to Bravery (17:4-9)
(4)   Combat Engagement of the Second Troop
       (17:10-17+)
(C)   The Third to the Seventh Troops (17:?-18:3a)
(D)   Destruction of the Kittim (18:3b-6a)
(E)   Prayer of Thanksgiving (18:6b-19:8)
(F)   Ceremony after the Battle (19:9-13)

Principal Commentaries or Translations of 1QM
(beyond those listed in chapter VIII above)

Carmignac, J., *La règle de la guerre des fils de lumière contre les fils de ténèbres: Texte restauré, traduit, commenté* (Paris: Letouzey et Ané, 1958)

Carmignac, J., "La règle de la guerre," *Les textes de Qumran traduits et annotés* (ed. J. Carmignac et al.; Paris: Letouzey et Ané) 1 (1961) 81-125

Dupont-Sommer, A., "Règlement de la guerre des fils de lumière: Traduction et notes," *RHR* 148 (1955) 25-43, 141-80

Jones, R. G., *The Rules for the War of the Sons of Light with the Sons of Darkness* (?: Privately published, 1956)

Jongeling, B., *Le rouleau de la guerre des manuscrits de Qumrân* (Assen: Van Gorcum, 1962)

Ploeg, J. van der, *Le rouleau de la guerre: Traduit et annoté avec une introduction* (STDJ 2; Leiden: Brill, 1959)

Yadin, Y., *Mĕgillat milḥemet bĕnê ʾôr ûbĕnê ḥōšek* (Jerusalem: Bialik, 1955); *The Scroll of the War of the Sons of Light against the Sons of Darkness* (tr. C. Rabin; Oxford: OxfordUniversity, 1962)

THE TEMPLE SCROLL (11QTemple^a)

  (2) Prohibition of Pagan Mourning Practices (48:8-14)

  (3) Places outside the City for Lepers, etc. (48:14-17)

  (4) Purification from Leprosy (48:17-49:4)

  (5) Defilement from a Dead Person (49:5-50:9)

  (6) Defilement from the Stillborn (50:10-19)

  (7) Defilement from Impure Small Animals (50:19-51:10)

 (B) Judicial Regulations I (51:11-18)

 (C) Cultic Regulations (51:19-54:7)

  (1) Pagan Practices Forbidden (51:19-52:3)

  (2) Unsuitable Sacrifices (52:4-12)

  (3) Use of Domestic Animals (52:12-13)

  (4) Slaughter and Eating of Unclean Animals (52:13- 53:8)

  (5) About Vows and Oaths of Men and Women (53:9-54:7)

 (D) On Idolatry (54:8-55:20)

 (E) Judicial Regulations II (56:1-11)

 (F) The Statutes of the King (56:12-59:21)

  (1) Setting up a King in Israel (56:12-21)

  (2) The King's Soldiers (57:1-11)

  (3) The King's Council (57:12-15)

  (4) The King's Wife: No Polygamy, No Divorce (57:15-19)

  (5) The King's Obligation to Justice (57:19-58:2)

  (6) Warfare, Mobilization, Booty (58:3-17)

  (7) The High Priest's Role in the King's War (58:18-21)

  (8) Curses and Blessings (59:1-21)

 (G) Priestly and Levitical Perquisites (60:1-15)

 (H) Divination and Prophecy, False Prophecy, False Testimony (60:16-61:12)

 (I) Military Regulations (61:13-62:16)

 (J) Protection of the Land from Blood Guilt (63:2-9)

 (K) Family Regulations (63:10-64:6)

 (L) Penalties for Capital Crimes (64:7-13)

 (M) Laws to Safeguard the Israelites (64:13-66:11)

 (N) Laws about Incest (66:11-17)

Bibliography on 11QTemple[a] can be found in F. García Martínez, "El rollo del Templo (*11 Q Temple*): Bibliografía sistemática," *RevQ* 12 (1985-87) 425-40 [up to December 1985]. See further Z. Kapera, "A Review of East European Studies on the Temple Scroll," *Temple Scroll Studies* (JSPS 7; ed. G. J. Brooke; Sheffield, UK: JSOT, 1989) 275-86. Also:

Baumgarten, J. M., "The First and Second Tithes in the *Temple Scroll*," *Biblical and Related Studies Presented to Samuel Iwry* (ed. A. Kort and S. Morschauser; Winona Lake, IN: Eisenbrauns, 1985) 5-15.

Baumgarten, J. M., "The Calendars of the Book of Jubilees and the Temple Scroll," *VT* 37 (1987) 71-78.

Betz, O., "The Temple Scroll and the Trial of Jesus," *Southwestern Journal of Theology* 30 (1988) 5-8

Brin, G., "Concerning Some of the Uses of the Bible in the Temple Scroll," *RevQ* 12 (1986-87) 519-28

Brooke, G. J., "The Temple Scroll and the Archaeology of Qumran, ʿAin Feshkha and Masada," *RevQ* 13 (Mémorial Jean Carmignac, 1988) 225-37.

Broshi, M., "The Gigantic Dimensions of the Visionary Temple in the Temple Scroll," *BARev* 13/6 (1987) 36-37

Callaway, P., "Exegetische Erwägungen zur Tempelrolle XXIX, 7-10," *RevQ* 12 (1985-87) 95-104.

Callaway, P., "Source Criticism of the Temple Scroll: The Purity Laws," *RevQ* 12 (1985-87) 213-22.

Callaway, P., "*ʾrbyh* in the Temple Scroll xxiv, 8," *RevQ* 12(1985-87) 269-70.

Callaway, P. R., "The Temple Scroll and the Canonization of Jewish Law," *RevQ* 13 (Mémorial Jean Carmignac, 1988) 239-50

Delcor, M., "Réflexions sur l'investiture sacerdotale sans onction à la fête du Nouvel An d'après le *Rouleau du Temple* (XIV 15-17)," *Hellenica et judaica: Hommage à Valentin Nikiprowetzky zʾl* (ed. A. Caquot; Louvain: Peeters, 1986) 155-64.

Delcor, M., "Réflexions sur la fête de la xylophorie dans le rouleau du Temple et les textes parallèles," *RevQ* 12 (1985-87) 561-69.

Delcor, M., "La description du Temple de Salomon selon Eupolémos et le problème de ses sources," *RevQ* 13 (Mémorial Jean Carmignac, 1988) 251-71.

Dion, P. E., "Early Evidence for the Ritual Significance of the 'Base of the Altar' around Deut 12:27 LXX," *JBL* 106 (1987) 487-90.

Emerton, J. A., "A Consideration of Two Recent Theories about Bethso in Josephus' Description of Jerusalem and a Passage in the Temple Scroll," *Text and Context: Old Testament and Semitic Studies for F. C. Fensham* (ed. W. Claasen; JSOTSup 48; Sheffield, UK: JSOT, 1988) 93-104.

Hengel, M., J. H. Charlesworth and D. Mendels, "The Polemical Character of 'On Kingship' in the Temple Scroll: An Attempt at Dating 11QTemple," *JJS* 37 (1986) 28-38.

McCready, W. O., "A Second Torah at Qumran?" *SR* 14 (1985) 5-15.

Mink, H.-A., "The Use of Scripture in the Temple Scroll and the Status of the Scroll as Law," *SJOT* 1 (1987) 20-50.

Mink, H.-A., "Tempel und Hofanlagen in der Tempelrolle," *RevQ* 13 (Mémorial Jean Carmignac, 1988) 273-85.

Patrich, J., "The *Mesibbah* of the Temple according to the Tractate *Middot*," *IEJ* 36 (1986) 215-33 (+ pl. 27A).

Qimron, E., "Further New Readings in the Temple Scroll," *IEJ* 37 (1987) 31-35.

Qimron, E., "Column 14 of the Temple Scroll," *IEJ* 38 (1988) 44-46.

Reeves, J. C., "The Meaning of *Moreh Ṣedeq* in the Light of 11QTorah," *RevQ* 13 (Mémorial Jean Carmignac, 1988) 287-98

Rofé, A., "Qumranic Paraphrases, the Greek Deuteronomy and the Late History of the Biblical *nśyʾ*," *Textus* 14 (1988) 163-74.

Rosen, D. and A. Salvesen, "A Note on the Qumran Temple Scroll 56:15-18 and Psalm of Solomon 17:33," *JJS* 38 (1987) 99-101.

Schiffman, L. H., "Exclusion from the Sanctuary and the City of the Sanctuary in the Temple Scroll," *Biblical and Other Studies in Memory of Shelomo D. Goitein* (ed. R. Ahroni; Hebrew Annual Review 9; Columbus, OH: Ohio State University, 1986) 301-20.

Schiffman, L. H., "The Laws of War in the Temple Scroll," *RevQ* 13 (Mémorial Jean Carmignac, 1988) 299-311

Shanks, H., "Intrigues and the Scroll—Behind the Scenes of Israel's Acquisition of the Temple Scroll," *BARev* 13/6 (1987) 23-27

Stegemann, H., "Is the Temple Scroll a Sixth Book of the Torah—Lost for 2,500 Years?" *BARev* 13/6 (1987) 28-35.

Stegemann, H., "The Origins of the Temple Scroll," *Congress Volume, Jerusalem 1986* (VTSup 40; ed. J. A. Emerton; Leiden: Brill, 1988) 235-56

Sweeney, M. A., "Midrashic Perspective in the Torat Ham-Melek of the Temple Scroll," *Hebrew Studies* 28 (1987) 51-66.

Wilk, R., "Ywḥnn Hwrqnws hrʾšwn wmgylt hmqdš (John Hyrcanus I and the Temple Scroll)," *Shnaton* 9 (1987) 221-30.

Wise, M. O., "A New Manuscript Join in the 'Festival of Wood Offering' (Temple Scroll XXIII)," *JNES* 47 (1988) 113-21.

X

SELECT BIBLIOGRAPHY ON SOME TOPICS
OF DEAD SEA SCROLLS STUDY

SELECT BIBLIOGRAPHY ON SOME TOPICS OF
DEAD SEA SCROLLS STUDY

The purpose of this section is to guide the student to the more important writings on various topics that have become areas of research in the study of the Dead Sea Scrolls. No effort is made here to be exhaustive on any of the topics, since it suffices to list the more important materials, which will of themselves contain references and guides to further literature. In some instances the literature on a topic is more abundant than others; but that is not to be taken as a gauge of the importance of the topic. Sometimes the literature has grown about a topic simply because of an extrinsic reason, e.g., the piecemeal fashion in which some of the texts have been published. The areas for special bibliographies are the following:

    I.   Palaeography of the Dead Sea Scrolls
    II.   Archaeology of the Dead Sea Scrolls
    III. The Old Testament at Qumran and Murabbaᶜat
    VI. Old Testament Interpretation in Qumran Literature
    V.   Qumran Theology
    VI. Qumran Messianism
    VII. The New Testament at Qumran ?
    VIII. The Qumran Scrolls and the New Testament
         A. Qumran Literature and Pauline Writings
         B. Qumran Literature and Johannine Writings
    IX. The Qumran Calendar and Related Problems
    X.   History of the Qumran Community

I. PALAEOGRAPHY OF THE DEAD SEA SCROLLS

The two most fundamental studies are those of:

Avigad, N., "The Palaeography of the Dead Sea Scrolls and Related
    Documents," *Aspects of the Dead Sea Scrolls* (Scripta hierosoly-
    mitana 4; Jerusalem: Magnes, 1958) 56-87.
Cross, F. M., "The Development of the Jewish Scripts," *The Bible and
    the Ancient Near East: Essays in Honor of William Foxwell
    Albright* (Anchor Books A431; Garden City, NY: Doubleday,
    1965) 170-264.

See further:

Eissfeldt, O., "Ansetzung der Rollen nach paläographischen
    Kriterien," *TLZ* 74 (1949) 226-28
Birnbaum, S. A., *The Qumrân (Dead Sea) Scrolls and Palaeography*
    (*BASOR* Supplementary Studies 13-14; New Haven: American
    Schools of Oriental Research, 1952)
Cross, F. M., "The Oldest Manuscripts from Qumran," *JBL* 74 (1955)
    147-72
Cross, F. M., "Excursus on the Palaeographical Dating of the Copper
    Document," *Les 'Petites Grottes' de Qumrân* (DJD 3) 217-21
Cross, F. M., "Epigraphic Notes on Hebrew Documents of the
    Eighth-Sixth Centuries B.C.: II. The Murabbaʿat Papyrus and
    the Letter Found near Yabneh-Yam," *BASOR* 165 (1962) 34-46
Hanson, R. S., "Paleo-Hebrew Scripts in the Hasmonean Age,"
    BASOR 175 (1964) 26-42
Hanson, R. S., "Jewish Palaeography and Its Bearing on Text Critical
    Studies," *Magnalia Dei: The Mighty Acts of God: Essays in
    Memory of G. E. Wright* (ed. F. M. Cross et al.; Garden City, NY:
    Doubleday, 1976) 561-76
Haran, M., "Bible Scrolls from Qumran to the Middle Ages: Types
    and Dates of Jewish and Gentile Skins," *Tarbiz* 51 (1981-82)
    347-82 (in modern Hebrew)

II. ARCHAEOLOGY OF THE DEAD SEA SCROLLS

To be noted above all are the following surveys and preliminary or official reports on various caves that have been published to date (arranged according to the date of publication):

Lankester Harding, G. et al., "Archaeological Finds," *Qumran Cave I* (DJD 1; Oxford: Clarendon, 1955) 3-40 (official report)

Vaux, R. de et al., "Archéologie," *Les grottes de Murabba'ât* (DJD 2 [1961]) 1-63 (official report)

Vaux, R. de, *L'Archéologie et les manuscrits de la Mer Morte* (The Schweich Lectures of the British Academy 1959; London: Oxford University, 1961). This appeared in a revised translation as *Archaeology and the Dead Sea Scrolls* (London: Oxford University, 1973). Vaux, R. de, "Archéologie," *Les 'Petites Grottes' de Qumran* (DJD 3 [1962]) 1-36 (with an appendix by J. T. Milik, "Deux jarres inscrites d'une grotte de Qumrân," 37-41) (official report)

Aviram, J. et al., "The Expedition to the Judean Desert, 1960,"*IEJ* 11 (1961) 3-72

Avigad, N. et al., "The Expedition to the Judean Desert, 1961,"*IEJ* 12 (192) 169-262 (This and the preceding entry are preliminary reports)

Yadin, Y., *The Finds from the Bar-Kokhba Period in the Cave of Letters* (Judaean Desert Studies 1; Jerusalem: Israel Exploration Society, 1963) (official report; a second volume is to present the texts found there now; see p. 87 above)

Yadin, Y., "The Excavation of Masada —1963/64: Preliminary Report," *IEJ* 15 (1965) 1-120

Yadin, Y., *Masada: Herod's Fortress and the Zealots' Last Stand* (London: Weidenfeld and Nicolson; New York: Random House, 1966) (A popular presentation of the excavation and finds)

Yadin, Y., *Bar Kokhba: The Rediscovery of the Legendary Hero of the Second Jewish Revolt against Rome* (London: Weidenfeld and Nicolson, 1971) (A popular presentation, which gives much information about the as yet unpublished texts)

Laperrousaz, E.-M, *Qoumrân: L'Etablissement essénien des bords de la Mer Morte: Histoire et archéologie du site* (Paris: Picard, 1976).

(An interpretation of the archaeology of Qumran that differs from that of de Vaux in some respects.)

Bar-Adon, P., "Another Settlement of the Judean Desert Sect at ʿEn el-Ghuweir on the Shores of the Dead Sea," *BASOR* 227 (1977) 1-25; cf. Eretz-Israel 10 (1971) 72-89; cf. R. de Vaux, *Archaeology*, 88-90.

Davies, P. R., *Qumran* (Cities of the Biblical World; Guilford, Surrey, UK: Lutterworth; Grand Rapids, MI: Eerdmans, 1982)

Preliminary Reports on the Qumran Area

These reports have often been superseded by the official ones, but at times they preserve details that become important because of subsequent developments. The most important preliminary reports are the following (arranged according to the date of publication):

Vaux, R. de, "Post-scriptum: La cachette des manuscrits hébreux,"*RB* 56 (1949) 234-37 (Report of the excavation of Qumran Cave 1)

Vaux, R. de, "La grotte des manuscrits hébreux," *RB* 56 (1949) 586-609

Vaux, R. de, "A propos des manuscrits de la Mer Morte," *RB* 57 (1950) 417-29 (De Vaux's initial dating of the pottery, which proved to be too early)

Lankester Harding, G., "Khirbet Qumran and Wady Murabbaʿat," *PEQ* 84 (1952) 104-9

Vaux, R. de, "Fouille au Khirbet Qumrân: Rapport préliminaire,"*RB* 60 (1953) 83-106 (Report on the first campaign of excavation at the Qumran community center)

Vaux, R. de, "Exploration de la région de Qumrân," *RB* 60 (1953) 540-61 (Report on the search for further caves, in which the Ecole Biblique and other archaeological institutions in Jerusalem were involved in 1952; see further the two following entries).

Reed, W. L., "The Qumrân Caves Expedition of March, 1952," *BASOR* 135 (1954) 8-13

Vaux, R. de, "Fouilles au Khirbet Qumrân: Rapport préliminaire sur la deuxième campagne," *RB* 61 (1954) 206-36 (Second campaign)

Vaux, R. de, "Chronique archéologique: Khirbet Qumrân," *RB* 61 (1954) 567-68 (Third campaign)

Vaux, R. de, "Chronique archéologique: Khirbet Qumrân," *RB* 63 (1956) 73-74 (Fourth campaign)

Vaux, R. de, "Fouilles de Feshkha: Rapport préliminaire," *RB* 66 (1959) 225-55

Vaux, R. de, "Une hachette essénienne," *VT* 9 (1959) 399-407

Vaux, R. de, "Excavations at ʿAin Feshka," *ADAJ* 4-5 (1960) 7-11.

Other Important Archaeological or Scientific Articles

Burton, D., J. B. Poole, and R. Reed, "A New Approach to the Dating of the Dead Sea Scrolls," *Nature* 184 (No. 4685, 15August 1959) 533-34

Duhaime, J. L., "Remarques sur les dépôts d'ossements d'animaux à Qumrân," *RevQ* 9 (1977-78) 245-51.

Laperrousaz, E.-M. and G. Odent, "La datation d'objets provenant de Qoumran, en particulier par la méthode utilisant les propriétés du carbone 14," *Sem* 27 (1977) 83-98.

Laperrousaz, E.-M., "A propos des dépôts d'ossements d'animaux trouvés à Qumrân," *RevQ* 9 (1977-78) 569-78 (comments on the article of Duhaime)

Laperrousaz, E.-M., "Brèves remarques archéologiques concernant la chronologie des occupations esséniennes de Qoumrân," *RevQ* 12 (1985-87) 199-212

Lapp, P. W., *Palestinian Ceramic Chronology 200 B.C. — A.D. 70* (New Haven: American Schools of Oriental Research, 1961)

Libby, W. F., "The Accuracy of Radiocarbon Dates," *Antiquity* 37 (1963) 213-19 (reprinted from *Science* 140 [No. 3564, 19 April [1963] 278-80)

Poole, J. B. and R. Reed, "The 'Tannery' of ʿAin Feshkha," *PEQ* 93 (1961) 114-23

Poole, J. B. and R. Reed, "The Preparation of Leather and Parchment by the Dead Sea Scrolls Community," *Technological Culture* 3 (1962) 1-26

Reed, R. and J. B. Poole, "A Study of Some Dead Sea Scroll and Leather Fragments from Cave 4 at Qumran: Part II, Chemical Examination," *Proceedings of the Leeds Philosophical and Literary Society*, Scientific Section 9/6 (1964) 171-82.

Sellers, O. R., "Radiocarbon Dating of Cloth from the ʿAin Feshkha Cave," *BASOR* 123 (1951) 24-26.

Strobel, A., "Die Wasseranlagen der Hirbet Qumrān: Versuch einer Deutung," *ZDPV* 88 (1972) 55-86.

Schulz, S., "Chirbet kumrān, ʿĒn Feschcha und die bukēʿa: Zugleich ein archäologischer Beitrag zum Felsenaquädukt und zur Strasse durch das wādi kumrān," *ZDPV* 76 (1960) 50-72

Stuckenrath R., "On the Care and Feeding of Radio-carbon Dating," *Archaeology* 18 (1965) 277-81.

Zeuner, F. E., "Notes on Qumran," *PEQ* 92 (1960) 27-36.

Controversial Aspects of the Archaeology of Qumran

Vaux, R. de, "Archaeology and the Dead Sea Scrolls," *Antiquity* 37 (1963) 126-27 (Reaction to J. L. Teicher)

Vaux, R. de, "Essenes or Zealots," *NTS* 13 (1966-67) 89-104 (Reaction to G. R. Driver)

Haas, N. and H. Nathan, "Anthropological Survey on the Human Skeletal Remains from Qumran," *RevQ* 6 (1967-69) 345-52.

Steckoll, S. H., "Preliminary Excavation Report in the Qumran Cemetery," *RevQ* 6 (1967-69) 323-44

Steckoll, S. H., "Marginal Notes on the Qumran Excavations," *RevQ* 7 (1969-71) 33-44. (On the last entries, note the comments of R. de Vaux, *Archaeology*, 47-48: "The authorities of the Israeli occupation have forbidden this Sherlock Holmes of archaeology [Steckoll] to continue his researches at Qumran.")

Davies, P. R., "How Not to Do Archaeology: The Story of Qumran," *BA* 51 (1988) 203-7

III. THE OLD TESTAMENT AT QUMRAN AND MURABBAᶜAT

Albright, W. F., "New Light on Early Recensions of the Hebrew Bible," *BASOR* 140 (1955) 27-33.

Cross, F. M., "The Scrolls and the Old Testament," *Christian Century* 73 (1955) 920-22.

Cross, F. M., "The History of the Biblical Text in the Light of Discoveries in the Judaean Desert," *HTR* 57 (1964) 282-99.

Cross, F. M., *ALQ*, 161-94; *Die antike Bibliothek von Qumran* (see chapter IV above), 154-79.

Cross, F. M., "The Contribution of the Qumran Discoveries to the Study of the Biblical Text," *IEJ* 16 (1966) 81-95.

Cross, F. M., "The Evolution of a Theory of Local Texts," *1971 Proceedings, International Organisation for Septuagint and Cognate Studies* (Septuagint and Cognate Studies 2; Missoula, MT: Society of Biblical Literature, 1972) 108-26.

Cross, F. M. and S. Talmon (eds.), *Qumran and the History of the Biblical Text* (Cambridge, MA: Harvard University, 1975)

Cross, F. M., "I. The Text behind the Text of the Hebrew Bible,"*Bible Review* 1 (1985) 12-25.

Delcor, M., "Zum Psalter von Qumran," *BZ* ns 10 (1966) 15-29.

Freedman, D. N., "The Massoretic Text and the Qumran Scrolls: A Study in Orthography," *Textus* 2 (1962) 87-102.

Freedman, D. N., "The Old Testament at Qumran," *NDBA*, 117-26.

Goshen-Gottstein, M. H., "The Hebrew Bible in the Light of Qumran Scrolls and the Hebrew University Bible," *Congress Volume, Jerusalem 1986* (VTSup 40; ed. J. A. Emerton; Leiden: Brill, 1988) 42-53.

Greenberg, M., "The Stabilization of the Text of the Hebrew Bible, Reviewed in the Light of the Biblical Materials from the Judean Desert," *JAOS* 76 (1956) 157-67.

Hoenig, S. B., "The Dead Sea Scrolls and the Bible," *JQR* 48 (1958) 304-6.

Howard, G., "Frank Cross and Recensional Critisism [sic]," *VT* 21 (1971) 440-50.

Kahle, P., *The Cairo Geniza* (2d ed.; Oxford: Blackwell, 1959)

Kutscher, E. Y., *The Language and Linguistic Background of the Isaiah Scroll (1 Q Isaᵃ)* (STDJ 6; Leiden: Brill, 1974)

Mansoor, M., "The Massoretic Text in the Light of Qumran,"*Congress Volume, Bonn 1962* (VTSup 9; Leiden: Brill, 1963) 305-21

Orlinsky, H. M., "Studies in the St. Mark's Isaiah Scroll," *JBL* 69 (1950) 149-66; *HUCA* 25 (1954) 85-92.

Orlinsky, H. M., "Qumran and the Present State of Old Testament Text Studies: The Septuagint Text," *JBL* 78 (1959) 26-33.

Orlinsky, H. M., "The Textual Criticism of the Old Testament," *The Bible and the Ancient Near East: Essays in Honor of William Foxwell Albright* (ed. G. E. Wright; Anchor Books A431; Garden City, NY: Doubleday, 1965) 140-69.

Purvis, J. D., *The Samaritan Pentateuch and the Origin of the Samaritan Sect* (HSM 2; Cambridge, MA: Harvard University, 1968)

Rabin, C., "The Dead Sea Scrolls and the History of the O. T. Text," *JTS* ns 6 (1955) 174-82

Roberts, B. J., "The Dead Sea Scrolls and the Old Testament Scriptures," *BJRL* 36 (1953-54) 75-96

Roberts, B. J., "The Old Testament Canon: A Suggestion," *BJRL* 46 (1963) 164-78

Sanders, J. A., *DSPS*, 143-55 (Catalogue of pre-Masoretic Psalms); cf. *CBQ* 27 (1965) 114-23

Sanders, J. A., "Cave 11 Surprises and the Question of Canon," *McCormick Quarterly* 21 (1968) 1-15 (repr, *NDBA*, 101-16)

Sanders, J. A., "The Qumran Psalms Scroll (11QPs[a]) Reviewed," *On Language, Culture, and Religion: In Honor of Eugene A. Nida* (ed. M. Black and W. A. Smalley; The Hague: Mouton, 1974) 79-99

Skehan, P. W., "The Qumran Manuscripts and Textual Criticism,"*Volume du congrès, Strasbourg 1956* (VTSup 4; Leiden: Brill, 1957) 148-60

Skehan, P. W., "The Period of the Biblical Texts from Khirbet Qumrân," *CBQ* 19 (1957) 435-40

Skehan, P. W., "Two Books on Qumran Studies," *CBQ* 21 (1959) 71-78

Skehan, P. W., "Qumran and the Present State of Old Testament Text Studies: The Masoretic Text," *JBL* 78 (1959) 21-25

Skehan, P. W., "The Scrolls and the Old Testament Text," *NDBA*, 89-100

Skehan, P. W., "Qumran, IV. Littérature de Qumran—A. Textes bibliques," *DBSup* 9 (1978) 805-28.

Skehan, P. W., "Qumran and Old Testament Criticism," *Qumrân: Sa piété, sa théologie et son milieu* (BETL 46; ed. M. Delcor; Gembloux: Duculot; Louvain: Leuven University, 1978) 163-82 (This important article lists not only the variants in 4QPs^{a-s} [over against BHS], but also the psalms and verses in the canonical psalter that are represented, as well as the palaeographical dating of the texts.)

Sundberg, A. C., *The Old Testament of the Early Church* (HTS 20; Cambridge: Harvard University, 1964); cf. *HTR* 51 (1958) 205-26; "The 'Old Testament': A Christian Canon," *CBQ* 30 (1968) 143-55

Talmon, S., "Aspects of the Textual Transmission of the Bible in the Light of Qumran Manuscripts," *Textus* 4 (1964) 95-132

Talmon, S., "The Old Testament Text," *Cambridge History of the Bible* (ed. P. R. Ackroyd and C. F. Evans; Cambridge, UK: University Press) 1 (1970) 159-99

Tov, E. and J. Cook, "A Computerized Database for the Qumran Biblical Scrolls with an Appendix on the Samaritan Pentateuch," *JNSL* 12 (1984) 133-37.

Tov, E., "The Orthography and Language of the Hebrew Scrolls Found at Qumran and the Origin of These Scrolls," *Textus* 13 (1986) 31-57.

Tov, E., "Hebrew Biblical Manuscripts from the Judaean Desert: Their Contribution to Textual Criticism," *JJS* 39 (1988) 5-37 (a very important article)

Ulrich, E., "Horizons of Old Testament Textual Research at the Thirtieth Anniversary of Qumran Cave 4," *CBQ* 46 (1984) 613-36.

IV. OLD TESTAMENT INTERPRETATION IN QUMRAN LITERATURE

Betz, O., *Offenbarung und Schriftforschung in der Qumransekte* (WUNT 6; Tübingen: Mohr [Siebeck], 1960)

Brooke, G. J., *Exegesis at Qumran: 4QFlorilegium in Its Jewish Context* (JSOTSup 29; Sheffield, UK: JSOT, 1985) [the sub-title is more accurate than the main title]

Brownlee, W. H., "Biblical Interpretation among the Sectaries of the Dead Sea Scrolls," *BA* 14 (1951) 54-76

Bruce, F. F., *Biblical Exegesis in the Qumran Texts* (Grand Rapids, MI: Eerdmans, 1959)

Efird, E. M. (ed.), *The Use of the Old Testament in the New and Other Essays: Studies in Honor of William Franklin Stinespring* (Durham, NC: Duke University, 1972)

Fitzmyer, J. A., "The Use of Explicit Old Testament Quotations in Qumran Literature and in the New Testament," *NTS* 7 (1960-61) 297-333; revised form, *ESBNT*, 3-58

Gottstein, M. H., "Bible Quotations in the Sectarian Dead Sea Scrolls," *VT* 3 (1953) 79-82

Horgan, M. P., *Pesharim: Qumran Interpretations of Biblical Books* (CBQMS 8; Washington, DC: Catholic Biblical Association of America, 1979)

Osswald, E., "Zur Hermeneutik des Habakuk-Kommentar," *ZAW* 68 (1956) 243-56

Ploeg, J. van der, "Bijbelverklaring te Qumrân," *Mededelingen der koninklijke Akademie van Wetenschappen*, Afd. Letterkunde, nieuwe reeks, deel 23, No. 8 (1960) 207-29

Roth, C., "The Subject Matter of Qumran Exegesis," *VT* 10 (1960) 51-65

Schwarz, O. J. R., *Der erste Teil der Damaskusschrift und das Alte Testament* (Diest: Lichtland, 1965)

Talmon, S., "DSI[a] as a Witness to Ancient Exegesis of the Book of Isaiah," *ASTI* 1 (1962) 62-72

Trever, J. C., "The Qumran Covenanters and Their Use of Scripture," *Personalist* 39 (1958) 127-38

Vermes, G., "A propos des commentaires bibliques découverts à Qumrân," *RHPR* 33 (1955) 95-102

Vermes, G., *Scripture and Tradition in Judaism: Haggadic Studies* (SPB 4; Leiden: Brill, 1961)

Vermes, G., "The Qumran Interpretation of Scripture in Its Historical Setting," ALUOS 6 (1966-68) 85-97

Waard, J. de, *A Comparative Study of the Old Testament Text in the Dead Sea Scrolls and in the New Testament* (STDJ 4; Leiden: Brill, 1965)

Wernberg-Møller, P., "Some Reflections on the Biblical Material in the Manual of Discipline," *ST* 9 (1955) 40-66

Wieder, N., "The Dead Sea Scrolls Type of Biblical Exegesis among the Karaites," *Between East and West* (1958) 75-106

162   The Dead Sea Scrolls

V. QUMRAN THEOLOGY

For articles on various aspects of Qumran theology or religion, see the topical bibliographies of W. S. LaSor and B. Jongeling and the yearly bibliography of P. Nober or R. North (chapter III above), as well as *NTA* (ed. D. J. Harrington; Cambridge: Weston School of Theology [3 times a year]) and *IZBG* (ed. F. Stier; B. Lang; Düsseldorf: Patmos [issued once a year]). Listed below are merely the more important books on the general topic.

Altmann, A. (ed.), *Biblical Motifs: Origins and Transformations* (Philip W. Lown Institute for Advanced Judaic Studies, Brandeis University, Texts and Studies 3; Cambridge, MA: Harvard University, 1966)

Betz, O., *Der Paraklet: Fürsprecher im häretischen Spätjudentum, im Johannesevangelium und in neu gefundenen gnostischen Schriften* (Leiden: Brill, 1963)

Denis, A.-M., *Les thèmes de connaissance dans le Document de Damas* (Studia hellenistica 15; Louvain: Publications universitaires, 1967)

Garnet, P., *Salvation and Atonement in the Qumran Scrolls* (WUNT 2/3; Tübingen: Mohr [Siebeck], 1977)

Huppenbauer, H. W., *Der Mensch zwischen zwei Welten: Der Dualismus der Texte von Qumran (Höhle I) und der Damaskusfragmente: Ein Beitrag zur Vorgeschichte des Evangeliums* (Zurich: Zwingli, 1959)

Jeremias, G., *Der Lehrer der Gerechtigkeit* (Göttingen: Vandenhoeck & Ruprecht, 1963)

Jeremias, J., *Die theologische Bedeutung der Funde am Toten Meer* (Göttingen: Vandenhoeck & Ruprecht, 1962) (translated as "Qumrân et la théologie," *NRT* 85 [1963] 674-90)

Klinzing, G., *Die Umdeutung des Kultus in der Qumrangemeinde und im Neuen Testament* (SUNT 7; Göttingen: Vandenhoeck & Ruprecht, 1971)

Merrill, E. H., *Qumran and Predestination: A Theological Study of the Thanksgiving Hymns* (STDJ 8; Leiden: Brill, 1975)

Nickelsburg, G. W. E., *Resurrection, Immortality and Eternal Life in Intertestamental Judaism* (Cambridge, MA: Harvard University; London: Oxford University, 1972)

Nötscher, F., *Zur theologischen Terminologie der Qumran-Texte* (BBB 10; Bonn: Hanstein, 1956)

Nötscher, F., *Gotteswege und Menschenwege in der Bibel und in Qumran* (BBB 15; Bonn: Hanstein, 1958)

Osten-Sacken, P. von der, *Gott und Belial: Traditionsgeschichtliche Untersuchungen zum Dualismus in den Texten aus Qumran* (SUNT 6; Göttingen: Vandenhoeck & Ruprecht, 1969)

Ringgren, H., *The Faith of Qumran: Theology of the Dead Sea Scrolls* (tr. E. T. Sander; Philadelphia: Fortress, 1963)

Schiffman, L. H., *The Halakhah at Qumran* (SJLA 16; Leiden: Brill, 1975)

Schubert, K., *Die Gemeinde vom Toten Meer: Ihre Entstehung und ihre Lehren* (Munich/Basel: E. Reinhardt, 1958)

Strobel, A., *Untersuchungen zum eschatologischen Verzögerungsproblem auf Grund der spätjüdisch-urchristlichen Geschichte von Habakuk 2:2ff.* (NovTSup 2; Leiden: Brill, 1961)

VI. QUMRAN MESSIANISM

Beasley-Murray, G. R., "The Two Messiahs in the Testaments of the Twelve Patriarchs," *JTS* 48 (1947) 1-12

Black, M., "The Messiah of the Testament of Levi XVIII," *ExpTim* 60 (1948-49) 321-22; 61 (1949-50) 157-58

Black, M., "Messianic Doctrine in the Qumran Scrolls," *Studia patristica 1* (= TU 63; ed. K. Aland and F. L. Cross; Berlin: Akademie-V., 1957), 1. 441-59

Blidstein, G. J., "A Rabbinic Reaction to the Messianic Doctrine of the Scrolls," *JBL* 90 (1971) 330-32

Brown, R. E., "The Messianism of Qumran," *CBQ* 19 (1957) 53-82

Brown, R. E., "The Teacher of Righteousness and the Messiah(s)" *The Scrolls and Christianity* (ed. M. Black; SPCK Theological Collections 11; London: SPCK, 1969) 37-44, 109-12

Brown, R. E., "J. Starcky's Theory of Qumran Messianic Development," *CBQ* 28 (1966) 51-57

Brownlee, W. H., "Messianic Motifs of Qumran and the New Testament," *NTS* 3 (1956-57) 12-30, 195-210

Burrows, M., "The Messiahs of Aaron and Israel (DSD IX, 11," *ATR* 34 (1952) 202-6

Caquot, A., "Ben Sira et le messianisme," *Sem* 16 (1966) 43-68

Caquot, A., "Le messianisme qumrânien," *Qumrân: Sa piété, sa théologie et son milieu* (BETL 46; ed. M. Delcor; Gembloux: Duculot; Louvain: Leuven University, 1978) 231-47

Croatto, J. S., "De messianismo qumranico," *VD* 35 (1957) 279-86, 344-60

Deichgräber, R., "Zur Messiaserwartung der Damaskusschrift," *ZAW* 78 (1966) 333-43

Delcor, M., "Un psaume messianique de Qumrân," *Mélanges bibliques rédigés en l'honneur de André Robert* (Paris: Bloud et Gay, 1957) 334-40

Donaldson, T. L., "Levitical Messianology in Late Judaism: Origins, Development and Decline," *JETS* 24 (1981) 193-207.

Ehrlich, E. L., "Ein Beitrag zur Messiaslehre der Qumransekte," *ZAW* 68 (1956) 234-43

Fitzmyer, J. A, "The Aramaic 'Elect of God' Text from Qumran Cave 4," *CBQ* 27 (1965) 348-72; slightly revised in *ESBNT*, 127-60

Fritsch, C. T ., "The So-called 'Priestly Messiah' of the Essenes," *JEOL* 6 (1959-66) 69-72

Giblet, J., "Prophétisme et attente d'un messie prophète dans l'ancien Judaïsme," *L'attente du Messie* (RechBib 1; ed. B. Rigaux; Bruges: Desclée de Brouwer, 1958) 85-130

Gnilka, J., "Die Erwartung des messianischen Hohenpriesters in den Schriften von Qumran und im Neuen Testament," *RevQ* 2 (1959-60) 395-426

Gnilka, J., "Bräutigam spätjüdisches Messiasprädikat?" *TTZ* 69 (1960) 298-301

Gordis, R., "The 'Begotten' Messiah in the Qumran Scrolls," *VT* 7 (1957) 191-94

Greig, J. C. G., "Gospel Messianism and the Qumran Use of Prophecy," *SE I* (= TU 73; Berlin: Akademie-V., 1959) 593-99

Grelot, P., "Le messie dans les apocryphes de l'Ancien Testament," *La venue du Messie: Messianisme et eschatologie* (RechBib 6; Bruges: Desclée de Brouwer, 1962) 19-50

Grundmann, W., "Die Frage nach der Gottessohnschaft des Messias im Lichte von Qumran," *Bibel und Qumran: Beiträge zur Erforschung der Beziehungen zwischen Bibel- und Qumran-wissenschaft: Hans Bardtke zum 22. 8. 1966* (Berlin: Evangelische Haupt-Bibelgesellschaft, 1968) 86-111

Grundmann, W., F. Hesse, M. de Jonge, and A. S. van der Woude," *Chriō, Christos. . . ," TDNT* 9 (1974) 493-580, esp. 509-20

Héring, J., "Encore le messianisme dans les écrits de Qoumran," *RHPR* 41 (1961) 160-62

Higgins, A. J. B., "Priest and Messiah," *VT* 3 (1953) 321-36

Higgins, A. J. B., "The Priestly Messiah," *NTS* 13 (1966-67) 211-39

Higgins, A. J. B., "Jewish Messianic Belief in Justin Martyr's *Dialogue with Trypho*," *NovT* 9 (1967) 298-305

Jonge, M. de, "The Use of the Word 'Anointed' in the Time of Jesus," *NovT* 8 (1966) 132-48

Jonge, M. de, "Jewish Expectations about the 'Messiah' according to the Fourth Gospel," *NTS* 19 (1972-73) 246-70

Kuhn, K. G., "Die beiden Messias Aarons und Israels," *NTS* 1 (1954-55) 168-79; translated and adapted in K. Stendahl (ed.), *The Scrolls and the New Testament* (see chapter X/VIII) 54-64

Kuhn, K. G., "Die beiden Messias in den Qumrantexten und die Messiasvorstellung in der rabbinischen Literatur," *ZAW* 70 (1958) 200-208

Laperrousaz, E.-M., *L'Attente du Messie en Palestine à la veille et au début de l'ère chrétienne* (Collection Empreinte; Paris: Picard, 1982)

Laperrousaz, E.-M., *Les Esséniens selon leur témoignage direct* (Religion et culture; Paris: Desclée, 1982)

LaSor, W. S., "'The Messiahs of Aaron and Israel,'" *VT* 6 (1956) 425-29

LaSor, W. S., "The Messianic Idea in Qumran," *Studies and Essays in Honor of Abraham A. Neuman* (ed. M. Ben-Horin et al.; Leiden: Brill, 1962) 343-64

Laurin, R. B., "The Problem of Two Messiahs in the Qumran Scrolls," *RevQ* 4 (1963-64) 39-52

Liver, J., "The Doctrine of the Two Messiahs in the Sectarian Literature in the Time of the Second Commonwealth," *HTR* 52 (1959) 149-85

Lohse, E., "Der König aus Davids Geschlecht: Bemerkungen zur messianischen Erwartung der Synagoge," *Abraham unser Vater: Juden und Christen im Gespräch über die Bibel: Festschrift für Otto Michel zum 60. Geburtstag* (AGJU 5; ed. O. Betz et al.; Leiden: Brill, 1963) 337-45

Mariès, L., "Le Messie issu de Lévi chez Hippolyte de Rome," *Mélanges J. Lebreton* (*RSR* 39/1 [1951]) 385-88

Pearce Higgins, A. G. McL., "A Few Thoughts on the Dead Sea Scrolls," *Modern Churchman* 13 (1970) 198-201

Priest, J. F., "Mebaqqer, Paqid, and the Messiah," *JBL* 81 (1962) 55-61

Priest, J. F., "The Messiah and the Meal in 1QSa," *JBL* 82 (1963) 95-100

Prigent, P., "Quelques testimonia messianiques: Leur histoire littéraire de Qoumran aux Pères de l'église," *TZ* 15 (1959) 419-30

Ragot, A., "Messie essénien et messie chrétien," *Cahiers du cercle Ernest Renan* 37 (1963) 1-10

Rivkin, E., "The Meaning of Messiah in Jewish Thought," *USQR* 26 (1971) 383-406

Sabbe, M., "Het thema van de Messias, profeet zoals Mozes," *Collationes brugenses* 50 (1954) 148-65

Sabugal, S., "1 Q Regla de la comunidad IX, 11: Dos ungidos, un Mesias," *RevQ* 8 (1972-75) 417-23

Schubert, K., "Zwei Messiasse aus dem Regelbuch von Chirbet Qumran," *Judaica* 11 (1955) 216-35

Schubert, K., "Der alttestamentliche Hintergrund der Vorstellung von den beiden Messiassen im Schrifttum von Chirbet Qumran," *Judaica* 12 (1956) 24-28

Schubert, K., "Die Messiaslehre in den Texten von Chirbet Qumran," *BZ* ns 1 (1957) 177-97

Schubert, K., "Die Messiaslehre in den Testamenten der 12 Patriarchen im Lichte der Texte von Chirbet Qumran," *Akten des 24. internationalen Orientalisten-Kongresses München 28. August bis 4. September 1957* (Wiesbaden: F. Steiner, 1959) 197-98

Segert, S., "Der Messias nach neueren Auffassungen," *Communio viatorum* 2 (1959) 343-53

Silberman, L. H., "The Two 'Messiahs' of the Manual of Discipline," *VT* 5 (1955) 77-82

Smith, M., "'God's Begetting the Messiah' in 1QSa," *NTS* 5 (1958-59) 218-24

Smith, M., "What Is Implied by the Variety of Messianic Figures?" *JBL* 78 (1959) 66-72

Smyth, K., "The Dead Sea Scrolls and the Messiah," *Studies* 45 (1956) 1-14

Starcky, J., "Les quatre étapes du messianisme à Qumran," *RB* 70 (1963) 481-505

Stefaniak, L., "Messianische oder eschatologische Erwartungen in der Qumransekte?" *Neutestamentliche Aufsätze: Festschrift J. Schmid* (Regensburg: Pustet, 1962) 294-302

Villalón, J. R., "Sources vétéro-testamentaires de la doctrine des deux Messies," *RevQ* 8 (1972-75) 53-63

Wcela, E. A., "The Messiah(s) of Qumrân," *CBQ* 26 (1964) 340-49

Wieder, N., "The Doctrine of the Two Messiahs among the Karaites," *JJS* 6 (1955) 14-25

Winter, P., "The Holy Messiah," *ZNW* 50 (1959) 275

Woude, A. S. van der, *Die messianischen Vorstellungen der Gemeinde von Qumran* (Studia semitica neerlandica 3; Assen: Van Gorcum, 1957)

Woude, A. S. van der, "Le Maître de Justice et les deux messies de la communauté de Qumrân," *La secte de Qumrân et les origines chrétiennes* (RechBib 4; Bruges: Desclée de Brouwer, 1959) 121-34

VII. THE NEW TESTAMENT AT QUMRAN ?

This issue has been raised by the writings of José O'Callaghan apropos of the Greek fragments of Qumran Cave 7. He has identified 7Q4 as 1 Tim 3:16; 4:1,3; 7Q5 as Mark 6:52-53; 7Q6 1 as Mark 4:28; 7Q6 2 as Acts 28:38; 7Q7 as Mark 12:17; 7Q8 as Jas 1:23-24; 7Q9 as Rom 5:11-12; 7Q10 as 2 Pet 1:15; and 7Q15 as Mark 6:48. Though most scholars have been skeptical about the claims that O'Callaghan has been making, the issue cannot be simply dismissed. He has not yet proved his case, and it seems most likely that the frgs. 7Q3-18 are nothing more than copies of some Old Greek translation of the OT. The entries that follow are intended simply to give students access to the material that he has published and to the reactions of noted NT scholars. Favorable reactions to the claims have come only from uncritical sources.

The Writings of José O'Callaghan
(according the date of publication)

"¿Papiros neotestamentarios en la cueva 7 de Qumrān?" *Bib* 53 (1972) 91-100 (Engl. tr. by W. L. Holladay, "New Testament Papyri in Qumrân Cave 7?" Supplement to *JBL* 91/2 [1972] 1-14)

"Tres probables papiros neotestamentarios en la cueva 7 de Qumrān," *SP* 11 (1972) 83-89

"¿1 Tim 3,16; 4,1.3 en 7Q4?" *Bib* 53 (1972) 362-67

"Die griechischen Papyri aus der Höhle 7 von Qumran," *Bibel und Liturgie* 45 (1972) 121-22

"¿Un fragmento del Ev. de s. Marcos en el papiro 5 de la cueva 7 de Qumran?" *Arbor* 81/316 (1972) 429-31

"Notas sobre 7Q tomadas en el 'Rockefeller Museum' de Jerusalén,"*Bib* 53 (1972) 517-33

"Sobre los papiros de la cueva 7 de Qumrān," *Boletín de la asociación española de orientalistas* 8 (1972) 205-6

"Les papyrus de la grotte 7 de Qumrân," *NRT* 95 (1973) 188-95

"El ordenador, 7Q5 y Homero," *SP* 12 (1973) 73-79

"La identificación de papiros literarios (bíblicos)," *SP* 12 (1973) 91-100

"El cambio *d* > *t* en los papiros bíblicos," *Bib* 54 (1973) 415-16

Los papiros griegos de la cueva 7 de Qumrân (BAC 353; Madrid: Editorial católica, 1974)

"El ordenador, 7Q5 y los autores griegos (Apolonio de Rodas, Aristóteles, Lisias)," *SP* 13 (1974) 21-29

"Sobre la identificación de 7Q4," *SP* 13 (1974) 45-55

"Nota sobre 7Q4 y 7Q5," *SP* 13 (1974) 61-63

"¿El texto de 7Q5 es Tuc. I 41,2? *SP* 13 (1974) 125 (+ pl.) [Tuc.= Thucydides]

"Paleografía herculanense en algunos papiros griegos de Qumran,"*Homenaje a Juan Prado: Miscelanea de estudios bíblicos y hebráicos* (ed. L. Alvarez Verdes et al.; Madrid: C.S.I.C., Instituto "B. Arias Montano," 1975) 529-32

"The Identifications of 7Q," *Aegyptus* 56 (1976) 287-94

"7Q5: Nuevas consideraciones," *SP* 16 (1977) 41-47

"Verso le origini del Nuovo Testamento," *Civiltà cattolica* 139 (1988) 269-72

Secondary Literature on O'Callaghan's Publications

Could One Small Fragment Shake the World? (= *Eternity* 23/6 [Philadelphia, PA: Evangelical Foundation, 1972] 1-14)

Aland, K., "Neue neutestamentliche Papyri? Ein Nachwort zu den angeblichen Entdeckungen von Prof. O'Callaghan," *Bibel und Kirche* 28 (1973) 19-20

Aland, K., "Neue neutestamentliche Papyri III," *NTS* 20 (1973-74) 357-81

Baillet, M., "Les manuscrits de la grotte 7 de Qumrân et le Nouveau Testament," *Bib* 53 (1972) 508-16; 54 (1973) 340-50

Baillet, M., "Les fragments grecs de la grotte 7 de Qumrân et le Nouveau Testament," *Orient chrétien: Actes du xxixe congrès international des orientalistes* (Paris: Asiathèque, 1975) 4-10

Bartina, S., "Identificación de papiros neotestamentarios en la cueva 7 de Qumrân," *Cultura bíblica* 29 (1972) 195-206

Bartina, S., "La cueva séptima de Qumrán y sus papiros neotestamentarios," *EstEcl* 48 (1973) 87-91

Benoit, P., "Note sur les fragments grecs de la grotte 7 de Qumrân," *RB* 79 (1972) 321-24

Benoit, P., "Nouvelle note sur les fragments grecs de la grotte 7 de Qumrân, *RB* 80 (1973) 5-12

Bernardi, J., "L'Evangile de Saint Marc e la grotte 7 de Qumrân,"*ETR* 47 (1972) 453-56

Briend, J., "La grotte 7 de Qumran et le Nouveau Testament," *BTS* 143 (1972) 24

Chmiel, J., "Papirusy groty 7 Qumran," *Ruch Biblijny i Liturgiczny* 26 (1973) 85-93

Duplacy, J., "Bulletin de critique textuelle du Nouveau Testament, V (1ère partie)," *Bib* 54 (1973) 79-114, esp. 92-93

Estrada, D., "On the Latest Identification of New Testament Documents," *WTJ* 34 (1972) 109-17

Fee, G., "Some Dissenting Notes on 7Q5 = Mark 6:52-53," *JBL* 92 (1973) 109-12

Fisher, E., "New Testament Documents among the Dead Sea Scrolls," *TBT* 61 (1972) 835-41

Fitzmyer, J. A., "A Qumran Fragment of Mark?" *America* 126/25 (24 June 1972) 647-50

Focant, C., "Un fragment du second évangile à Qumran: 7Q5 = Mc 6,52-53?" *RTL* 16 (1985) 447-54 [on Thiede's publications]

Garnet, P., "O'Callaghan's Fragments: Our Earliest New Testament Texts?" *EvQ* 45 (1973) 6-12

Gasque, W. W., "The Gospel of Mark and 'The Scrolls': An Introductory Word," *Christianity Today* 17 (1973) 1284-85

Ghiberti, G., "Dobbiamo anticipare la data di composizione dei Vangeli?" *Parole di vita* 17 (1972) 303-6

Hemer, C. J., "New Testament Fragments at Qumran?" *Tyndale Bulletin* 23 (1972) 125-28

Hemer, C. J., "7Q5: A Correction," *SP* 16 (1977) 39-40

Legrand, L., "The New Testament at Qumran," *Indian Ecclesiastical Studies* 11 (1972) 157-66

Martini, C., "Note sui papiri della grotta 7 di Qumrân," *Bib* 53 (1972) 101-4 (Engl. tr. by W. L. Holladay, "Notes on the Papyri of Qumran Cave 7," Supplement to *JBL* 91/2 [1972] 15-20)

Martini, C., "Testi neotestamentari tra i manoscritti del deserto di Giuda?" *Civiltà cattolica* 123 (1972) 156-58; cf. *Rocca* (Assisi) 11 (1 June 1972) 26-27

Mejía, J., "Un problema bíblico: La antigüedad del Nuevo Testamento," *Criterio* (Buenos Aires) 45 (1972) 270-73

Nebe, G. W., "7Q4—Möglichkeit und Grenze einer Identifikation," *RevQ* 13 (Mémorial Jean Carmignac, 1988) 629-33

Noack, B., "Note om påståede stumper af det Nye Testamente i Qumran," *DTT* 36 (1973) 152-55

[Orchard, B.], "A Fragment of St. Mark's Gospel Dating from before AD 50?" *Biblical Apostolate* (Rome) 6 (1972) 5-6

Parker, P., "7 Q 5: Enthält das Papyrusfragment 5 aus der Höhle 7 von Qumran einen Markustext?" *Erbe und Auftrag* 48 (1972) 467-69

Reicke, B., "Fragmente neutestamentlicher Papyri bei Qumrân?" *TZ* 28 (1972) 304

Roberts, C. H., "On Some Presumed Papyrus Fragments of the New Testament from Qumran," *JTS* ns 23 (1972) 446-47

Roberts, C. H., "A Papyrus Fragment," *London Times*, 7 April 1972, p. 15

Rohrhirsch, F., "Das Qumranfragment 7Q5," *NovT* 30 (1988) 97-99

Rosenbaum, H.-U., "Cave 7Q5! Gegen die erneute Inanspruchnahme des Qumran-Fragments 7Q5 als Bruckstück der ältesten Evangelien-Handschrift," *BZ* 31 (1987) 189-205 (against Thiede; good survey of earlier opinions)

Sabourin, L., "Un papyrus de Marc à Qumran?" *Bulletin de théologie biblique* 2 (1972) 309-13; Engl. transl., "A Fragment of Mark at Qumran," *BTB* 2 (1972) 308-12.

Sacchi, P., "Scoperta di frammenti neotestamentari in una grotta di Qumran," *Rivista di storia e letteratura religiosa* 8 (1972) 429-31

Salvoni, F., "Qumran e le Pastorali," *Ricerche bibliche e religiose* 7 (1972) 147-48

Spottorno, M. V., "Nota sobre los papiros de la cueva 7 de Qumran," *Estudios clásicos* 15 (1972) 261-63

Thiede, C. P., "7Q —Eine Rückkehr zu den neutestamentlichen Papyrusfragmenten in der siebten Höhle von Qumran," *Bib* 65 (1984) 538-59

Thiede, C. P. *Die älteste Evangelien-Handschrift? Das Markus-Fragment von Qumran und die Anfänge der schriftlichen Überlieferung des Neuen Testaments* (Wuppertal: Brockhaus, 1986)

Urbán, A. C., "Observaciones sobre ciertos papiros de la cueva 7 de Qumran," *RevQ* 8 (1972-74) 233-51

Urbán, A. C., "La identificación de 7Q4 con Núm 14,23-24 y la restauración de textos antiguos," *EstBib* 32 (1973) 219-44.

Vardaman, J., "The Earliest Fragments of the New Testament?" *ExpTim* 83 (1971-72) 374-76

Vardaman, J., "The Gospel of Mark and 'The Scrolls,'" *Christianity Today* 17 (1973) 1284-87

Vermes, G., "A Papyrus Fragment," *London Times*, 1 April 1972, p. 15

Vogt, E., "Entdeckung neutestamentlicher Texte beim Toten Meer?"*Orientierung* 36 (1972) 138-40

Voulgaris, C. S., "*Nea heurēmata apospasmatōn bibliōn tēs Kainēs Diathēkēs*," *Theologia* (Athens) 43 (1972) 458-63

White, W., Jr., "A Layman's Guide to O'Callaghan's Discovery," *Eternity* 23/6 (1972) 27-31

White, W., Jr., "O'Callaghan's Identifications: Confirmation and Its Consequences," *WTJ* 35 (1972) 15-20

White W., Jr., "Notes on the Papyrus Fragments from Cave 7 at Qumran," *WTJ* 35 (1972-73) 221-26

Zurro, E., "El importante hallazgo del P. O'Callaghan," *Vida nueva* 828 (15 April 1972) 22-25

Zurro, E., "El P. Alonso Schökel comenta el hallazgo escrituristico de O'Callaghan," *Vida nueva* 828 (15 April 1972) 26-29

VIII. THE QUMRAN SCROLLS AND THE NEW TESTAMENT

Much has been written about the bearing of the Qumran texts on books of the NT. No attempt is made here to cover that relationship in a comprehensive way. For articles on various aspects of the relationship between these two bodies of literature, one should consult the topical bibliographies of W. S. LaSor and B. Jongeling and the yearly bibliography of P. Nober and R. North (see chapter III above), as well as *NTA* (ed. D. J. Harrington; Cambridge, MA: Weston School of Theology [3 times a year]) and the *IZBG* (ed. F. Stier; B. Lang; Düsseldorf: Patmos [issued once a year]). Listed below are merely the more important books on the general topic and on two specific areas of it (in the latter cases, some of the more important articles are included).

Black, M., *The Scrolls and Christian Origins: Studies in the Jewish Background of the New Testament* (New York: Scribner,1961)

Black, M. (ed.), *The Scrolls and Christianity* (SPCK Theological Collections 11; London: S.P.C.K., 1969)

Braun, H., *Spätjüdisch-häretischer und frühchristlicher Radikalismus: Jesus von Nazareth und die essenische Qumransekte* (2 vols.; BHT 24; Tübingen: Mohr [Siebeck], 1957; 2d ed.,1969)

Braun, H., *Qumran und das Neue Testament* (2 vols.; Tübingen: Mohr [Siebeck], 1966). Vol. 1 is a reprint of articles that appeared in *TRu* 28-30 (1962-64) and constituted an analytical survey of literature on Qumran in the preceding ten years; vol. 2 is a synthetic approach to many topics related to the NT. This is a fundamental, indispensable work for the period surveyed.

Brown, R. E., "Second Thoughts, X: The Dead Sea Scrolls and the New Testament," *ExpTim* 78 (1966-67) 19-23.

Carmignac, J., *Christ and the Teacher of Righteousness: The Evidence of the Dead Sea Scrolls* (Baltimore: Helicon, 1962)

Casciaro Ramírez, J. M., *Qumran y el Nuevo Testamento: Aspectos eclesiológicos y soteriológicos* (Pamplona: Ediciones Universidad de Navarra, 1982)

Daniélou, J., *The Dead Sea Scrolls and Primitive Christianity* (2d ed.; Baltimore: Helicon, 1963); revised French edition, *Les manuscrits de la Mer Morte et les origines du christianisme* (Paris: Editions de l'Orante, 1974)

Fitzmyer, J. A., *ESBNT*, 3-89, 127-60, 187-354, 435-80; *TAG*, 79-111, 125-46; *WA*, 85-160

Fitzmyer, J. A., "The Qumran Scrolls and the New Testament after Forty Years," *RevQ* 13 (= Mémorial Jean Carmignac, 1988) 609-20

Graystone, G., *The Dead Sea Scrolls and the Originality of Christ* (New York: Sheed and Ward, 1956)

Jeremias, J., *Die theologische Bedeutung der Funde am Toten Meer* (2d ed.; Göttingen: Vandenhoeck & Ruprecht, 1962)

LaSor, W. S., *The Dead Sea Scrolls and the New Testament* (Grand Rapids, MI: Eerdmans, 1972)

Mowry, L., *The Dead Sea Scrolls and the Early Church* (Chicago: University of Chicago, 1962)

Ploeg, J. van der (ed.), *La secte de Qumrân et les origines du Christianisme* (RechBib 4; Bruges: Desclée de Brouwer, 1959)

Praag, H. van (ed.), *Studies on the Jewish Background of the New Testament* (Assen: Van Gorcum, 1969)

Rowley, H. H., *The Dead Sea Scrolls and the New Testament* (London: S.P.C.K., 1957)

Rowley, H. H., "The Qumran Sect and Christian Origins," *BJRL* 44 (1961) 119-56; repr. separately (Manchester, UK: John Rylands Library, 1961)

Schelkle, K. H., *Die Gemeinde von Qumran und die Kirche des Neuen Testaments* (Die Welt der Bibel; 2d ed.; Düsseldorf: Patmos, 1965)

Stauffer, E., *Jesus und die Wüstengemeinde am Toten Meer* (Calwer Hefte 9; 2d ed.; Stuttgart: Calwer V., 1960)

Stendahl, K. (ed.), *The Scrolls and the New Testament* (New York: Harper, 1957)

Thiering, B. E., *The Gospels and Qumran: A New Hypothesis* (Australian and New Zealand Studies in Theology and Religion; Sydney: Theological Explorations, 1981); see the reviews by J. C. VanderKam, *CBQ* 45 (1983) 512-14; C. Y. Lambert, *REJ* 145 (1986) 431-32.

Thiering, B. E., *The Qumran Origins of the Christian Church* (Australian and New Zealand Studies in Theology and Religion; Sydney: Theological Explorations, 1983); see the reviews by A. Caquot, *RHR* 202 (1985) 309; B. A. Mastin, *RevQ* 12 (1985-87) 125-28

Vermes, G., "The Impact of the Dead Sea Scrolls on the Study of the New Testament," *JJS* 27 (1976) 107-16

A. *Qumran Literature and Pauline Writings*

In addition to the literature surveyed in H. Braun, *Qumran und das Neue Testament* (see above), 1. 169-240; 2. 165-80, and that collected in K. Stendahl (ed.), *The Scrolls and the New Testament*, 65-113, 157-82, one should note in particular the following title:

Murphy-O'Connor, J. (ed.), *Paul and Qumran: Studies in New Testament Exegesis* (Chicago: Priory, 1968)

See further:

Barré, M. L., "Qumran and the 'Weakness' of Paul," *CBQ* 42 (1980) 216-27

Braun, H., "Römer 7,7-25 und das Selbstverständnis des Qumran-Frommen" *ZTK* 56 (1959) 1-18

Brown, R. E., *The Semitic Background of the Term "Mystery" in the New Testament* (Facet Books, Biblical series 21; Philadelphia: Fortress, 1968)

Cadbury, H. J., "A Qumran Parallel to Paul," *HTR* 51 (1958) 1-2; cf. J. A. Fitzmyer, *NTS* 4 (1957-58) 48-58; *ESBNT*, 187-204

Casciaro Ramirez, J. M., "Los 'himnos' de Qumrān y el 'misterio' paulino," *Scripta theologica* 8 (1976) 9-56

Derrett, J. D. M., "New Creation: Qumran, Paul, the Church, and Jesus," *RevQ* 13 (Mémorial Jean Carmignac, 1988) 597-608

Fitzmyer, J. A., "Qumrân and the Interpolated Paragraph in 2 Cor 6,14-7,1," *CBQ* 23 (1961) 271-80; slightly revised, *ESBNT*, 205-17; tr. into German: *Qumran* (ed. K. E. Grözinger et al.; WF 410; Darmstadt: Wissenschaftliche Buchgesellschaft, 1981) 385-98

Grundmann, W., "Der Lehrer der Gerechtigkeit von Qumran und die Frage nach der Glaubensgerechtigkeit in der Theologie des Apostels Paulus," *RevQ* 2 (1959-60) 237-59

Kertelge, K., *Rechtfertigung bei Paulus: Studien zur Struktur und zum Bedeutungsgehalt des paulinischen Rechtfertigungsbegriffs* (NTAbh ns 3; 2d ed.; Münster: Aschendorff, 1967)

Kuhn, K.-G., "Der Epheserbrief im Lichte der Qumrantexte," *NTS* 7 (1960-61) 334-46

Osborne, R. E., "Did Paul Go to Qumran? *CJT* 10 (1964) 15-24

Penna, A., "Testi d'Isaia in S. Paolo," *RivB* 5 (1957) 25-30, 163-79

Penna, A., "L'elezione nella lettera ai Romani e nei testi di Qumran," *Divinitas* 2 (1958) 597-614

Rad, G. von, "Die Vorgeschichte der Gattung vom 1. Kor. 13,4-7,"*Festschrift Albrecht Alt zum 70. Geburtstag* (BHT 16; Tübingen: Mohr [Siebeck], 1953) 153-68

Sabugal, S., "El primer autotestimonio de Pablo sobre su conversión: Gál 1,1.11-17 (Damasco [1,17]: ¿Ciudad de Siria o región de Qumrán?)," *Augustinianum* 15 (1975) 429-43

Sabugal, S., *Análisis exegético sobre la conversión de San Pablo: El problema teológico et histórico* (Barcelona: Editorial Herder, 1976) [title on cover resembles the title of the preceding entry]

Sanders, J. A., "Habakkuk in Qumran, Paul, and the Old Testament," *JR* 39 (1959) 232-44

Sanders, J. A., "Dissenting Deities and Philippians 2:1-11," *JBL* 88 (1969) 279-90

Schneider, G., "Die Idee der Neuschöpfung beim Apostel Paulus und ihr religionsgeschichtlicher Hintergrund," *TTZ* 68 (1959) 257-70

Schulz, S., "Zur Rechtfertigung aus Gnaden in Qumran und bei Paulus: Zugleich ein Beitrag zur Form und Überlieferungsgeschichte der Qumrantexte," *ZTK* 56 (1959) 155-85

Schweizer, E., "Röm. 1,3f. und der Gegensatz von Fleisch und Geist vor und bei Paulus," *EvT* 12 (1952-53) 563-71

Schweizer, E., "Zur Interpretation des Römerbriefes," *EvT* 22 (1962) 105-7

Stendahl, K., "Hate, Non-Retaliation, and Love (1QS X, 17-20 and Rom. 12:19-21)," *HTR* 55 (1962) 343-55

Stuhlmacher, P., *Gerechtigkeit Gottes bei Paulus* (FRLANT 87; Göttingen: Vandenhoeck & Ruprecht, 1965)

Thierry, J. J., "Der Dorn im Fleische (2 Kor. XII 7-9)," *NovT* 5 (1962) 301-10

Wibbing, S., *Die Tugend- und Lasterkataloge im Neuen Testament und ihre Traditionsgeschichte unter besonderer Berücksichtigung der Qumrantexte* (BZNW 25; Berlin: Töpelmann, 1959)

Wood, J. E., "Pauline Studies and the Dead Sea Scrolls," *ExpTim* 78 (1966-67) 308-10

Yamauchi, E., "Qumran and Colossae," *BSac* 121 (1964) 141-52

Zedda, S., "Il carattere gnostico e giudaico dell'errore colossese nella luce dei manoscritti del Mar Morto," *RivB* 5 (1957) 31-56

B.   *Qumran Literature and Johannine Writings*

Again in addition to the literature surveyed in H. Braun, *Qumran und das Neue Testament* (see above), 1. 96-138, 290-326; 2.118-44, and that collected in K. Stendahl (ed.), *The Scrolls and the New Testament*, 183-207, one should note in particular the following title: Charlesworth, J. H. (ed.), *John and Qumran* (London: Chapman, 1972)

See further:

Baumbach, G., *Qumrān und das Johannes-Evangelium* (Aufsätze und Vorträge zur Theologie und Religionswissenschaft 6; Berlin: Evangelische Verlagsanstalt, 1957)

Bergmeier, R., "Glaube als Werk? Die 'Werke Gottes' in Damaskusschrift II, 14-15 und Johannes 6, 28-29," *RevQ* 6 (1967-69) 253-60

Böcher, O., *Der johanneische Dualismus im Zusammenhang des nachbiblischen Judentums* (Gütersloh: Mohn, 1965)

Boismard, M.-E., "Qumrán y los escritos de s. Juan," *Cultura bíblica* 12 (1955) 250-64

Braun, F.-M., "L'Arrière-fond judaïque du quatrième évangile et la communauté de l'alliance," *RB* 62 (1955) 5-44

Brown, R. E., "John and Qumran," *The Gospel According to John* (AB 29; Garden City, NY: Doubleday, 1966) lxii-lxvi

Cullmann, O., "Secte de Qumran, Hellénistes des Actes et quatrième évangile," *Les manuscrits de la Mer Morte: Colloque de Strasbourg 25-27 mai 1955* (Paris: Presses universitaires de France, 1957) 61-74, 135-36

Cullmann, O., "L'Opposition contre le Temple de Jérusalem, motif commun de la théologie johannique et du monde ambiant," *NTS* 5 (1958-59) 157-73

Grelot, P., "Jean 8, 56 et Jubilés 16, 16-29," *RevQ* 13 (Mémorial Jean Carmignac, 1988) 621-28

Kuhn, K. G., "Johannesevangelium und Qumrantexte," *Neotestamentica et patristica* (Festschrift O. Cullmann; Leiden: Brill, 1962) 111-22

Lákatos, E., "El cuarto evangelio y los descubrimientos de Qumran," *Revista de teología* 21 (1956) 67-77

Leaney, A. R. C., "John and Qumran," *SE VI* (TU 112; Berlin: Akademie, 1973) 296-310

Mowry, L., "The Dead Sea Scrolls and the Gospel of John," *BA* 17 (1954) 78-97

Roloff, J., "Der johanneische 'Lieblingsjünger' und der Lehrer der Gerechtigkeit," *NTS* 15 (1968-69) 129-51

Teeple, H. M., "Qumran and the Origin of the Fourth Gospel," *NovT* 4 (1960) 6-25

IX. THE QUMRAN CALENDAR AND RELATED PROBLEMS

A.   *The Qumran Calendar*
        Basic Discussions:

Barthélemy, D., "Notes en marge de publications récentes sur les manuscrits de Qumrân," *RB* 59 (1952) 187-218, esp. 200-202

Jaubert, A., "Le calendrier des Jubilés et de la secte de Qumrân: Ses origines bibliques," *VT* 3 (1953) 250-64

Milik, J. T., "Le travail d'édition des manuscrits du Désert de Juda," *Volume du Congrès, Strasbourg, 1956* (VTSup 4; Leiden: Brill, 1957) 17-26, esp. 24-25

Talmon, S., "The Calendar Reckoning of the Sect from the Judaean Desert," *Aspects of the Dead Sea Scrolls* (Scripta hierosolymitana 4; Jerusalem: Magnes, 1958) 162-99

Further Discussions:

Baumgarten, J. M., "The Beginning of the Day in the Calendar of Jubilees," *JBL* 77 (1958) 355-60

Baumgarten, J. M., "The Counting of the Sabbath in Ancient Sources," *VT* 16 (1966) 277-86

Baumgarten, J. M., "Some Problems of the Jubilees Calendar in Current Research," *VT* 32 (1982) 485-89

Beckwith, R. T., "The Modern Attempt to Reconcile the Qumran Calendar with the True Solar Year," *RevQ* 7 (1969-71) 379-96

Beckwith, R. T., "The Qumran Calendar and the Sacrifices of the Essenes," *RevQ* 7 (1969-71) 587-91

Beckwith, R. T., "St. Luke, the Date of Christmas and the Priestly Courses at Qumran," *RevQ* 9 (1977-78) 73-94

Beckwith, R. T., "The Significance of the Calendar for Interpreting Essene Chronology and Eschatology," *RevQ* 10 (1979-81)167-202

Beckwith, R. T., "The Earliest Enoch Literature and Its Calendar: Marks of Their Origin, Date and Motivation," *RevQ* 10 (1979-81) 365-403.

Burgmann, H., "Ein Schaltmonat nach 24,5 Jahren im chasidischen Sonnenkalender?" *RevQ* 8 (1972-75) 65-73

Burgmann, H., "Die Interkalation in den sieben Jahrwochen des Sonnenkalenders," *RevQ* 10 (1979-81) 67-81

Ettisch, E. E., "Die Gemeinderegel und der Qumrankalender," *RevQ* 3 (1961-62) 125-33

Jaubert, A., "Le calendrier des Jubilés et les jours liturgiques de la semaine," *VT* 7 (1957) 35-61

Kimbrough, S. T., "The Concept of Sabbath at Qumran," *RevQ* 5 (1964-66) 483-502

Kutsch, E., "Der Kalender des Jubiläenbuches und das Alte und das Neue Testament," *VT* 11 (1961) 39-47

Leach, E. R., "A Possible Method of Intercalation for the Calendar of the Book of Jubilees," *VT* 7 (1957) 392-97

Meysing, J., "L'énigme de la chronologie biblique et qumrânienne dans une nouvelle lumière," *RevQ* 6 (1967-69) 229-51

Morgenstern, J., "The Calendar of the Book of Jubilees: Its Origin and Its Character," *VT* 5 (1955) 34-76

Obermann, J., "Calendaric Elements in the Dead Sea Scrolls," *JBL* 75 (1956) 285-97

Pelletier, A., "La nomenclature du calendrier juif à l'époque hellénistique," *RB* 82 (1975) 218-33 (+ pl. XVII)

Rook, J. T., "A Twenty-eight-day Month Tradition in the Book of Jubilees, *VT* 31 (1981) 83-87.

Strobel, A., "Zur kalendarisch-chronologischen Einordnung der Qumran-Essener," *TLZ* 86 (1961) 179-84

Strobel, A., "Zur Funktionsfähigkeit des essenischen Kalenders," *RevQ* 3 (1961-62) 395-412

Strobel, A., "Der 22. Tag des XI. Monats im essenischen Jahr,"*RevQ* 3 (1961-62) 539-43

VanderKam, J. C., "The Origin, Character, and Early History of the 364-Day Calendar: A Reassessment of Jaubert's Hypotheses," *CBQ* 41 (1979) 390-411

VanderKam, J. C., "A Twenty-Eight Day Month Tradition in the Book of Jubilees?" *VT* 32 (1982) 504-6

Vogt, E ., "Antiquum kalendarium sacerdotale" *Bib* 36 (1955) 403-8

Vogt, E., "Kalenderfragmente aus Qumran," *Bib* 39 (1958) 72-77

Wacholder, B. Z., "The Calendar of Sabbatical Cycles during the Second Temple and the Early Rabbinic Period," *HUCA* 44 (1973) 153-96

The Dead Sea Scrolls

The Qumran Calendar:

Instead of the luni-solar calendar of 354 days, apparently officially used in the Jerusalem Temple, the Essenes of Qumran employed an older solar calendar of 364 days see (11QPs[a] DavComp 27:6, "songs to sing ... for all the days of the year, 364"); cf. *Jub.* 6:38. For the importance of the calendar, see 1QS 1:14-15; 10:3-8; 1QH 1:15-20; CD 6:18-19; 3:13-15; 16:1-5; 1QpHab 11:4-8 [the last text indicates a difference of calendar being used by the Qumran community and the Wicked Priest of Jerusalem who persecuted it].

Day of the Week								Months							
	I	IV	VII	X		II	V	VIII	XI		III	VI	IX	XII	
4 (Wed.)	1	8	15	22	29		6	13	20	27		4	11	18	25
5 (Thur.)	2	9	16	23	30		7	14	21	28		5	12	19	26
6 (Fri.)	3	10	17	24		1	8	15	22	29		6	13	20	27
7 (Sabb.)	4	11	18	25		2	9	16	23	30		7	14	21	28
1 (Sun.)	5	12	19	26		3	10	17	24		1	8	15	22	29
2 (Mon.)	6	13	20	27		4	11	18	25		2	9	16	23	30
3 (Tues.)	7	14	21	28		5	12	19	26		3	10	17	24	31
		(30)					(30)					(31)			

B.   The Qumran Calendar and the Date of Passover in the NT

   (1)   The Problem of the Date of the Last Supper

(a) Jesus' Death Recorded on the Eve of a Sabbath: Mark 15:42
   ("when evening had come, since it was the day of Preparation,
   that is, the day before the Sabbath, Joseph of Arimathea . . .");
   Matt 27:62 ("Next day, that is, after the day of Preparation");
   Luke 23:54 ("It was the day of Preparation, and the Sabbath
   was beginning" [see 23:56]); John 19:31, 42 ("since it was the
   day of Preparation, in order to prevent the bodies from
   remaining on the cross on the Sabbath (for that Sabbath was a
   high day, . . .").
        Paraskeuē is here understood as the Preparation Day for
   the Sabbath (= *prosabbaton*)

(b) John 18:28 implies that this *paraskeuē* was the Preparation Day
   for the Passover — probably the reason for his parenthetical
   remark in 19:31, the coincidence of Passover and the
   beginning of the Sabbath. Hence *paraskeuē* is 14 Nisan (up to
   sundown [on Friday]). But this would mean that Jesus ate the
   Last Supper on Thursday, roughly at the beginning of 14
   Nisan, a day early. Cf. John 19:14.

(c) Mark 14:12 ("on the first day of Unleavened Bread, when they
   sacrificed the Passover lamb, his disciples said to him, 'Where
   will you have us go and prepare for you to eat the Passover'");
   16 ("they prepared the Passover"); cf. Matt 26:17-19; Luke
   22:7-13. These passages suggest that Jesus ate the Last Supper
   as a Passover meal, i.e., prepared on the 14 Nisan, eaten at
   sundown (roughly), at the beginning of 15 Nisan.

   (2)   Solutions of the Problem

(a) *Theological Solutions:*
   The Synoptics place the Last Supper of Jesus with the Twelve at
   the beginning of 15 Nisan to give it the character of a Passover
   meal (most explicit in Luke 22, but probably also intended in
   Mark and Matthew as well). John places it on the Preparation
   Day to depict Jesus slain about the same time as the slaughter of

the Passover lambs, thus giving his death a special connotation (he dies as the Lamb of God).

(b) *Calendaric Solutions:*

Different calendars were used by the Synoptics and John. Before the discovery of the Qumran calendar, it was often said that the difference was one of Pharisaic and Sadducee calendars, but the evidence for that difference was not really forthcoming. Since the discovery of the Qumran (Essene) calendar, the explanation of two calendars, which were then in use, has been proposed to solve this classic problem of gospel interpretation. It was mainly proposed by A. Jaubert, *La date de la Cène, calendrier biblique et liturgie chrétienne* (EBib; Paris; Gabalda, 1957); *The Date of the Last Supper* (Staten Island, NY: Alba House, 1965).

		SOLAR CALENDAR	LUNI-SOLAR (official) CALENDAR
Tues.	—Before Sundown	14 Nisan: Preparation for Passover (Mark 14:12-16)	
	About Sundown	15 Nisan: Last Supper (Passover meal, Mark 14:17-25)	12 Nisan:
	Night	Arrest; Interrogation before Annas (Mark 14: 53a; John 18:13), Peter's Denial Jesus led to Caiaphas (John 18:24)	
Wed.	—Before Sundown	15 Nisan: First Appearance before Sanhedrin (Mark 14:55)	12 Nisan:

		16 Nisan:	13 Nisan:
	At Sundown	16 Nisan:	13 Nisan:
Thurs.	—Before Sundown	16 Nisan: Second Appearance before Sanhedrin (Mark 15:1a) Jesus led to Pilate (Mark 15:1b) Jesus sent to Herod (Luke 23:7-11) People stirred up to demand Barabbas' release (Mark 15:11)	13 Nisan:
	At Sundown Night	17 Nisan: Dream of Pilate's wife (Matt 27:19)	14 Nisan:
Fri.	—Before Sundown	17 Nisan: Jesus led to Pilate again (Luke 23:11) Barabbas released (Mark 15:15) Jesus delivered to be crucified; death (Mark 15:15-37)	14 Nisan: Prepa- ration for Passover (John 18:28)
	At Sundown	18 Nisan: Sabbath Jesus in the tomb (Mark 15:42-46)	15 Nisan: Sabbath and Passover (John 19:31)
Sat.	—Before Sundown	18 Nisan: Sabbath Jesus in the Tomb	15 Nisan: Sabbath

According to this solution, Jesus would have eaten the Last Supper according to the solar calendar (about sundown on 15 Nisan, Tuesday evening) and been crucified according to the luni-solar calendar (on 14 Nisan, the Preparation Day for the Passover). Thus the Synoptics dated the Last Supper according to the old solar calendar, and John records his death according to the official calendar.

Initial favorable reactions to the proposed solution came mainly from OT scholars and conservative NT interpreters. Problems with the solution are mainly two: (a) Is there ever an indication elsewhere in the gospel tradition that Jesus followed the solar calendar in opposition to the luni-solar (official) calendar? (b) The harmonization of Synoptic and Johannine material in the proposal rides roughshod over the long-accepted analyses of many of the passages according to form-critical methods and betrays a fundamentalist concern.

Further discussions of the proposal:

Blinzler, J., "Qumran-Kalender und Passionschronologie," *ZNW* 49 (1958) 238-51

Braun, H., *Qumran und das Neue Testament* (see chapter X/VIII above), 2. 43-54

Carmignac, J., "Les apparitions de Jésus ressuscité et le calendrier biblico-qumranien," *RevQ* 7 (1969-71) 483-504

Carmignac, J., "Comment Jésus et ses contemporains pouvaient-ils célébrer la Pâque à une date non officielle?" *RevQ* 5 (1964-66) 59-79 (with bibliography on this topic)

Cortés Quirant, J., "La nueva fecha de la última cena, *EstBib* 17 (1958) 47-81

Hoehner, H. W., "Chronological Aspects of the Life of Christ,"*BSac* 131 (1974) 241-64

Jaubert, A., "Le mercredi où Jésus fut livré," *NTS* 14 (1967-68)145-64

Kuhn, K. G., "Zum essenischen Kalender," *ZNW* 52 (1961) 65-73

Mann, C. S., "The Chronology of the Passion and the Qumran Calendar," *Church Quarterly Review* 160 (1959) 446-56

Ruckstuhl, E., *Chronology of the Last Days of Jesus: A Critical Study* (New York: Desclée, 1965). (A poor translation of *Die Chronologie des letzten Mahles und des Leidens Jesu* [Biblische Beiträge; Einsiedeln: Benziger, 1963])

Skehan, P. W., "The Date of the Last Supper," *CBQ* 20 (1958) 192-99

Strobel, A., "Der Termin des Todes Jesu: Überschau und Lösungsvorschlag unter Einschluss des Qumrankalenders," *ZNW* 51 (1960) 69-101

Walker, N., "The Dating of the Last Supper," *JQR* 47 (1957) 293-95

Walther, J. A., "The Chronology of Passion Week," *JBL* 77 (1958) 116-22

X. HISTORY OF THE QUMRAN COMMUNITY

Allegro, J., *The Dead Sea Scrolls: A Reappraisal* (Pelican Books A376; Baltimore: Penguin, 1964) 103-9

Beckwith, R. T., "The Pre-History and Relationships of the Pharisees, Sadducees and Essenes: A Tentative Reconstruction," *RevQ* 11 (1982-84) 3-46

Bowman, J., "Contact between Samaritan Sects and Qumran?" *VT* 7 (1957) 184-89

Burgmann, H., *Vorgeschichte und Frühgeschichte der essenischen Gemeinden von Qumrân und Damaskus* (Arbeiten zum Neuen Testament und Judentum 7; Frankfurt am M./Bern/New York: P. Lang, 1987)

Callaway, P. R., *The History of the Qumran Community: An Investigation* (JSPSup 3; Sheffield, UK: JSOT Press, 1988)

Carnevale, L., "Le fonti storiche in 'Khirbet Qumrân,'" *Euntes docete* 35 (1982) 233-48

Charlesworth, J. H., "The Origin and Subsequent History of the Authors of the Dead Sea Scrolls: Four Transitional Phases among the Qumran Essenes," *RevQ* 10 (1979-81) 213-33

Cross, F. M., *ALQ*, 49-160

Cross, F. M., "The Early History of the Qumran Community," *NDBA*, 3-79

Denis, A. M., *Les thèmes de connaissance* (see chapter X/V above)

Dequeker, L., "1 Chronicles XXIV and the Royal Priesthood of the Hasmoneans," *OS* 24 (1986) 94-106

Dionisio, F., "A Qumran con gli Esseni," *BeO* 30 (1988) 3-34, 85-100

Dupont-Sommer, A., *The Essene Writings from Qumran* (see chapter VIII above), 339-67

Fritsch, C. T., "Herod the Great and the Qumran Community," *JBL* 74 (1955) 175-81

García Martínez, F., "Orígenes apocalípticos del movimiento esenio y orígenes de la secta qumránica," *Communio* 18 (1985) 353-68.

García Martínez, F., "Essénisme qumranien: Origines, caractéristiques, héritage," *Atti del congresso tenuto a S. Miniato dal 12 al 15 novembre 1984: Associazione italiana per lo studio del giudaismo, Testi e studi* (Rome: Carucci, 1987) 37-57

Ginzberg, L., *Eine unbekannte jüdische Sekte: Erster Teil*(Hildesheim: Olms, 1972 [reprint of 1922 ed.]); *An UnknownJewish Sect* (New York: Jewish Theological Seminary of America, 1976)

Iwry, S., "Was There a Migration to Damascus? The Problem of *šby yśrʾl*," *W. F. Albright Volume* (Eretz Israel 9; Jerusalem: Israel Exploration Society, 1969) 80-88

Jeremias, G., *Der Lehrer der Gerechtigkeit* (see chapter X/Vabove)

Kister, M., "Ltwldwt kt hʾysyym: ʿywnym bḥzwn hḥywt spr hywblymw bryt Dmśq (On the History of the Essene Sect: Studies in the Animal Apoclypse, the Book of Jubilees, and the Damascus Document)," *Tarbiz* 56 (1986-87) 1-18

Milik, J. T., *Ten Years* (see chapter IV above) 44-97

Murphy-O'Connor, J., "The Essenes and Their History," *RB* 81 (1974) 215-44

Murphy-O'Connor, J., "The Essenes in Palestine," *BA* 40 (1977) 100-24

Murphy-O'Connor, J., "Demetrius I and the Teacher of Righteousness (*I Macc.*, x, 25-45)," *RB* 83 (1976) 400-20

Rabinowitz, I., "Sequence and Dates of the Extra-Biblical Dead Sea Scroll Texts and 'Damascus' Fragments," *VT* 3 (1953) 175-85

Rowley, H. H., "The History of the Qumran Sect," *BJRL* 49 (1966-67) 203-32

Stegemann, H., *Die Entstehung der Qumrangemeinde* (Dissertation, Bonn, 1965; privately published, 1971).

Thiering, B. E., *Redating the Teacher of Righteousness* (Australian and New Zealand Studies in Theology and Religion 1; Sydney: Theological Explorations, 1979); see the reviews by J. Murphy-O'Connor, *RB* 87 (1980) 425-30; M. P. Horgan, *CBQ* 43 (1981) 143-45; B. Z. Wacholder, *JBL* 101 (1982) 147-48

Vermes, G., "The Essenes and History," *JJS* 32 (1981) 18-31

Woude, A. S. van der, "Wicked Priest or Wicked Priests? Reflections on the Identification of the Wicked Priest in the Habakkuk Commentary," *JJS* 33 (1982) 349-59

XI

THE COPPER PLAQUE MENTIONING BURIED TREASURE (3QTREASURE, 3Q15)

THE COPPER PLAQUE MENTIONING BURIED TREASURE
(3QTREASURE, 3Q15)

This copper plaque, which is also variously referred to as the "Copper Scroll" or the "Copper Rolls" (because it was found in two parts rolled up to resemble scrolls), is really not a scroll at all. It was found in Qumran Cave 3 in 1952. The archaeological institutions, which were involved that year in the exploration of the cliffs along the northwest shore of the Dead Sea, entrusted the publication of it to J. T. Milik. Attempts to unroll the brittle oxidized copper were unsuccessful; the attempts to restore it to a supple copper form were on the verge of success when it was decided to saw it open in strips at Manchester in England. J. M. Allegro was on the spot at the time and published the first reading of the text with a translation (see below). Milik's publication of the text in DJD 3 is, however, the official publication and is to be regarded as the *editio princeps*, despite Allegro's prior making known of the text to the public.

Though it was found in Qumran Cave 3, it most likely had nothing to do with the Qumran community. It resembles the rest of the Qumran writings neither in palaeography nor in language (being an early form of Mishnaic Hebrew).

3Q Treasure,　　　　3Q15　　　Milik, J. T., "Le rouleau de cuivre provenant de la grotte 3 (3Q15)," DJD 3. 199-302

See further:
Kuhn, K. G., "Les rouleaux de cuivre de Qumrân," *RB* 61 (1954) 193-205
Kuhn, K. G., "Die Kupferrollen von Qumran und ihr Inhalt," *TLZ* 79 (1954) 303-4
Baker, H. W., "Notes on the Opening of the 'Bronze' Scrolls from Qumran," *BJRL* 39 (1956) 45-56 (see also DJD 3. 203-10)
Kuhn, K. G., "Bericht über neue Qumranfunde und über die Öffnung der Kupferrolle," *TLZ* 81 (1956) 541-46
Milik, J. T., "The Copper Document from Cave III, Qumran," *BA* 19 (1956) 532

Dupont-Sommer, A., "Les rouleaux de cuivre trouvés à Qoumrân,"
    RHR 151 (1957) 22-35

Mowinckel, S., "The Copper Scroll—An Apocryphon," *JBL* 76 (1957)
    261-65

Milik, J. T., "Le rouleau de cuivre de Qumran (3Q15): Traduction et
    commentaire topographique," *RB* 66 (1959) 321-57

Milik, J. T., "Notes d'épigraphie et de topographie palestiniennes,"
    RB 66 (1959) 550-75, esp. 567-75; 67 (1960) 354-67

Milik, J. T., "The Copper Document from Cave III of Qumran:
    Translation and Commentary," ADAJ 4-5 (1960) 137-55

Allegro, J. M., *The Treasure of the Copper Scroll* (Garden City, NY:
    Doubleday, 1960) (A translation and commentary that are to
    be used with caution; see R. de Vaux, *RB* 68 [1961] 146-47; J. A.
    Fitzmyer, *TS* 22 [1961] 292-96)

Jeremias, J., "The Copper Scroll from Qumran," *ExpTim* 71 (1959-60)
    227-28

Jeremias, J., "Remarques sur le rouleau de cuivre de Qumrân,"*RB* 67
    (1960) 220-22

Milik, J. T., "Observations," *RB* 67 (1960) 222-23 (on the article of J.
    Jeremias)

Silberman, L. H., "A Note on the Copper Scroll," *VT* 10 (1960) 77-79
    (see also the postscript by P. Grelot, pp. 37-38)

Laperrousaz, E.-M., "Remarques sur l'origine des rouleaux de
    cuivre découverts dans la grotte 3 de Qumrân," *RHR* 159
    (1961) 157-72

Nötscher, F., "Die Kupferrolle von Qumran (3 Q 15)," *BZ* 5 (1961)
    292-97

Cross, F. M., "Excursus on the Palaeographical Dating of the Copper
    Document," DJD 3. 217-21

Lurie, B. Z., Měgillat han-něḥōšet mimmidbar Yěhûdāh (Publications
    of the Israel Bible Research Society 14; Jerusalem: Kirjath-
    Sepher, 1963)

Lehmann, M. R., "Identification of the Copper Scroll Based on Its
    Technical Terms," *RevQ* 5 (1964-66) 97-105

Jeremias, J., *The Rediscovery of Bethesda: John 5:2* (NT Archaeology
    Monograph 1; Louisville: Southern Baptist Theological
    Seminary, 1966)

Jeremias, J., *Abba: Studien zur neutestamentlichen Theologie und
    Zeitgeschichte* (Göttingen: Vandenhoeck & Ruprecht, 1966) 361-
    64

Pixner, B., "Unravelling the Copper Scroll Code: A Study on the Topography of 3 Q 15," *RevQ* 11 (1982-84) 323-66 (with further bibliography)

Thorion, Y., "Beiträge zur Erforschung der Sprache der Kupfer-Rolle," *RevQ* 12 (1985-87) 163-76

Wolters, A., "The Fifth Cache of the Copper Scroll: 'The Plastered Cistern of Manos,'" *RevQ* 13 (Mémorial Jean Carmignac, 1988) 167-76

Dalman, G., "The Search for the Temple Treasure at Jerusalem,"*Palestine Exploration Fund Quarterly Statement* 1912-13, 35-39

XII

INDEXES

I. INDEX OF MODERN AUTHORS
(Numbers refer to pages of this book)

202 *The Dead Sea Scrolls*

II. INDEX OF BIBLICAL PASSAGES

The following list not only supplies references to pages in this book (in parentheses on the right) but also gives information as to where one can find the biblical texts that are quoted in the Dead Sea Scrolls. Included are not only such texts as 1QIsa[a], 1QIsa[b], 11QPs[a] (with their detailed listings), but also the isolated quotations of the OT in various scrolls. The purpose of this index is to enable the student to ascertain what the form of an OT text was in the Qumran or other writings among the DSS. For the psalter in these writings, one should also consult J. A. Sanders, *DSPS*, 146-49; his list may be fuller than that given below, because he also lists the Psalms that are known to exist but that have not yet been fully published. The list of psalm passages given below is mostly limited to those that have been published or are shortly to be published. In the following list col. 1 gives the passages of biblical books, col. 2 the commonly used Qumran (Murabbaʿat, etc.) siglum, col. 3 the numbered siglum in the DJD series, and col. 4 the page(s) of this book on which information is given where the Qumran or other text can be found.

Genesis

1:18-21	1QGen	1Q1	(15)
1:27	CD 4:21		(92)
1:28(?)	pap4QJub?	4Q483	(53, 65)
3:11-14	1QGen	1Q1	(15)
6:8-9	1QapGen		(14)
6:13-21	6QpaleoGen	6Q1	(27)
7:9	CD 5:1		(92)
9:2-3,4,20	1QapGen		(14)
10?	1QapGen		(14)
10:6,20(?)	6QGen(?) ar	6Q19	(28)
12:8-15:4	1QapGen		(14)
17:12-19	8QGen	8Q1	(30)
18:20-25	8QGen	8Q1	(30)
19:27-28	2QGen	2Q1	(20)
22:13-15	1QGen	1Q1	(15)
23:17-19	1QGen	1Q1	(15)
24:4-6	4QBibPar	4Q158	(63)
24:22-24	1QGen	1Q1	(15)

25:9,7-8	2QJub^a	2Q19	(21)
32:4-5,30	MurGen	Mur 1	(79)
32:25-32,31(?)	4QBibPar	4Q158	(63)
32:33-33:1	MurGen	Mur 1	(79)
33:18-34:3	Mur(?)Gen		(84)
34:5-7	MurGen	Mur 1	(79)
34:30-35:1,4-7	MurGen	Mur 1	(79)
35:6-10	?HevGen		(85)
36:5-12	?HevGen		(85)
36:6,35-37	2QGen	2Q1	(20)
46:7-11	MasGen		(77)
49:10	4QPBless	omitted	(56)
50:26,22	2QJub^b	2Q20	(21)

Exodus

1:1-5	4QExod^b		(31)
1:7	2QJub^b	2Q20	(21)
1:11-14	2QExod^a	2Q2	(20)
3:12	4QBibPar	4Q158	(49)
4:27-28	4QBibPar	4Q158	(63)
4:28-31	MurExod	Mur 1	(79)
4:31	2QExod^b	2Q3	(20)
5:3	MurExod	Mur 1	(79)
5:3-5	2QExod^c	2Q4	(20)
6:5-11	MurExod	Mur 1	(79)
6:25-7:19	4QpaleoExod^m		(31)
7:1-4	2QExod^a	2Q2	(20)
7:16-19	4QpaleoExod^m		(31)
7:29-8:1,12-18	4QpaleoExod^m		(31)
8:19-22	4QpaleoExod^m		(31)
9:5-16,19-21	4QpaleoExod^m		(31)
9:27-29	2QExod^a	2Q2	(20)
9:35-10:1,2-5	4QpaleoExod^m		(31)
10:5-12,19-24	4QpaleoExod^m		(31)
10:25-28	4QpaleoExod^m		(31)
11:3-7	2QExod^a	2Q2	(20)
11:8-12:2	4QpaleoExod^m		(31)
12:6-8,13-15,17-22	4QpaleoExod^m		(31)
12:26-27(?)	2QExod^b	2Q3	(20)
12:31-32,34-39	4QpaleoExod^m		(31)
12:32-41	2QExod^a	2Q2	(20)

20:7-12	4Qmez[a]	4Q149	(44)
20:11	8Qphyl	8Q3	(30)
20:12,16,17	4QBibPar	4Q158	(63)
20;18-19	4QpaleoExod[m]		(32)
20:19ff.	4QBibPar	4Q158	(63)
20:19-22 (Sam.)	4QBibPar	4Q158 frg. 6	(63)
20:21 (Sam.)	4QTestim	4Q175	(59, 64)
(20:21-21:4),5-6	4QpaleoExod[m]		(32)
20:22-26	4QBibPar	4Q158	(63)
20:25-21:1,4-5	1QExod	1Q2	(15)
21:1,3,4,6,8,10	4QBibPar	4Q158	(63)
21:13-14,22-32	4QpaleoExod[m]		(32)
21:15,16,18,20, 22,25,32,34,35-37	4QBibPar	4Q158	(63)
21:18-20(?)	2QExod[a]	2Q2	(20)
21:37-22:2,15-19	2QExod[b]	2Q3	(20)
22:1-11,13	4QBibPar	4Q158	(63)
22:3-4,6-7,11-13, 16-18	4QpaleoExod[m]		(32)
22:20-30	4QpaleoExod[m]		(32)
23:7	1QS 5:15		(15)
23:15-16	4QpaleoExod[m]		(32)
23:29-31	4QpaleoExod[m]		(32)
24:1-4,6-11	4QpaleoExod[m]		(32)
24:4-6	4QBibPar	4Q158	(49)
25:11-12,20-22	4QpaleoExod[m]		(32)
25:22-29,31-34	4QpaleoExod[m]		(32)
26:8-15,21-30	4QpaleoExod[m]		(32)
26:11-13	2QExod[a]	2Q2	(20)
(26:35, 30:1-9),10, (26:36-37)	4QpaleoExod[m]		(32)
27:1-2,9-14	4QpaleoExod[m]		(32)
27:17-19	2QExod[b]	2Q3	(20)
27:18-19	4QpaleoExod[m]		(32)
28:3-4,8-11	4QpaleoExod[m]		(32)
28:4-7	7QLXXExod gr	7Q1	(29)
28:22-24,26-28, 30-39	4QpaleoExod[m]		(32)
28:39-29:5	4QpaleoExod[m]		(32)
29:20,22-25,31-34	4QpaleoExod[m]		(32)
29:34-41,(42-46)	4QpaleoExod[m]		(32)

29:38-41	11QTemple^a 13		(72)
(30:11),12-18	4QpaleoExod^m		(32)
30:21(?),23-25	2QExod^a	2Q2	(20)
30:29-31,34-38	4QpaleoExod^m		(32)
30:32,34	4QBibPar	4Q158	(72)
31:1-7	4QpaleoExod^m		(32)
31:7-8,13-15	4QpaleoExod^m		(32)
31:16-17	2QExod^b	2Q3	(20)
32:2-9	4QpaleoExod^m		(32)
32:10-19,25-30	4QpaleoExod^m		(32)
32:32-34	2QExod^a	2Q2	(20)
33:12-15	4QpaleoExod^m		(32)
33:16-34:3,10-13	4QpaleoExod^m		(32)
34:10	2QExod^b	2Q3	(20)
34:11-16	11QTemple^a 2		(72)
34:15-18,20-24, 27-28	4QpaleoExod^m		(32)
(35:1-37:9)	4QpaleoExod^m		(32)
37:9-16	4QpaleoExod^m		(32)
40:8-27	4QExod^f		(31)
Leviticus			
2:3-5,7	4QLXXLev^b	4Q120	(42)
3:4,9-13	4QLXXLev^b	4Q120	(42)
4:3-8	MasLev		(77)
4:4-8,10-11, 18-20,26-29	4QLXXLev^b	4Q120	(42)
4:24-26	11QpaleoLev		(68)
5:8-10,18-24	4QLXXLev^b	4Q120	(42)
6:2-4	4QLXXLev^b	4Q120	(42)
8:12-13	6QpaleoLev	6Q2	(27)
9:23-10:2	11QLev		(68)
10:4-7	11QpaleoLev		(68)
11	11QTemple^a 48		(72)
11:10-11	1QpaleoLev	1Q3	(15)
11:22-29	2QpaleoLev	2Q5	(20)
11:27-32	11QpaleoLev		(68)
11:29-40	11QTemple^a 50		(72)
13	4QD^a		(50)
13-14	11QTemple^a 48		(72)
13:3-9	11QpaleoLev		(68)

13:39-43	11QpaleoLev		(68)
13:58-59	11QLev		(68)
14:16-21	11QpaleoLev		(68)
14:53-15:5/16:2-4	11QpaleoLev		(68)
15	4QD[a]		(50)
15:3	11QpaleoLev		(68)
16	11QTemple[a] 25		(72)
16:12-15,18-21	4QtgLev	4Q156	(45)
16:34-17:5	11QpaleoLev		(68)
17:2-4	11QpaleoLev		(68)
18:12-13	11QTemple[a] 66		(72)
18:13	CD 5:8-9		(92)
18:27-19:4	11QpaleoLev		(68)
19:16	11QTemple[a] 64		(72)
19:17,18	CD 9:7-8		(92)
19:30-34	1QpaleoLev	1Q3	(15)
20:1-6	11QpaleoLev		(68)
20:2-3	11QpaleoLev		(68)
20:17	11QTemple[a] 66		(72)
20:19	11QTemple[a] 66		(72)
20:20-24	1QpaleoLev	1Q3	(15)
20:21	11QTemple[a] 66		(72)
21:6-9	11QpaleoLev		(68)
21:24-22:6	1QpaleoLev	1Q3	(15)
21:6-11	11QpaleoLev		(68)
22:20-22	11QTemple[a] 52		(72)
22:21-27	11QpaleoLev		(68)
22:22-25	11QpaleoLev		(68)
22:28	11QTemple[a] 52		(72)
23:1-3	2QNum[d(?)]	2Q9	(20)
23:4-8	1QpaleoLev	1Q3	(15)
23:5-8	11QTemple[a] 17		(72)
23:10-14,15-21	11QTemple[a] 18		(72)
23:22-29	11QpaleoLev		(68)
23:23	11QTemple[a] 25		(72)
23:4-8	1QpaleoLev	1Q3	(15)
23:27-32	11QTemple[a] 25		(72)
23:33-36	11QTemple[a] 27		(72)
23:38	CD 11:17-18		(92)
24:9-10	11QpaleoLev		(68)
24:9-14	11QpaleoLev		(68)

22:21	4QNum^b		(32)
22:37-38	4QNum^b		(32)
22:41-23:4	4QNum^b		(32)
23:6,13-15,21-22	4QNum^b		(32)
23:13	4QNum^b		(32)
23:27	4QNum^b		(32)
23:27-24:10	4QNum^b		(32)
24:15-17	4QTestim	**4Q175**	(59, 63)
24:17	CD 7:18-21		(92)
24:17-19	1QM 11:5-7		(15)
25:4-8,16-18	4QNum^b		(32)
26:1-5,7-10,12, 14-34	4QNum^b		(32)
26:62-27:5	4QNum^b		(32)
27:7-8,10,18-19, 21-23b	4QNum^b		(32)
28:3-5	11QTemple^a 13		(72)
28:13-17,28,30-31	4QNum^b		(32)
28:16	11QTemple^a 17		(72)
28:26-31	11QTemple^a 18		(72)
29:1-6	11QTemple^a 25		(72)
29:7-11	11QTemple^a 25		(72)
29:10-13,16-18, 26-30	4QNum^b		(32)
29:12-38	11QTemple^a 27		(72)
30:1-3,5-9,15-16	4QNum^b		(32)
30:3-6	11QTemple^a 53		(72)
30:7-10	11QTemple 54		(72)
30:17	CD 7:8-9		(92)
31:2-6,21b-25, 30-33,35-36	4QNum^b		(32)
31:25	4QNum^b		(32)
31:28	4QNum^b		(32)
31:38,43-44	4QNum^b		(32)
31:46-32:1	4QNum^b		(32)
31:48	4QNum^b		(32)
32:7-10,13-17,19, 23-30,35	4QNum^b		(32)
32:37-39,41	4QNum^b		(32)
33:1-4,23,25,28, 31,45,47-48,50-52	4QNum^b		(32)

5:24-32	4Qphyl^j	4Q137	(44)
5:27-6:3	4Qphyl^a	4Q128	(43)
5:27-6:9	4Qmez^c	4Q151	(45)
5:28-29	4QTestim	4Q175	(59, 63)
5:28-31	4QDeut^k		(33)
5:29 (Sam.)	4QBibPar	4Q158 frg. 6	(63)
5:29-33	4QDeut^j		(33)
5:30-31	4QBibPar	4Q158	(63)
5:33-6:5	4Qphyl^m	4Q140	(44)
6:1-3	4QDeut^j		(33)
6:1-3	8Qphyl	8Q3	(30)
6:2-3	4Qphyl^j	4Q137	(44)
6:4-6,8-10	4QDeut^p		(33)
6:4-9	4Qphyl^c	4Q130	(43)
6;4-9	8Qphyl	8Q3	(30)
6:4-9	Murphyl	Mur 4	(79)
6:5-6	4Qmez^b	4Q150	(44)
6:6-7(?)	4Qphyl^i	4Q136	(44)
6:7-9	4Qphyl^o	4Q142	(44)
7:9	CD 19:1		(92)
7:12-16	4QDeut^e		(33)
7:15-24	5QDeut	5Q1	(25)
7:19-22	4QDeut^m		(33)
7:21-22	1QM 10:1-2		(15)
7:21-8:4	4QDeut^e		(33)
7:25-26	11QTemple^a 2		(72)
8:5-10	4QDeut^j		(33)
8:5-10	4QDeut^n		(33)
8:5-16	4QDeut^e		(33)
8:5-9:2	5QDeut	5Q1	(25)
8:8-9	1QDeut^b	1Q5	(16)
8:18-19	1QDeut^a	1Q4	(16)
9:5	CD 8:14-16		(92)
9:10	1QDeut^b	1Q5	(16)
9:23	CD 3:7		(92)
9:27-28	1QDeut^a	1Q4	(16)
10:1-3	MurDeut	Mur 2	(79)
10:8-12	2QDeut^c	2Q12	(21)
10:12,14	4QDeut^l		(33)
10:12-19	8Qphyl	8Q3	(30)
10:12-30	4Qmez^c	4Q151	(44)

15:14-15	1QDeut[b]	1Q5	(16)
15:19-23	11QTemple[a] 52		(72)
16:1	11QTemple[a] 17		(72)
16:4,6-7	1QDeut[a]	1Q4	(16)
16:18-20	11QTemple[a] 51		(72)
16:21-22	11QTemple[a] 51		(72)
17:1	11QTemple[a] 52		(72)
17:2-5	11QTemple[a] 55		(72)
17:5-20	11QTemple[a] 56		(72)
17:12-15	2QDeut[b]	2Q11	(21)
17:16	1QDeut[b]	1Q5	(16)
17:17	CD 5:2		(92)
18:9-19	11QTemple[a] 60		(72)
18:18-19	4QTestim	4Q175	(59, 63)
18:18-20,22	4QBibPar	4Q158	(63)
18:20-22	11QTemple[a] 60		(72)
19:8-16	4QDeut[k]		(33)
19:15-21	11QTemple[a] 61		(72)
19:21	4QDeut[h]		(33)
20:1-18	11QTemple[a] 61-62		(72)
20:2-5	1QM 10:2-5		(15)
20:6-19	4QDeut[k]		(33)
21:1-9	11QTemple[a] 63		(72)
21:8-9	1QDeut[b]	1Q5	(16)
21:10-14	11QTemple[a] 63-64		(72)
21:15-17	11QTemple[a] 64		(72)
22:1	11QTemple[a] 64		(72)
22:5-8	11QTemple[a] 65		(72)
22:10	11QTemple[a] 52		(72)
22:13-21	11QTemple[a] 65		(72)
22:22-29	11QTemple[a] 66		(72)
23:1	11QTemple[a] 66		(72)
23:21-23	11QTemple[a] 53		(72)
23:22-24:3	4QDeut[k]		(33)
23:24	CD 16:6-7		(92)
24:10-16	1QDeut[b]	1Q5	(16)
25:4	11QTemple[a] 52		(72)
25:13-18	1QDeut[b]	1Q5	(16)
25:19-26:4	4QDeut[k]		(33)
26:18-19	4QDeut[k]		(33)

40-42,40-43, 48-49	1QJudg	1Q6	(16)

Ruth

2:13-14,14-19,19-22	2QRuth^a	2Q16	(21)
2:22-3:3.4-8	2QRuth^a	2Q16	(21)
3:13-18	2QRuth^b	2Q17	(21)
4:3-4	2QRuth^a	2Q16	(21)

1 Samuel

1:11-13,22-28	4QSam^a		(34)
1:22b-2:6	4QSam^a		(34)
2:1-6,8-11,13-36	4QSam^a		(34)
2:16-25	4QSam^a		(34)
3:1-4,18-20	4QSam^a		(34)
3:14-17	4QVisSam	4Q160	(63)
4:9-12	4QSam^a		(34)
5:8-12	4QSam^a		(34)
6:1-7,12-13, 16-18,20-21	4QSam^a		(34)
7:1	4QSam^a		(34)
8:9-20	4QSam^a		(34)
9:6-8,11-12,16-24	4QSam^a		(34)
10:3-18,25-27	4QSam^a		(34)
11:1,7-12	4QSam^a		(34)
12:7-8,14-19	4QSam^a		(34)
14:24-25,28-34, 47-51	4QSam^a		(34)
15:24-32	4QSam^a		(34)
16:1-11	4QSam^b		(35)
17:3-6	4QSam^a		(34)
18:17-18	1QSam	1Q7	(16)
19:10-17	4QSam^b		(35)
21:3-10	4QSam^b		(35)
23:9-17	4QSam^b		(35)
24:4-5,8-9,14-23	4QSam^a		(34)
25:3-12,20-21, 25-26,39-40	4QSam^a		(34)
25:30-32	4QSam^c		(35)
26:10-12,21,23	4QSam^a		(34)
27:8-12	4QSam^a		(34)

3:12-14	6QKgs	6Q4	(27)
7:31-41	4QKgs^a		(35)
8:1-9,16-18	4QKgs^a		(35)
12:28-31	6QKgs	6Q4	(27)
22:28-31	6QKgs	6Q4	(27)
2 Kings			
5:26	6QKgs	6Q4	(27)
6:32	6QKgs	6Q4	(27)
7:8-10	6QKgs	6Q4	(27)
7:20-8:5	6QKgs	6Q4	(27)
9:1-2	6QKgs	6Q4	(27)
10:19-21	6QKgs	6Q4	(27)
1 Chronicles			
17:9-13	4QFlor	4Q174	(63)
Tobit			
1:17	4QTob ar^a		(35)
1:19-2:2,3	4QTob ar^a		(35)
3:5,9-15,17	4QTob ar^a		(35)
3:6-8	4QTob ar^b		(35)
3:6,10-11	4QTob hebr		(36)
4:2-3,5-7	4QTob ar^a		(35)
4:3-9	4QTob hebr		(36)
4:21-5:1	4QTob ar^a		(35)
4:21-5:1,12-14	4QTob ar^b		(36)
5:2	4QTob hebr		(36)
5:3,9	4QTob ar^a		(35)
5:8-13	4QPs^s		(38)
5:19-6:12,12-18	4QTob ar^b		(36)
6:1	4QPs^s		(38)
6:6-8,13,15-28	4QTob ar^a		(35)
6:18-7:6,13	4QTob ar^a		(35)
6:18-7:10	4QTob ar^b		(36)
7:11	4QTob ar^d		(36)
8:17-19	4QTob ar^b		(36)
8:21-9:4	4QTob ar^b		(36)
10:7-9	4QTob hebr		(36)
11:10-14	4QTob hebr		(36)
12:18-22	4QTob ar^a		(35)

38:3-13	11QtgJob		(70)
38:23-34	11QtgJob		(70)
39:1-11	11QtgJob		(70)
39:20-29	11QtgJob		(70)
40:5-14(15?)	11QtgJob		(70)
40:23-31	11QtgJob		(70)
41:7-17	11QtgJob		(70)
41:25-42:6	11QtgJob		(70)
42:9-11	11QtgJob		(70)

Psalms

	4QPs^a-q		(36)
	4QPs^a-s		(36)
1:1	4QFlor	**4Q174**	(63)
2:1	4QFlor	**4Q174**	(63)
2:1-8	11QPs^c		(69)
2:6-7	3QPs	**3Q2**	(23)
5:8-13	4QPs^s		(38)
5:9-13	4QPs^a		(36)
6:1	4QPs^s		(38)
6:1-4	4QPs^a		(36)
7:8-9	11QMelch 10		(72)
7:14-31:22	5/6HevPs		(85)
9:3-7	11QPs^c		(69)
12:5-13:6	11QPs^c		(69)
14:1-6	11QPs^c		(69)
15:1-5	5/6HevPs		(85)
16:1	5/6HevPs		(85)
16:7-9	4QPs^c		(37)
17:1(?)	4QPs^c		(37)
17:5-9,14	8QPs	**8Q2**	(30)
17:9-15	11QPs^c		(69)
18:1-12	11QPs^c		(69)
18:3-4,16-17,33-41	4QPs^c		(37)
18:6-9,10-13	8QPs	**8Q2**	(30)
18:10-13	8QPs	**8Q2**	(30)
18:15-16	11QPs^c		(69)
22:15-17	4QPs^f		(37)
25:15	4QPs^a		(36)
26:7-12	4QPs^r		(38)
27:1	4QPs^r		(38)

57:1,4	1QpPs	**1Q16**	(17)
59:5-8	11QPs^d		(69)
60:8-9	4QpPs^a	**4Q171**	(63)
62:13(?) + 63:2-4	4QPs^a		(36)
66:16-20	4QPs^a		(36)
67:1-8	4QPs^a		(36)
68:1-5,16-18	11QPs^d		(69)
68:12-13,26-27, 30-31	1QpPs	**1Q16**	(17)
69:1-19	4QPs^a		(36)
74:1-14	4QPs^a		(36)
76:10-12	4QPs^e		(37)
77:1	4QPs^e		(37)
77:18-78:1	11QPs^c		(69)
78:5-12	11QPs^d		(69)
78:6-7,31-33	4QPs^e		(37)
78:36-37(?)	6QPs	**6Q5**	(27)
79:2-3	4QTanh	**4Q176**	(58, 64)
81:2-3	4QPs^e		(37)
81:3-85:10	MasPs		(77)
81:4-10	11QPs^d		(69)
82:1	11QMelch 10		(72)
82:2	11QMelch 11		(72)
86:5-8	1QPs^a	**1Q10**	(16)
86:10-11	4QPs^e		(37)
86:11-14	11QPs^c		(69)
88:1-5	4QPs^e		(37)
88:15-17	4QPs^s		(38)
89:20-22,26,23, 27-28,31	4QPs89	**4Q236**	(38)
89:44-47,50-53	4QPs^e		(37)
91:1-16	11QPsAp^a		(69)
91:5-8,12-15	4QPs^b		(36)
92:4-8,13-15	4QPs^b		(36)
92:12-14	1QPs^a	**1Q10**	(16)
93:1-3	11QPs^a col. xxii		(74)
93:3-5	4QPs^m		(38)
94:1-4,8-9,10-14, 17-18,21-22	4QPs^b		(36)
94:16	1QPs^a	**1Q10**	(16)
95:3-7	4QPs^m		(38)

115:1-4	4QPs^o		(38)
115:2-3	4QPs^b		(37)
115:15-18	4QPs^e		(37)
116:1-3	4QPs^e		(37)
116:5-10	4QPs^o		(38)
116:17-19	4QPs^b		(37)
118:1(?),15-16	11QPs^b		(69)
118:1-3,6-11, 18-20,23-26,29	4QPs^b		(37)
118:1(?),15,16, 8,9,?,29(?)	11QPs^a		(74)
118:25-29	11QPs^a frg. E i		(73)
118:26-27(?)	4QpPs^b	4Q173	(48, 63)
119:1-6	11QPs^a col. vi		(74)
119:10-21	4QPs^h		(37)
119:15-28	11QPs^a col. vii		(74)
119:31-34,43-48, 77-79	1QPs^a	1Q10	(16)
119:37-49	11QPs^a col viii		(74)
119:37-43,44-46, 49-50,73-74, 81-83,90-92	4QPs^g		(37)
119:59-73	11QPs^a col. ix		(74)
119:82-96	11QPs^a col. x		(74)
119:99-101,104, 113-20,138-42	5QPs	5Q5	(25)
119:105-20	11QPs^a col. xi		(74)
119:128-42	11QPs^a col. xii		(74)
119:150-64	11QPs^a col. xiii		(74)
119:171-76	11QPs^a col. xiv		(74)
120:6	4QPs^e		(37)
121:1-8	11QPs^a col. iii		(74)
122:1-9	11QPs^a col. iii		(74)
122:1-9	4QPs122		(38, 74)
123:1-2	11QPs^a col. iii		(74)
124:7-8	11QPs^a col. iv		(74)
125:1-5	11QPs^a col. iv		(74)
125:2-5	4QPs^e		(37)
126:1-5	4QPs^e		(37)
126:1-6	11QPs^a col. iv		(74)

147:18-20	11QPs^a frg. E iii		(73)
148:1-12	11QPs^a col. ii		(74)
149:7-9	11QPs^a col. xxvi		(74)
150:1-6	11QPs^a col. xxvi		(74)
150:1-6	MasPs		(77)
51A:3-12 (Syr Ps I)	11QPs^a col. xxviii		(74)
151B:13-14 (Syr Ps I)	11QPs^a col. xxviii		(74)
154:3-19 (Syr Ps II)	11QPs^a col. xviii		(74)
155:1-18 (Syr Ps III)	11QPs^a col. xxiv		(74)

Proverbs

1:27-2:1	4QProv^a		(38)
chaps. 14-15	4QProv^a		(38)
15:8	CD 11:20-21		(92)

Qoheleth (Ecclesiastes)

5:13-17	4QQoh^a		(39)
6:3-8	4QQoh^a		(39)
7:7-9	4QQoh^a		(39)

Canticle of Canticles (Song of Songs)

1:1-6,6-7	6QCant	6Q6	(27)

Sirach

1:19-20	2QSir	2Q18	(21)
6:14-15(?)	2QSir	2Q18	(21)
6:20-31	2QSir	2Q18	(21)
39:27-44:17c	MasSir		(77)
51:13-20b	11QPs^a		(74)
51:30	11QPs^a		(74)

Isaiah

1-66	1QIsa^a		(11)
?	1QIsa^b	1Q8 frg. 7	(13)
1:1	3QpIsa	3Q4	(23)
1:1(?)	4QpIsa^e	4Q165	(47, 62)
1:1-3	4QIsa^a		(39)

22:13d-23:6a	4QIsa^a		(39)
22:24-23:4	1QIsa^b	*DSSHU* frg. 5	(12)
23:1-12	4QIsa^a		(39)
24:17	CD 4:12-18		(92)
24:18-25:8	1QIsa^b	1Q8 6:1-15	(12, 16)
26:1-5	1QIsa^b	*DSSHU* frg. 6	(13)
28:15-19	1QIsa^b	*DSSHU* frg. 6	(13)
29:1-8	1QIsa^b	*DSSHU* frg. 7	(13)
29:10-11,15-16, 19-23	4QpIsa^c	4Q163	(47, 62)
30:1-5,15-18	4QpIsa^c	4Q163	(47, 62)
30:10-14	1QIsa^b	*DSSHU* frg. 8	(13)
30:19-21	4QpIsa^c	4Q163	(47, 62)
30:21-16	1QIsa^b	*DSSHU* frg. 9	(13)
31:1	4QpIsa^c	4Q163	(47, 62)
31:8	1QM 11:11-12		(15)
32:5-6	4QpIsa^c	4Q163	(47, 62)
32:5-7	4QpIsa^e	4Q165	(47, 62)
35:4-6	1QIsa^b	*DSSHU* frg. 10	(13)
37:8-12	1QIsa^b	*DSSHU* frg. 11	(13)
38:12-39:8	1QIsa^b	*DSSHU* col. 1 + frg. 12	(13)
40:1-5	4QTanh	4Q176	(58, 64)
40:2-3	1QIsa^b	*DSSHU* col. 1 + frg. 12	(13)
40:3	1QS 8:13-16		(15)
40:12	4QpIsa^e	4Q165	(47, 62)
40:16,18-19	5QIsa	5Q3	(25)
41:3-23	1QIsa^b	*DSSHU* col. 2	(13)
41:8-9	4QTanh	4Q176	(58, 64)
43:1-2,4-6	4QTanh	4Q17	(58, 64)
43:1-13,23-27	1QIsa^b	*DSSHU* col. 3 + frg. 13	(13)
44:21-28	1QIsa^b	*DSSHU* col. 4	(13)
45:1-13	1QIsa^b	*DSSHU* col. 4	(13)
46:3-13	1QIsa^b	*DSSHU* col. 5	(13)
47:1-14	1QIsa^b	*DSSHU* col. 5	(13)
48:17-22	1QIsa^b	*DSSHU* col. 6	(13)
49:1-15	1QIsa^b	*DSSHU* col. 6	(13)
49:7,13-17	4QTanh	4Q176	(58, 64)
50:7-11	1QIsa^b	*DSSHU* col. 7	(13)

14:4-7	4QJer^a		(39)
15:1-2	4QJer^a		(39)
17:8-26	4QJer^a		(39)
18:15-19:1	4QJer^a		(39)
parts of 19-22	4QJer^c		(40)
22:4-16	4QJer^a		(39)
32:24-25(?)	2QJer	2Q13	(21)
parts of 25-27	4QJer^c		(40)
parts of 30-33	4QJer^c		(40)
42:7-11,14	2QJer	2Q13	(21)
43:2-10	4QJer^d		(39)
43:3-9	4QJer^b		(39)
43:8-11	2QJer	2Q13	(21)
44:1-3,12-14	2QJer	2Q13	(21)
46:27-47:7	2QJer	2Q13	(21)
48:2-4,41-42	2QJer	2Q13	(21)
48:7,25-39,43-45	2QJer	2Q13	(21)
49:10	2QJer	2Q13	(21)
50:4-6	4QJer^e		(39)

Lamentations

1 and 4	4QapLam^a	4Q179	(48)
1:1-6,6-10,10-16	4QLam^a		(40)
1:10-12	3QLam	3Q3	(23)
3:53-62	3QLam	3Q3	(23)
4:5-8,11-15, 15-16,19-20	5QLam^a	5Q6	(25)
4:17-20	5QLam^b	5Q7	(25)
4:20-5:3,4-12, 12-13,16-17	5QLam^a	5Q6	(25)

Epistle of Jeremy (Baruch 6)

43-44	7QLXXEpJer	7Q2	(29)

Ezekiel

1:10,11-12,13, 16-17,20-24	4QEzek^b		(40)
4:3-5	11QEzek		(69)
4:16-5:1	1QEzek	1Q9	(16)
5:11-17	11QEzek		(69)
7:9-12	11QEzek		(69)

3:4	CD 20;15-17		(92)
4:16	CD 1:13-14		(92)
5:10	CD 19:15-16		(92)
5:13-15	4QpHos^b	**4Q167**	(47, 62)
6:4,7,9-10	4QpHos^b	**4Q167**	(47, 62)
6:9	4QpIsa^c	**4Q163**	(47, 62)
8:6-7,13-14	4QpHos^b	**4Q167**	(47, 62)
13:15b-14:1a,3-6	4QXII(?)		(41)
?	4QXII^c		(40)

Joel

2:20	MurXII	Mur 88	(83)
2:26-4:16	MurXII	Mur 88	(83)
?	4QXII^c		(40)

Amos

1:3-5	5QAmos	5Q4	(25)
1:5(?)	8HevXII gr frg. 2		(85)
1:5-2:1	MurXII	Mur 88 iii	(83)
5:26-27	CD 7:14-15		(92)
6	MurXII	Mur 88 vi	(83)
7:3-8:7	MurXII	Mur 88 vii	(83)
8:11-9:15	MurXII	Mur 88 viii	(83)
9:11	4QFlor	**4Q174**	(63)
9:11	CD 7:15-16		(92)
?	4QXII^c		(40)

Obadiah

1-21	MurXII	Mur 88 ix	(83)

Jonah

1:1-3:2	MurXII	Mur 88 x	(83)
1:14-16	8HevXII gr ii		(86)
2:1-7	8HevXII gr ii		(86)
3:2	MurXII	Mur 88 xi	(83)
3:2-5	8HevXII gr iii		(85, 86)
3:7-10	8HevXII gr iii		(86)
4:1-2,5	8HevXII gr iii		(86)
?	4QXII^f		(41)

1:6-17	1QpHab		(14)
1:14-17	8HevXII gr xvii		(86)
2:1-8a	8HevXII gr xvii		(86)
2:1-20	1QpHab		(14)
2:13-20	8HevXII gr xviii		(86)
2:18-3:19	MurXII	Mur 88 xix	(83)
3:9-15	8HevXII gr xix		(86)

Zephaniah

1:1	MurXII	Mur 88 xix	(83)
1:1-6a	8HevXII gr xx		(86)
1:11-3:6	MurXII	Mur 88 xx	(83)
1:12-13	4QpZeph	4Q170	(47, 62)
1:13-18	8HevXII gr xxi		(86)
1:18-2:2	1QpZeph	1Q15	(17)
2:9-10	8HevXII gr xxii		(86)
3:6-7	8HevXII gr xxiii		(86)
3:8-20	MurXII	Mur 88 xxi	(83)
?	4QXII^c		(40)

Haggai

1:1-11	MurXII	Mur 88 xxi	(83)
1:12-2:10	MurXII	Mur 88 xxii	(83)
2:12-23	MurXII	Mur 88 xxiii	(83)

Zechariah

1:1-4	8HevXII gr xxviii		(83, 86)
1:4	MurXII	Mur 88 xxiii	(83)
1:12-15	8HevXII gr xxix		(86)
1:19-2:4	8HevXII gr xxx		(86)
2:7-12	8HevXII gr xxx		(86)
2:11-12	8HevXII gr frg. 9		(86)
2:16-17	8HevXII gr xxxi		(86)
3:1-2	8HevXII gr frg. 7		(86)
8:19-23a	8HevXII gr B1		(86)
8:23b-9:5	8HevXII gr B2		(86)
11:11	4QpIsa^c	4Q163	(47, 62)
13:7	CD 19:7-9		(92)
13:9	4QTanh	4Q176	(58, 64)
?	4QXII^g		(41)

New Testament Passages Referred to

III. INDEX OF EXTRABIBLICAL PASSAGES

239

IV. INDEX OF THE DEAD SEA SCROLLS ACCORDING TO SIGLA, A

11QBer	(71)	MirdA	(91)
11QDeut	(68)	MirdActs cpa	(91)
11QEzek	(68)	MirdAmul cpa	(91)
11QHalakha	(71)	Miš gr	(90)
11QHym^{a-b}	(71)	MurABC	(79)
11QJN ar	(71)	MurDeut	(79)
11QJub	(71)	MurEpBarC^{a-b}	(81)
11QLev	(68)	MurEpBethMashiko	(81)
11QMelch	(72)	MurEpJonathan	(81)
11QpaleoLev	(68)	MurExod	(79)
11QPs^{a-e}	(69, 73, 74)	MurGen	(79)
11QPsAp^a	(69)	MurIsa	(79)
11QŠirŠabb	(72)	MurMez	(79)
11QTemple^a	(72)	MurNum	(79)
11QTemple^b	(73)	MurPalimp^{a-b}	(80)
11QtgJob	(70)	MurPhyl	(79)
XQphyl 1-4	(76)	P. Yadin 18	(88)
CD	(92)	34ṢeEp	(89)
CSir	(92)	34Ṣe gr 1-8	(89)
CTLevi ar	(92, 93)	34ṢePhyl	(89)
?HevGen	(85)		
5/6HevA nab	(87)		
5/6Hev B ar	(87)		
5/6Hev BA	(87)		
5/6Hev C ar	(87)		
5/6HevEp 1-15	(87)		
5/6HevEp gr	(88)		
5/6HevNum	(85)		
5/6HevPs	(85)		
8HevEp gr	(88)		
8HevXII gr	(85, 86)		
MasDeut	(77)		
MasEp gr	(78)		
MasExod	(77)		
MasEzek	(77)		
MasGen	(77)		
MasJub	(78)		
Mas lat	(78)		
MasOstr	(78)		
MasPs	(77)		
MasSir	(77)		
MasŠirŠabb	(78)